Reconstructing Desire

RECONSTRUCTING DESIRE

The Role of
the Unconscious
in Women's
Reading and Writing

by Jean Wyatt

The
University
of North
Carolina Press

Chapel Hill
and London

Library of Congress Cataloging-in-Publication Data
Wyatt, Jean.
   Reconstructing desire : the role of the unconscious in women's
reading and writing / by Jean Wyatt.
      p.   cm.
   Includes bibliographical references.
   ISBN 0-8078-1915-8 (alk. paper).—ISBN 0-8078-4285-0
(pbk. : alk. paper)
   1. English fiction—Women authors—History and criticism.
2. American fiction—Women authors—History and criticism.
3. Subconsciousness in literature.   4. Psychoanalysis and
literature.   5. Women—Books and reading.   6. Fantasy in
literature.   7. Desire in literature.   8. Women in literature.
I. Title.
PR830.W6W93   1990
823.009'353—dc20   90-12010
                                                            CIP

The paper in this book meets the guidelines for permanence and
durability of the Committee on Production Guidelines for Book
Longevity of the Council on Library Resources.

Design by April Leidig-Higgins

Manufactured in the United States of America

94 93 92 91 90   5 4 3 2 1

Chapter 1 appeared in somewhat different form in *Tulsa Studies
in Women's Literature* 4 (1985): 199–216, and in *Critical Essays
on Charlotte Brontë*, edited by Barbara Timm Gates. Boston:
G. K. Hall, 1990. © 1990 by Barbara Timm Gates.

Portions of Chapter 7 appeared in *Perspectives on Contemporary
Literature* 11 (1985): 37–45, under the title, "Escaping Literary
Designs: The Politics of Reading and Writing in Margaret Drabble's
The Waterfall."

for Bob

Contents

Acknowledgments

I HAVE BEEN FORTUNATE in having friends who not only read my work and listened to my ideas but developed a personal stake in this book's progress.

My thanks go to Gayle Greene for her help in solving problems great and small over several years of writing and for the insights that her reading of the whole manuscript produced. To Janice Rossen for her wisdom on the shaping of books and the importance of finishing them. To Lynn Ross-Bryant for the untiring energy and goodwill with which she read each chapter as I completed it. To Sara van den Berg for her generosity in reading the whole manuscript and helping me discover its structure. To Susan Grayson for initiating our collaborative reading and discussion of Lacan and for suggesting changes in several chapters. To Jane Jaquette for giving me workspace in her garage and reading what I wrote there. To Phyllis Lindquist for discussions of Joanna Field's work and for her enthusiastic commitment to my writing. To Leslie Rabine for giving my chapter on *The Awakening* the benefit of her expertise on Julia Kristeva. To John Swift for help both creative and critical, in particular for the idea that sparked my theory of an imaginary confusion between the reader's "I" and the "I" in a text. To Warren Montag for sharing his wide knowledge of Lacan with me. To Dan Fineman for a tough and helpful reading of my first drafts. To Marshall Alcorn, who read my chapters on reader response, cheered me on, and helped me in a variety of ways to understand the intersection between reading and psychoanalytic theory. To Adrienne Hamcke, who combined accuracy in the work of assembling the bibliography and adjusting the notes with a passionate commitment to the subject of my study. I am grateful to the Louis and Hermione Brown Humanities Support Fund at Occidental College for funding Adrienne Hamcke's assistance in preparing the manuscript. To my editor, Sandra Eisdorfer, for her unfailing patience, support, and understanding, especially in the matter of missed deadlines. Also to Laura Oaks for the sympathy of her reading and the elegance of her copyediting. The perspicacity of numerous students in Women and Literature classes at Occidental College over the years both gave me the energy to continue writing and moved my ideas along.

I would not have written this book had I not attended the 1981 National Endowment for the Humanities Summer Seminar on Feminism and Modernism conducted by Susan Gubar and Sandra Gilbert. The circle of supportive women in that seminar gave each of us the confidence that what we had to say was worth writing down. Reading novels by women, we felt we were participants in a tradition of women who wrote in spite of social and psychological obstacles similar to the ones we faced; and Susan and Sandra, by their presence, example, and encouragement, stirred up creative energy that overflowed into our writing. I especially want to thank Sandra Gilbert, Susan Gubar, Linda Mizejewski, Gail Mortimer, Caryn Musil, Alice Reich, and Melody Zajdel for their readings of very early drafts of these chapters. And the book is much better as a result of Anne Goodwyn Jones's careful reading of the completed manuscript. I am grateful for her combination of alert and informed criticism with a sympathetic grasp of what I wanted to say.

Most of all I am grateful for the constant nurturing support of my husband, Bob, who made me feel that I could do it, during good writing times and bad.

Reconstructing
Desire

Introduction

THIS BOOK IS ABOUT the possibilities for change—change through practices not usually regarded as revolutionary because, located in the private sphere, they do not carry the blazon of social change: reading, writing, sexual intimacy, and creative work. How can one change one's mind, from within the confines of that same mind? Even to begin to see the assumptions that support one's own conceptual framework, it would be necessary to move outside the limits of that mental frame. But outside the mind is only the inscrutable territory of the unconscious, where our own desires are patterned according to designs that are dark to us, apparently beyond the compass of any conscious will to change.

Myra Jehlen, confronting the problem of changing one's mind from within the limits of that same mind, claims that "somewhat like Archimedes, who to lift the earth with his lever required someplace else on which to locate himself and his fulcrum, feminists questioning the presumptive order of both nature and history—and thus proposing to remove the ground from under their own feet—would appear to need an alternative base . . . a standpoint off this world altogether" (190). In fact, patriarchy itself has constructed this ground for an alternative epistemological framework—not in some radical outside, but within its own system and within each individual produced by it. The child-rearing arrangements that make women responsible for domestic maintenance and child care may free men to regulate public institutions and define cultural norms, but they also construct a private sphere within the public sphere that breeds a different kind of thinking. The prolonged closeness of mother-child relations constructs ways of knowing the self and the world that shatter the dominant cultural definition of the individual as separate and self-contained. Freud describes the infantile outlook on the world as the "oceanic feeling."

An infant at the breast does not as yet distinguish his ego from the external world. . . . originally the ego includes everything, later it separates off an external world from itself. Our present ego-feeling is, therefore, only a shrunken residue of a much more inclusive—indeed, an all-embracing—feeling which corresponded to a more intimate

> bond between the ego and the world about it. If we may assume that there are many people in whose mental life this primary ego-feeling has persisted to a greater or less degree, it would exist in them side by side with the narrower and more sharply demarcated ego-feeling of maturity, like a kind of counterpart to it. In that case, the ideational contents appropriate to it would be precisely those of limitlessness and of a bond with the universe—the . . . "oceanic" feeling. (Freud, *Civilization*, 66–68)

Identity is not singular, then, but twofold: beside the clearly defined "mature" ego-feeling, bounded by the outline of the body and closed off from the world, exists the shadowy sense of a self continuous with the world; this other self-image is sustained by dim memories from a time of global wholeness before boundaries and difference emerged. If persons were only what Western culture mirrors back to us—coherent selves, unique and consistent "individuals"—we would presumably be entirely subject to the cultural values that surround us from birth. But because each of us is simultaneously a subject constructed by social discourse and the locus of an "other scene" where different desires play and different cognitive possibilities arise, there is in everyone a source of contradictory energy capable of challenging social formations—including the social formation of one's own conscious self.

Freud's description of an infant's perspective catches the main theme of preoedipal fantasy: the sense of continuity between self and other, self and world. Probably a young child's view of the world is not thus uniform: D. W. Winnicott, Nancy Chodorow, and Jessica Benjamin have elaborated the notion of the preoedipal, in ways that the following chapters explore, to encompass all the oscillations between symbiosis and differentiation, between "being one" and "being together," that a child experiences in relation to its mother in the first few years of life.[1]

The fluidity of self-definition implicit in preoedipal modes threatens the cornerstone of Western patriarchal systems: the distinct and unified individual who stands separate and self-contained is at the heart of syntax (as "I", the subject of enunciation), at the center of bourgeois democratic ideology (as the individual citizen), and at the top of the developmental ladder constructed by post-Freudian orthodoxy (the separate, self-contained ego). This study deals with the revolutionary and transformational potential of the preoedipal in novels by women. Part 1 focuses on the disruptions in narrative discourse, and hence in the mind of the reader, that preoedipal contradictions introduce into language. Part 2 examines the many ways that recapturing the indeterminacy between self and other can enhance creativity. And part 3 explores the possibility, reflected in contemporary women's novels, of imagining alternative family relations based on preoedipal patterns—family circles whose fluidity of interchange challenges the rigid gender and generational hierarchies of the patriarchal family.

Women writers of course have no monopoly on fantasies of the self joined to the world: Freud's description makes it clear that this fantasy is available to everyone whose first sense of self emerged within the diffuse, enveloping presence of a mother (or primary caretaker). An ecstatic return to unity with the natural world is at the heart of Keats's and Wordsworth's poetic vision, and the characters in D. H. Lawrence's *The Rainbow* experience various diffusions of identity out into the surrounding world. And certainly, no one has described an identity more enmeshed in his mother's than Proust.[2] But Nancy Chodorow's work on female psychosexual development has convinced many feminist theorists, including myself, that because girls remain unconsciously connected to their mothers well past infancy, women are more apt than men to feel at ease in regressing to a state of identity diffusion, where the boundary between self and other becomes indistinct. In a situation of exclusive mothering, Chodorow explains, boys must insist on a rather violent separation from their mothers in order to establish themselves as "not-female." But girls need not wrench themselves away from their mothers to establish gender identity and so tend to continue defining themselves in connection with her; indeed, many girls maintain an unconscious sense of continuity with their mothers throughout their lives (*Mothering*, 108–10; 166–70). Reasoning that "if girls and boys experience the process of differentiation from this early stage differently, . . . it seems likely that its resonances will echo differently in the male and female literary voice" (Lidoff, 44), critics Marianne Hirsch, Roberta Rubenstein, Joan Lidoff, and myself in an earlier article, have studied the traces of fluid boundaries in the plots, characters, and style of women's fiction. The present study likewise locates female textual difference in an adherence to values of "fusion, fluidity, mutuality, continuity and lack of differentiation" (Hirsch, "Spiritual *Bildung*," 27); but it focuses more specifically than other studies on the marks of the preoedipal in language and in readers' unconscious fantasy structures—on both sides of a reading process, then, that may lead to change.

The Preoedipal in Language

To propose reading and writing as paths toward change, as this study does, is to encounter a problem central to feminist debates: both reading and writing require an engagement with linguistic structures that carry patriarchal values. Using language means submitting to forms of logic that are also forms of authority and control; it means being interpellated into the "structures and entailments" of patriarchal discourse (Treichler, "Wallpaper," 323)—categories and divisions that pretend to be neutral while organizing thought in hierarchical structures that support male dominance (Cixous, "Castration," 44). On the other hand, trying to escape male linguistic and social dominance by basing a new discourse on the preoedipal raises the objection that the preoedipal is by definition preverbal and so always outside social discourse. The idea that the preoedipal could introduce change seems preposterous, then, since it can only turn people inward, toward unnameable delights, leaving untouched the political sphere "of shared language, responsibility, community, and political agency, the domain where transformation is effected" (Flieger, 5).[3]

In part 1 I argue that preoedipal drive energies *can* get into language, and when they do they throw the fixed positions of language and the fixed categories of traditional epistemology into question. Language carries the fundamental assumptions underlying Western constructs of reality in its grammar and syntax, beginning with the singular pronouns that reflect the faith of Western culture that the individual is distinct, singular, unified. Texts that incorporate a preoedipal perspective undermine the cognitive foundations of Western epistemology. A novel like Marilynne Robinson's *Housekeeping*, for example, narrated from the point of view of a character mired in the preoedipal, challenges the notion of singular identity as the narrative "I" slides into "we," then locates its existence entirely in the mind of the other. Because the narrator is blind to the boundary definitions that delineate the contours of our reality, her account leaves out the spatial and temporal divisions that allow us to make sense of the physical world. The same can be said for logic: the narrator's conflation of the mutually exclusive categories of being and nothingness mocks the ontological and logical foundations of Western conceptions of reality. If language is power, imprinting on us patriarchal designs (Fetterley, *Resisting Reader*, xi–xii), language can also be revolution.

Julia Kristeva's *Revolution in Poetic Language* explains how preoedipal drive energies participate in language production. Language is never simply a matter of varying verbal elements within a fixed grammatical structure, Kristeva insists. Meaning is produced through a dialectic between "semiotic" processes, with their origins in preverbal times, and "symbolic" processes operated by the speaking subject inscribed in social and linguistic systems. The "symbolic" refers to the structure of signifiers that a conscious subject processes to arrive at a given message; the "semiotic" is a name for the preoedipal. Kristeva adapts Lacan's notion that when a child enters the symbolic, when it enters language, it splits into speaking subject and unconscious. The speaking subject is produced by language structures and the ideology that marks them; desires that cannot be encompassed within the linguistic and social order constitute the unconscious. Kristeva's unconscious differs from Lacan's in that he constructs an unconscious peopled not by raw drive energies but by configurations of signifiers that pattern the drives, whereas she imagines the unconscious as the *chora*, a receptacle for the flux of primitive drive energies. These preoedipal drives circulate beneath language, charging language with their energies from a place outside the symbolic order and its ideologically loaded forms. Semiotic energy is thus countercultural: when it invades language, it distorts the signifying chain, causing a "wandering" that "marks the workings of the drives (appropriation/rejection, orality/anality, love/hate, life/death" ("Identity," 136). Kristeva must be speaking about the production of texts, and so about competing discursive registers in authors' writing processes; but she describes the tension and combat between symbolic and semiotic as if it were taking place before a reader's eyes, in the text itself. Her model enables me to think about specific features of texts like Chopin's *The Awakening* and Alcott's *Little Women* and Robinson's *Housekeeping* that represent an influx of preoedipal energy.

Most obviously, the central drive of the preoedipal, the drive to regain the original unity with the mother's body, runs counter to the symbolic register's requirement that the speaking subject separate from his or her objects (initially, the mother) in order to make statements about them (Kristeva, *Revolution*, 47, 52). When the urge to recapture that primal unity enters the text, it disrupts the basis of linguistic structure, the singular position of speaking subject and the separate positions of her or his objects: thus the central character of *The Awakening*, re-merging with a maternal sea, loses the clear envelope of individuality that has been marking her out as an identity within the symbolic register.

The entry of preoedipal drive energies into a symbolic register of language that is constituted on the basis of their repression of course disrupts and explodes that order. But this is a "productive dissolving," Kristeva insists: "the semiotic processes themselves, far from being set adrift . . . set up a new formal construct: a so-called new formal or ideological 'writer's universe,' the never-finished, undefined production of a new space of significance" ("Identity," 135). In *The Awakening* the pull of preoedipal desire is felt through language that neglects syntax for rhythm. When the sea speaks its invitation to Edna to lose herself in its waters, words draw together on the basis of sonal affinities, disrupting grammatical order to accommodate patterns of assonance, alliteration, and repetition. Kristeva calls this "poetic language" and claims for it a subversive effect on the reader.

A discourse that privileges rhythms and sonal patterns over meaning awakens in the reader the site of preoedipal energies, for as an infant she/he responded rhythmically to the sounds of language; only later did language become a collection of signifiers asking to be transformed to- ward meaning. When sound displaces syntax as the governing principle of discourse, as in the voice of the sea passages in *The Awakening*, the reader loses the syntactic order that caught and held in place the reader's socially constructed self; that unified persona begins to dissolve, to be replaced by a preoedipal flux that responds to the sonal patterns rather than the sense of words. The unity of the speaking subject breaks down; this is a revolutionary moment, for the reader has to recognize his/her own heterogeneity and hence the inadequacy of the social construct of his or her own identity as singular and coherent. Thrown into a flux of drive energies, the reading subject becomes "a questionable *subject-in-process*" ("Identity," 135)—no longer fixed, but in transit toward a new construc- tion of identity. Hence, she/he is open to new possibilities; according to Kristeva, only such a "subject-in-process" is capable of participating in social change. Thus Kristeva's analysis answers the objection that the preoedipal is socially useless because it is always beyond language: it is precisely through its emergence into language that the preoedipal can precipitate change.

Of course, the preoedipal speaks many languages. Dwelling in the pre- oedipal meant dwelling there with all our senses, so that each of our senses presumably bears traces of that time. It is not only sounds that can awaken the preoedipal side of the reader, then, but visual cues that remind him or her of the maternal dialogue of mirroring faces, or the imagery of bodies touching or knowing each other through proximity that recalls the lost closeness to the mother's body. To encompass the range of possible reader responses to preoedipal eruptions in texts, I rely on a number of theorists who emphasize different sensual and cognitive reminders of the preoedipal. Thus Freud's construction of the unconscious as the preserve of pre-oedipal ways of processing information—the primary processes—enables me to hypothesize an unconscious reading process that functions quite differently from the conscious one: processing the subtext of corporeal imagery in some girlhood novels enables readers to assimilate new fantasy structures. Lacan's explanation of the confusions between self and other that take place in the "imaginary" dimension of human experience enables me to explore aspects of reader identification with the "I" of first-person narrative. *Housekeeping* in particular represents the whole range of confu-sions that result, first, from the infant's misrecognition of the self in the reflecting surface of the other's face, and, second, from the reader's mis-recognition of his or her own "I" in the mirroring "I" of first-person narrative. Winnicott's and Kohut's vision of psychosexual development as a kind of joint project between mother and child enables me to elucidate the dimension of intersubjectivity where the artist figures discussed in part 2 produce some of their best works. In order to present a rounded picture of the preoedipal, my analysis sometimes brings together theorists from different—even competing—camps. The reader may be startled to see Lacan and Winnicott shoulder to shoulder in the chapter on *Housekeeping*, for example, but both contribute to our insight into the search for the self in the mirroring presence of the other. Rather than develop a single au-thoritative theory of the preoedipal, this study tries out various theories on various novels in an effort to understand how the preoedipal continues to influence adult thinking, opening the subject up to change.

Can Reading Change the Reader?

The theory that reading a text with preoedipal appeal can cause an up-heaval in the reader's socially constructed identity rests on the assumption that a reader is split, so that different parts of the self respond to different registers of language. But if the reader did not have a split-off preoedipal side, the subversive messages of the novels I examine in this study would go unheard: the reader would be unable to "read" the language of touch, song, and facial reflection that unites the female family circle in *Little Women*, could not respond to the sea's appeal to dissolve the burden of separate individuality in *The Awakening*, could not understand the confusions of identity in the dialectic between self and mirror in *Housekeeping*. Dealing with unconscious reader responses to particular texts is always problematic because the unconscious is by definition unknown—and because Freud, characteristically, said different things about it at different times. Given this undecidability, it is necessary to confront various conflicting constructs of the unconscious before going on to theorize particular unconscious reading processes.

Freud wrote sometimes as if the unconscious were totally articulated by patterns that hold unconscious desire captive. In *The Interpretation of Dreams* he says that when a need is satisfied, the memory of the need is embedded together with the image of what satisfied it; when the need arises again, it comes bound to the images surrounding that initial gratification. According to this description, desire always leads backwards, as one seeks to recreate the circumstances of one's earliest satisfactions (565–66). In a similarly conservative vein Freud describes unconscious fantasies as fixed structures. "The unconscious ideas are organised into phantasies or imaginary scenarios to which the instinct becomes fixated and which may be conceived of as true *mises en scène* of desire" (Laplanche and Pontalis, *Language*, 475). The fantasy structure remains the same throughout development; only the actors change. Thus in "A Child Is Being Beaten," a fantasy reported by several of Freud's female patients, the fantasy originally expresses sibling rivalry: "My father is beating my brother." Later, as an expression of oedipal guilt and desire, the fantasy becomes, "My father is beating me." In latency the fantasy takes the form, "A teacher is beating a boy" (184–86). According to this account, unconscious fantasy life is fundamentally static: the dramatis personae change as new figures move into old slots, but the fundamental structures of desire remain the same.[4]

When Freud discussed unconscious *processes*, on the other hand, he emphasized the mobility of unconscious mental energy. In displacement, for instance, the emotional charge attached to one idea can be transferred entirely to a new idea. Then unconscious desire appears to be free, *not* bound to unchanging patterns (Laplanche and Pontalis, *Language*, 121).

Lacan builds on this idea of unconscious mobility, describing desire as "that derangement of the instincts that comes from being caught on the rails—eternally stretching forth towards the desire for something else—of metonymy [Lacan's transmutation of the term *displacement*]" ("Agency," 167). Kristeva and Cixous likewise stress the volatility of unconscious energy and so construct an unconscious radically free from the fixed ideological structures of the conscious mind. Anglo-American feminist readers of Freud, on the other hand, base their idea of the unconscious on his notion that desire is always encased in fantasy patterns that reflect the child's earliest experience. Thus Nancy Chodorow imagines an unconscious structured by family patterns (and the larger cultural patterns that family relations mediate).

> Family structure and process, in particular the asymmetrical organization of parenting, affect unconscious psychic structure and process. . . . A child comes to channel libido and aggression in patterned ways as a result of its relational experiences and its interactions with caretakers, that is, the id becomes patterned and constructed. . . . This history, dependent on the individual personalities and behavior of those who happen to interact with a child, is also socially patterned according to the family structure and prevalent psychological modes of a society. (*Mothering*, 49–50)

Taking in relational structures from the family reconstitutes society, first in the inner world of the individual and subsequently in the way she/he chooses to live. "Thus, society constitutes itself psychologically in the individual. . . . All aspects of psychic structure, character, and emotional and erotic life are social" (*Mothering*, 50). This analysis accounts for women's compulsion to perpetuate the structures of their own oppression: unconscious desire becomes enmeshed with the setting of their earliest experiences of satisfaction (or frustration) in the nuclear family; so desire always moves them (unconsciously) to reconstruct in their adult lives the patterns of their original family life. Other Anglo-American theorists share this view of the unconscious as a mirror of the social order, notably Juliet Mitchell: "it is within the Freudian unconscious that the law of this [social] order speaks . . . the [individual] has to find its place within the unconscious system, . . . in the order of human society that expresses itself in the unconscious, or rather that the unconscious *is*" (*Psychoanalysis*, 391).

Lacan sees a different Freud altogether: "For Lacan . . . Freud's most fundamental discovery [was] that the unconscious never ceases to challenge our apparent identity as subjects" (Rose, "Introduction," 30). In Lacan's account the unconscious, far from simply reflecting the social order, is the home of repressed signifiers that are systematically excluded from social formations. The unconscious is formed, at the same time that the infant enters language systems, by precisely those desires that cannot get into language and the social thinking that language articulates. Part of a child's need can be voiced: it can, for instance, ask its mother for milk. But the rest of what the child wants from the mother—to be the mother's desire, to be one with her body, to have her love and recognition absolutely—cannot be articulated in language and so falls into the unconscious. (If these examples seem bizarre, that is because they exceed the logic of language, based as it is on the notion of singular identity and the separation between speakers—precisely Lacan's point.)[5] As Rosalind Coward and John Ellis point out, where Mitchell's unconscious "must always serve a retrogressive function, . . . returning in the face of economic, political, and ideological contradictions as the form of patriarchal sexual construction," Lacan's analysis is "less pessimistic. . . . [The unconscious] is . . . made up of heterogeneous elements which are refused entry into consciousness in the production of the positioned subject to produce (ideological) meaning. . . . The unconscious can then emerge as a disruptive . . . force" (155).[6]

Since what goes on in the unconscious is anybody's guess—and is probably more various and complex than anybody's guess—it seems more useful to imagine a variety of unconscious reading processes than to elaborate a single unambiguous model. Thus in the opening chapters of this study I examine the structure of certain formative fantasies—girlhood novels that have over several generations evoked the passionate loyalty of young readers. Trying to understand the appeal of the underlying fantasy patterns in *Jane Eyre*, *Little Women*, *Heidi*, and *The Wizard of Oz* involves me in trying out first one version of the unconscious, then the other. The popularity of *Little Women* seems to confirm the French idea that the unconscious is the home of repressed energies that challenge the socially indoctrinated conscious subject. The parents' repeated homilies on proper female manners and morals, together with their daughters' answering statements of pious intent, speak a language of abstract signifiers to the conscious mind, the part of the reader committed to the cultural ideology of the good girl. But at the same time subversive corporeal images of banned "masculine" activities such as running, climbing, writing stories, and getting them published engage the primary processes that govern unconscious thinking. It seems that books like *Little Women* maintain their immense popularity by gratifying both sides of a split reader: the part of the reader that wants to be a good girl, and also the repressed drives for independence, power, and autonomy that linger alongside her compliant gender identity.

On the other hand, *Jane Eyre* presents a text that seems to be split in the opposite way. In lucid and compelling rhetoric, Jane advocates in speech after speech the emancipation of women from the domestic world into a wider field of endeavor; but a conservative undertow of images pulls the reader back into confinement in that world through the attractions of the patriarchal figure that Jane loves. The imagery of power and inaccessibility that surrounds Rochester and the final vision of absolute union with him can only retrace the patterns of desire imprinted by father-daughter relations and so push readers to recreate in their adult lives the asymmetrical structure of heterosexual relations they first experienced in their fathers' houses.[7]

The contradictory responses of readers imply that the unconscious is more complex and contradictory than either the French or the Anglo-American model allows. Each of these competing models of the unconscious leaves out the central informing principle of the other, but both contain elements that seem necessary to a full description of unconscious reading. To dismiss the Anglo-American account of the unconscious as a repository of patriarchal relations would be to disregard the evidence that women tend to reproduce in their adult lives the structures of male dominance in which they were raised. I think we have to acknowledge that some unconscious energy is contained within fantasy structures that tend to perpetuate the patriarchal family. But whereas Chodorow finds that relational patterns embedded both before and after the oedipal turn tend to shape individual desire to the uses of patriarchy, I would differentiate the revolutionary potential of preoedipal fantasies from the conservative tendency of oedipal fantasies.

Contemporary feminist psychoanalysts speak of the oedipal crisis as the moment "when the child comprehends the [sex-gender] system and his or her place in it; the crisis is resolved when the child accepts that place and accedes to it" (Rubin, 189). So, I argue, unconscious fantasies from the oedipal period contain individual desire in the relational patterns of patriarchy. Thus, for example, girls in a male-dominant family embed the fantasy of union with a strong, dominant, unattainable male figure (originally the father); this unconscious fantasy pattern engenders the structure of romantic love, with its subordination of all a woman's many desires and talents to the single goal of romantic marriage. Oedipal fantasies thus bind women to their places in the socioeconomic network while, in Althusser's words, blinding them to the real nature of their relation to that overarching structure (162–65).

But this is not to say that the unconscious is totally patterned by social designs. What the Chodorow-Mitchell interpretation of the unconscious ignores is the Freudian notion of repression: "Whatever is repressed from consciousness . . . remains intact and potentially operative in the unconscious" ("A Child Is Being Beaten," 128). In my own view, the unconscious also contains "the repressed of culture" (Cixous, "Castration," 52): those preoedipal desires that, falling outside patriarchal language and logic, also elude cultural scripts and so circulate unbound in the unconscious; and also those desires debarred at a later stage from the social code and the language that articulates it. For instance, there may be no place in a family's stories of female development for ambitions labeled "masculine"—desires for achievement, independence, aggression, self-assertion. These desires must then be forced into repression, together with the rage associated with their denial—a rage that must also be suppressed, given the demure passivity required of girls. Given such a complex and contradictory unconscious, readers can respond with passionate attachment both to texts that entangle oedipal desire in familiar structures and to texts that evoke the preoedipal energies that throw into flux the fixed positions and plots of cultural scripts.

The constitution of the unconscious bears on two issues central to this book: change and reading. If the circle between the self and the social were closed, as in the Anglo-American model that assumes unconscious processes reflect and support the established order, there would be no room for change—as indeed Ira Cohen, in his recent *Ideology and Unconsciousness*, asserts: "The interpenetration of social structure and character structure militate against the transformation of either" (203). The Lacanian and Kristevan idea of the unconscious, on the other hand, constructs a heterogeneous ground whence the impetus for change can come: "the child's submission to the discursive practices of society is challenged by the existence of another self which is not synonymous with the subject of discourse" (Belsey, 85).

If readers were all of a piece, equally vulnerable to cultural imprinting on conscious and unconscious levels, reading a novel would be like reading a primer of cultural values. In Stanley Fish's formulation, "If selves are constituted by the ways of thinking and seeing that inhere in social organizations, and if these constituted selves in turn constitute texts according to these same ways, then there can be no adversary relationship between text and self because they are necessarily related products of the same cognitive possibilities" (336). Such a unified reader would be able to latch onto only those structures in fiction that reproduce the social patterns inscribed in his/her unconscious; he or she would be unable to assimilate anything new from texts. Confronting the ideological contradictions exposed by a text—as in Margaret Drabble's *The Waterfall*—or stumbling upon something new, something left out of social representations of reality—as in *The Awakening*—such a reader would be unable to pursue the implications of the contradiction to his/her ideological formation, missing or dismissing it.

But the complex and contradictory nature of the unconscious makes for a more complex reading experience. *The Waterfall*, for example, interacts with several different levels of oedipal and preoedipal fantasy in its reader's mind: the first forty-six pages captivate the reader by means of narrowing life to a familiar line of rising intensity—"that sequence of discovery and recognition that I would call love" (47). But simultaneously Drabble introduces a sensual script that merges mother and baby, inner and outer worlds, in a fluidity that disrupts the fixed stages of the romance plot. The text thus calls into play competing paradigms in the reader's unconscious, putting them in motion against each other. When combined with the narrator's conscious efforts to dislodge the romantic love paradigm from its dominance over her own fantasy life, such a continuous upheaval and jolting of one pattern against another might actually shake the hold of romantic fantasy on the reader's unconscious mind, freeing up libidinal energy to seek new channels for desire. Maybe; at least there is hope for change.

The Preoedipal: Revolution or Regression?

When Freud described the "oceanic" feeling of unbounded connection to the world existing alongside the sense of a separate ego, he articulated a principle of psychoanalytic theory: earlier stages of development remain available to us throughout life. But theorists from different schools of thought disagree on the value of finding refuge in these earlier modes. A retreat to an earlier way of being in the world can be labeled a lapse into regression, a failure of maturation; or such flexibility can be viewed as creative, offering an individual the opportunity to integrate earlier and potentially creative ways of thinking. An orthodox Freudian like Cynthia Griffin Wolff views Edna's "dream of total fusion" (217) in *The Awakening* as regression pure and simple—"the arrest of Edna's libidinal energies at a pre-genital level . . . at an oral level" (208). Edna's self-division is thus seen as destructive, leading her inevitably toward death because in life the dream of total fusion cannot be realized: "Once released, the inner being cannot be satisfied. It is an orally destructive self, a limitless void whose needs can be filled, finally, only by total fusion with the outside world, a totality of sensuous enfolding. And this totality means annihilation of the ego" (211). Powerful as Wolff's argument is—and consistent as it is with Edna's final plunge into union with the sea—there is a more positive way to view the tug of the preoedipal.

Because my view of the preoedipal has been shaped by the revisions of feminist theorists who have written since Wolff, I view Edna's "hidden self" as positive at least insofar as it keeps her moving past the satisfactions available to a wife and mother within her patriarchal culture. Impulses heterogeneous to her own culturally constructed identity propel her toward change by suggesting new, if indistinct, possibilities.

In the course of discovering within psychoanalytic theory a different path of development for women, Nancy Chodorow revalued qualities that had been derogated and branded "immature" by orthodox Freudians. Thus she does not present the fluid ego boundaries that result from girls' extended period of primary identity with their mothers as a failure of maturation. Rather than measuring girls' ego strength against the male developmental norm of a separate, bounded autonomy, Chodorow presents a straightforward and nonderivative account of women's difference (see Gilligan, 8). In a family organized along the lines of a traditional sexual division of labor, with the mother given primary responsibility for child care, a mother tends to define her daughter unconsciously as an extension of herself, while she sees her son almost from the start as a male other. She then tends to reinforce her son's moves toward individuation while remaining closely identified with her daughter.

> Girls emerge from this [extended period of symbiosis] with a basis for "empathy" built into their primary definition of self in a way that boys do not. Girls emerge with a stronger basis for experiencing another's needs or feelings as one's own. . . . Furthermore, girls do not define themselves in terms of the denial of preoedipal relational modes to the same extent as do boys. Therefore, regression to these modes tends not to feel as much a basic threat to their ego. From very early, then, because they are parented by a person of the same gender . . . girls come to experience themselves as less differentiated than boys, as more continuous with and related to the external object-world. (*Mothering*, 167)

Chodorow's validation of female qualities associated with the preoedipal has given feminist thinkers like Carol Gilligan, Nancy Hartsock, and Evelyn Fox Keller a new ground from which to challenge and revise paradigms central to their respective disciplines. Thus Keller deconstructs "objectivity," the fundamental ethic of scientific inquiry, from a standpoint that endorses the value of an ambiguous borderland, a "creative ebb and flow," between the scientist and the object of his or her study; empathy can be a legitimate way of knowing. Gilligan similarly pinpoints the bias toward male developmental values of detachment and separation in Lawrence Kohlberg's equation of moral maturity with the ability to apply abstract, universalist criteria to ethical issues; she suggests that an equally valid "ethic of care" emerges from women's view of life as a network of intertwining personal connections. Hartsock has suggested substituting an epistemology based on the material processes of women's everyday domestic life—including the fluidity of interchange between mothers and children—for the reductive abstractions of a political theory based on the principle of exchange.

So Chodorow's *Reproduction of Mothering* has made it possible for a number of American feminist theorists to think differently, to create alternatives to the dominant cognitive frameworks of their disciplines. Yet Chodorow herself has understood women's immersion in the preoedipal not as liberating, but as perpetuating the status quo. A girl internalizes the prolonged diffuse relation with the mother and thereafter seeks that primary union with an other—first in marriage, where she seeks a return to fusion with her husband; and, when that effort inevitably fails (because the vicissitudes of growing up male in a situation of exclusive mothering embed in men a powerful resistance to any semblance of a return to the maternal merger), she seeks to reproduce the experience of total fusion by having a child. If the child is a girl, the cycle begins again. According to Chodorow, then, the preoedipal fantasy of merging is not transformational, but conservative. It only perpetuates the institution of exclusive mothering on which patriarchal social arrangements rest.

Jane Eyre points to a similar assimilation of preoedipal energies to the maintenance of social order. Jane's desire for fusion ultimately pours into the culturally endorsed channel of romantic love as she becomes one with Rochester—"absolutely bone of his bone and flesh of his flesh" (454). So preoedipal desires are revolutionary only in potential: they can be appropriated and transformed to the purposes of patriarchy.

It may also be objected that the preoedipal fantasy of merging leads not to change, as this study argues, but to stasis. If one is fused with an other, one cannot move—either toward effective action in the world or toward a new level of personal development. "The one doesn't stir without the other," as Luce Irigaray puts it in her essay on maternal merging. My chapters on Robinson's *Housekeeping* and Morrison's *Beloved* explore the problematics of the preoedipal, as characters who unquestioningly follow preoedipal impulses either consume the substance of the other (*Beloved*) or find it impossible (that is, self-annihilating) to move away from the reflection of the self in the other's face (*Housekeeping*). Jerry Aline Flieger, in a recent talk, has argued that the embrace of sameness implied in preoedipal modes thwarts change; it is, rather, the encounter with difference that gives people new ideas.

On the other hand, ideas and images retained from preoedipal days can suggest directions for self-renewal and self-expansion outside the social scripts for women's behavior. In *Little Women* the faces of her sisters mirror back to Jo the worth of her artistic achievements, replenishing her narcissistic supplies so that, emboldened, she can confidently invest in more creative projects. A preoedipal line of communication thus undoes the damage to female creativity inflicted by patriarchal prohibitions on ambitious female fantasies. Edna in *The Awakening* goes through romantic love only to go beyond it, finding like several other protagonists of women's novels that an expansion into the natural world is more fulfilling than the containment of merging impulses within the romantic couple.[8] Lily in Woolf's *To the Lighthouse*, Rennie in Atwood's *Bodily Harm*, and Violet Clay in Godwin's novel of that name similarly bypass the "genuine genital relationship" (Wolff, 213) that is our culture's definition of happiness for women in order to merge with the subjects of their paintings (or writings) and thus transform erotic energy in the direction of creativity.

It is in the sphere of creativity that we can see most clearly the advantages of "an ego to whom the earlier and deeper levels of ego-reality integration remain alive as dynamic sources of higher organization" (Loewald, 18; quoted in Keller, 84). Ernst Kris and Brewster Ghiselin have long held that a strategic retreat to primary-process thinking is necessary to the germination of a new idea. Without some such abandon of habitual thinking the consciousness will reduce any vague intimation or hunch from less organized levels of the mind to its own iron structures (Ghiselin, 25). The artist figures in the novels and autobiographical accounts explored in part 2 are able to reach back in order to move forward, using a lapse into preoedipal modes as a source of creative energy. Joanna Field's account of her own creative processes suggests that drawing works best when the artist's relation to her subject is flexible, so she can "plunge" past the boundaries between self and other into "the full imaginative experience of [the object]," then withdraw and see it detached, separate from the nimbus of her own projections and associations (25, 84). To catch the life of her subject, an artist needs the capacity to slip along the relational continuum that the child once traversed with her mother, a spectrum of relational possibilities stretching from primary identification to differentiation. In order to complete a work of art, too, an artist has to tolerate long stretches of "transitional" experience, when the created object is no longer simply a figment of the artist's imagination but is not yet a complete object on its own in the external world. Making something thus recaptures the transitional zone between inner and outer realities described by Winnicott, where an object's ontological status is understood to be simultaneously part of the self and part of the external object world—where the question "is that me or not-me?" is not even asked ("Transitional Objects," 12).

Boundary flexibility thus seems essential to many stages of the creative process. The issue of "changing one's mind," central to this book, then takes the form: how can one give up one's habitual orientation to reality, one's reliance on distinct categories of thought, to slide back into a less differentiated way of thinking? An adult used to defending the line between inner and outer worlds, between self and other, may need some special solvent to diffuse the habitual containments of mental and emotional life.

Otto Kernberg's definition of sexual passion as an experience of transcending ego boundaries into the other's subjective field suggests that sexuality may enable an adult to reenter the ambiguous space where the border between self and other loses its distinctness. Ideally, sexual intimacy enables an adult to recapture the indeterminate zone between child and mother where the child once played, freed by the protective presence of the mother to discover and acknowledge her own impulses and to explore imaginary worlds (Winnicott, "Capacity," 34; see also Perry, 7–8). In "How I Came to Write Fiction" George Eliot presents the bed she shared with George Henry Lewes as just such a creative space: Lewes's protective presence enables her to relax into a fantasy of writing a novel, to acknowledge that daydream, and, with his enthusiastic affirmation, to make it part of her ongoing self-definition.

But using sexual intimacy as a way back to less differentiated states of mind is problematic in a world governed by patriarchal sexual politics, as the three novels explored in part 2 make clear. Drabble's *The Waterfall* and Lessing's *The Golden Notebook* explore the unconscious and conscious struggles that the writers Jane and Anna wage not so much with their lovers as with their own tendencies to subordinate themselves to male dominance—Anna through accepting the roles that Saul gives her in his psychological dramas, Jane through adhering to the addictive excitements of romantic love. But on the other hand, the writing of both Jane and Anna improves as a result of crossing over into the psychological field of their lovers: their prose becomes more fluid, sensually immediate, and moving. *The Color Purple* escapes the specific problems arising from the structure of heterosexuality in our culture in part by making both lovers women. The lesbian relationship between Celie and Shug represents a kind of maternal erotics, a reciprocal nurturance of each other's creative potential. Each in turn provides material care for the other, nurtures the other's development toward autonomy, and creates the safe space where the other can relax into the uninhibited play of her creative powers.

A Note on the Sequence of Chapters

In keeping with this study's affirmation of the preoedipal, the sequence of my chapters defies the standard developmental progression. Beginning with a chapter that analyzes an oedipal fantasy, parts 1 and 2 work backward through what I claim are the liberatory possibilities of the preoedipal. The book as a whole follows the same ex-centric trajectory, from the extended analysis of damaging oedipal family relations in the opening chapter to the review of various preoedipal family configurations in part 3.

Part 1 begins with the oedipal fantasy that puts Jane Eyre in her place (and exerts a powerful attraction on the female reader to follow her there). Subsequent chapters in part 1 describe both preoedipal texts and preoedipal readings that have the potential to liberate women from oedipal structures—sexual and narrative. Part 2 begins with the fantasy of austere autonomy that I argue is also generated by oedipal pressures to conform. In this fantasy structure, central to a striking number of novels about female artists, a woman has to choose between husbanding all her energies for art and pouring all her energies into personal relationships. While the fantasy of romantic love, with its dependency on the excitement of a man's presence, reflects the "normal" oedipal resolution in which a girl gives up ambitious strivings to become the object of a man's affections, the fantasy of austere autonomy is the result of a "negative" oedipal resolution. That is, a girl who refuses the subordinate and self-effacing role carved out for her in the sex-gender system becomes involved in an impossible choice: she can strike out for autonomy, but only at the cost of defying her mother's gender definition; and that involves the risk of losing her mother's love. This early painful choice between nurturing love and stark, other-denying autonomy is reflected in the uncompromising harshness of the choice between love and autonomy that structures the majority of female artist novels by white middle-class authors. Subsequent chapters in part 2 explore exceptions to the rule—artist novels by women that picture sexual love nurturing creativity rather than eclipsing it.

The book as a whole follows a trajectory of hope, from the skewed power structure of the oedipal family in chapter 1 to a review, in part 3, of preoedipal fantasies about the family—fantasies that expand the remembered circle of mother-infant love to encompass change and difference. To imagine finding in preoedipal fantasy a principle of organization sufficiently reality-oriented to supplant the hard and present realities of the oedipal family may itself appear to be an indulgence in preoedipal fantasy. And indeed *Beloved* presents a wholesome corrective to idealizations of the preoedipal: when a family is governed by the desires of an actual preoedipal child—unreconstructed hunger for the mother, unqualified aggression against rivals for her attention, rejection of difference and the outside world—mother-child relations lose their nurturing aspect and become self-consuming. In *Beloved*'s family circle, no one is finally left standing. On the other hand, a preoedipal child's vision of family relations offers important structural alternatives to the power imbalance of the oedipal family, which tilts toward respect and awe of the father's word, the father's work, and the father. The mother, seen by a preoedipal child as the sole source of comfort and bliss—or deprivation—occupies a central position of power. Authors who reach back for inspiration to fantasies from this period tend to create family patterns that celebrate not only the mother's love but the mother's work. And that respect for maternal work— both the work of love and the work of domestic maintenance—results in another structural innovation. Others in the family circle step up to share the no longer derogated work of nurturing and making things for the home. So in place of the patriarchal family system, where one mother is burdened with meeting everybody's needs while neglecting her own, a circle of mothering persons emerges, each nurturing the others. In Alcott's *Little Women* and Walker's *The Color Purple*, especially, adults as well as children get the emotional support that each needs to develop his or her autonomy and creativity. The rigid divisions of both gender and generation begin to disappear in a more fluid mutuality. Jo and Meg "feed their mother like dutiful young storks" (Alcott, 266), moving from the one-way mothering of patriarchal arrangements toward reciprocity. And in *The Color Purple* gender lines are effectively eclipsed as Harpo, Jack, and Albert discover their domestic skills and Shug, Celie, and Squeak pursue their careers. Such an extended family circle, in which men and women enjoy taking care of children and men and women engage in exciting, creative work, would, it seems, offer their children alternatives beyond the crippling choices of the oedipal stage. Rather than being forced into a narrowly defined gender identity embodied by a single inescapable parent, the children of such a family could choose to identify selectively with a range of traits represented by a spectrum of male and female persons.

My view of families is of course colored by my growing up in a white middle-class heterosexual family structured along traditional gender lines. Even calling the family patterns reflected in Alice Walker's and Toni Morrison's novels alternatives reveals my position as an outsider to African American culture. This qualification extends to my understanding of the fascinations of certain novels to female readers. If female readers of a particular culture share certain fantasies, it is because particular child-raising patterns, shared across a culture, embed common fantasy structures in their daughters. A reader brought up in a different culture, with different child-raising practices, might not, for example, respond with passionate attachment to the patriarchal family relations reflected in a *Jane Eyre*. (Alice Walker, for example, in spite of finding in *Jane Eyre* a companion and support for the difficulties of adolescence, says in *In Search of Our Mothers' Gardens* that she could not "identify completely with a Jane Eyre or her author" (8).) But if the more hopeful side of my thesis is also true, if through practices like reading one can expand past the limits of unconscious fantasy, then reading novels from other cultures can stretch our minds, enabling us to imagine and even desire something new.

1 Reading toward Change

1

A Patriarch of One's Own

Oedipal Fantasy and
Romantic Love in *Jane Eyre*

CAN READING CHANGE the reader? This book seeks answers to this question by exploring the interactions between the fantasy structures of literature and the unconscious fantasy structures of readers. A key question in understanding what goes on when we read then becomes: what is the nature of the unconscious? Is unconscious energy bound into fantasy patterns fixed in early childhood, so that readers can become attached only to those patterns in novels that repeat their own infantile fantasies? Norman Holland's *Dynamics of Literary Response* is based on this premise. Or is the unconscious composed of the "repressed of culture" (Cixous, "Castration," 52), that which is closed out of the culturally structured conscious mind of the subject, as Lacan, Kristeva, and Cixous affirm? In that case, unconscious desire would be capable of attachment to the alternatives offered by fiction—plots culturally forbidden or images of self and community that contradict family configurations.

Charlotte Brontë's *Jane Eyre* is in fact rich in fantasies that address the pleasures and frustrations of growing up in a patriarchal nuclear family structure: fantasies of heroic rebellion against tyrannical parents, fantasies based on the split between good mother (Miss Temple) and bad mother (Mrs. Reed), and fantasies of revenge on more powerful brothers and prettier sisters (John and Georgiana Reed). Perhaps most appealing, Rochester offers Jane the excitement combined with frustration and enigma that characterize father-daughter interactions in a traditionally structured nuclear family.[1] Against the pull of its oedipal love fantasy, *Jane Eyre* presents an equally passionate protest against patriarchal authority. The contradiction, I claim, mirrors a female reader's ambivalence toward her father. Part of *Jane Eyre*'s appeal lies in the way it allows female readers to work out fantasies of desire for the father and rage against him, fantasies that stem from the power and inaccessibility of a father in a traditional nuclear family structure and his ambiguous position with regard to his daughter's sexuality.

If we ask the question, what accounts for the enormous popularity of *Jane Eyre* among women readers? this overview of the novel's fantasy subtext appears to support Holland's contention in *The Dynamics of Liter-*

ary Response: "The writer expresses and disguises childhood fantasies. The reader unconsciously elaborates the fantasy content of the literary work with his own versions of these fantasies . . . it is the management of these fantasies, both his own and the work's, that . . . gives literary pleasure" (52). If we are looking to novels for an impetus to change, Holland's account of the unconscious pleasures of reading is discouraging: if unconscious energy is always already bound into fantasy patterns derived from our earliest experiences of desire or frustration in the nuclear family, there is no energy roving free through the unconscious to invest in novel patterns of living. We are all stuck—doomed to repeat. Reading can only deepen the channels of desire already stenciled into the unconscious by early family configurations. In *Jane Eyre* a reader's vicarious experience of passion for a distant, inaccessible, worldly man who comes and goes while the young female protagonist stays cooped up in his house can only recirculate desire through old memory traces of love for a mobile, authoritative, distant father. Reading *Jane Eyre*, then, must reinforce women's tendency to recreate in their adult lives the structures of power and desire they first experienced in their fathers' houses.

Yet readers have for the most part seen the novel as revolutionary rather than reactionary. As early as 1848 Elizabeth Rigby wrote, "The tone of mind and thought which has fostered . . . rebellion is the same which has also written *Jane Eyre*" (quoted in Gilbert and Gubar, *Madwoman*, 337). In our own times Adrienne Rich has written gratefully of the alternative fantasy patterns that *Jane Eyre* gave her—fantasies emphatically *not* provided by family and culture ("Temptations").

One way of confronting the differences in readers' responses to *Jane Eyre* is to examine the different messages the novel addresses to the unconscious and conscious registers of a reader's mind. The disparity between the two levels of meaning leads directly to an inquiry into the relation between reading, unconscious desire, and social change.

Jane is given to reasoning out the causes and effects of women's confinement to the domestic world in a rhetoric that addresses the reader's intellect; but on the level of concrete image and action Bertha burns down the imprisoning house. If Bertha's mime provides a vehicle for the unconscious rage of female readers who have felt hemmed in by patriarchal domestic structures while they were growing up, can Jane's reasoned argument for a wider field for women's endeavors then capture that released energy? Can unconscious rage be transformed into the desire for social change?

A second problem of reader response likewise engages the issue of transforming unconscious desire toward change. Adrienne Rich states that "the wind that blows through this novel is the wind of sexual equality—spiritual and practical" ("Temptations," 105). Yet inequality characterizes Jane's and Rochester's relationship throughout the novel; Rich is presumably referring to the conclusion, when the power balance is righted by a number of carefully constructed adjustments of Jane's re- sources relative to Rochester's. But readers do not just skip to the end: for more than two hundred pages, they vicariously experience Jane's attrac- tion to a powerful, authoritative, distant man who is twice her age. Per- haps, however, this evocation of a reader's original hierarchical model of heterosexual relations can awaken the desire attached to the old father- daughter pattern of relationship, making that energy available for invest- ment in the revised model of egalitarian and reciprocal heterosexual love that ends the novel. Perhaps, in other words, literary fantasies that involve readers on the passionate level of infantile desire do not enable them to revel in primitive fantasy merely, but offer the added pleasure of releasing the energy buried in old, restrictive fantasies and channeling it into new, potentially liberating ones.

Finally, the disparity between talk and image in the novel's conclusion seems to undermine this movement toward new and liberating fantasies: beneath the conscious commitment to a relationship between equals runs a constant stream of images that makes Rochester, despite his blindness, into a Samson, a Vulcan, a strong oak of a man that a girl can lean on. Do the conscious politics of Jane's egalitarian marriage then merely enable a reader to enjoy without guilt the old unconscious fantasy of attachment to a strong, dominant man?

What is certain is that some readers have been drawn to *Jane Eyre* by a fantasy pattern that has nothing to do with daughterly acquiescence to patriarchal figures. "I am not an angel, . . . I will be myself," Jane tells Rochester at intervals (262; see also 271, 272, 317–19); indeed she refuses to let anyone in a superior position define her. Rich claims to have been inspired in a lasting way by Jane's model of female integrity: "As a child, she rejects the sacredness of adult authority; as a woman, she insists on regulating her conduct by the pulse of her own integrity" ("Tempta- tions," 106). Jane Lazarre likewise credits *Jane Eyre* with giving her the courage to assert her own rebel identity in defiance of patriarchal injunc- tions to be a good girl (223).

Jane Eyre's passionate commitment to romantic love is equaled only by her passionate commitment to autonomy; like her readers, she wants to have it all. These impulses, in literature as in life, are in some ways contradictory. Does the one succumb to the other in the course of the novel? What fantasy structures do female readers finally take away with them from reading *Jane Eyre*? What can explain the especially passionate note in readers' statements of enthusiasm for the novel? Lazarre refers to *Jane Eyre* as "that adored book of my childhood" (223), and Rich reports that she was "carried away as by a whirlwind" when she first read it, in adolescence; she returned to it in her twenties, her thirties, and again in her forties, drawn by "some nourishment I needed and still need today" ("Temptations," 68). Harriet Martineau, nearly a century earlier, wrote in her autobiography, "I was convinced that it was by some friend of my own, who had portions of my childish experience in his or her mind" (cited by Moers, 99). What kinds of interaction take place between the fantasy structures of the novel and the unconscious fantasy structures of the reader to generate such acknowledgments of affinity?

Romantic Love and Rochester's Fatherly Ways

The most obvious reason for *Jane Eyre*'s appeal is the intensity with which Brontë imagines the passionate love between Jane and Rochester. Rochester, with his brooding moodiness and enigmatic passions, is modeled on the Byronic heroes that dominated romance in Brontë's time (Moglen, 26–33; 67–73); and Brontë in turn "can be credited with inventing many of the characters and situations of the popular romantic mythos" (Modleski, 46). So the patterns of desire in *Jane Eyre* can tell us something about the mythos of romantic love as it evolved in Western culture.

"Love in the western world," as Denis de Rougemont analyzes it, has at its heart a desire for desire. A lover's self-definition depends on the intensity of his or her feelings. Since possession takes the edge off passion, bringing it down to the level of everyday experience, what the lovers need is not so much one another's presence as one another's absence. Freud concurs: "The value the mind sets on erotic needs instantly sinks as soon as satisfaction becomes readily obtainable. Some obstacle is needed to swell the tide of the libido to its height" ("Debasement in Love," 187).[2] Where do we get such delight in frustration? Little boys cannot have their mothers, little girls cannot have their fathers: one's first heterosexual love object is unattainable. A girl's oedipal wish is to have her father all to herself forever, yet insuperable barriers prevent his being hers. The irreconcilable tension between the dream of union and the reality of separation in this first love provides a pattern for later passions, a blueprint for wanting someone you cannot have and thus maintaining intact the intensity of desire.

Inaccessibility, of course, allows the lover's imagination boundless scope, since the reality of the beloved is not there to check idealizing embellishments. Again, romantic love imitates a feature of patriarchal family arrangements that assign mothers the principal responsibility for child care, fathers the task of making a living. Since her father works outside the home, in a mysterious world a child can only imagine, her love for him is less embedded in actual contact than her feeling for her mother and is therefore likely to involve fantasy and idealization. In fact, a girl's relation to her father trains her to idealize a distant and mysterious figure whose absences she can fill with glamorous projections.[3]

The relations between Rochester and Jane reproduce in many obvious ways the power structure of father-daughter relations in the patriarchal family. Mastery of the wide world, freedom, and autonomy are Rochester's: "I have . . . roamed over half the globe, while you have lived quietly with one set of people in one house" (137). Jane remains enclosed in his house, subordinate to him and subject to his orders, in a position parallel to a girl's in her father's household. He hardly needs to remind us, as he does periodically, "I am old enough to be your father" (137, 142, 439). Far above Jane in rank and power, Rochester seems inaccessible. His mysterious absences and even more mysterious broodings over his hidden inner life endow him with the glamour of the unknown, making him a target for idealization.

The hierarchy of their relationship generates odd patterns of communication between them, patterns that echo the convolutions and contradictions of father-daughter relations. Among the behaviors that speak directly to the quirks of a female unconscious patterned by life in a patriarchal family are waiting, flirting, and the oedipal triangle.

First, waiting. Chodorow and Contratto have singled out the father's homecoming as the exciting event of a child's day (Chodorow, *Mothering*, 80, 195; Contratto, "Father Presence," 143).[4] Studies have shown that fathers tend to play more roughly and wildly with their children than mothers do, so the father's return may be marked by physical stimulation. The father arrives trailing clouds of glory from the exciting outside world, injecting excitement into the daily round of domestic life. The daughter's part, then, is to wait, for "novelty, stimulation, outsideness" (Benjamin, 86) to enter her life attached to a male figure. That is the woman's part too, in the romantic scenario: "In song and story the young man . . . slays the dragon, he battles giants: she is locked in a tower, a palace, a garden, a cave, she is chained to a rock, a captive, sound asleep: she waits" (de Beauvoir, 328). And when *he* enters, of course, "real life" begins. As in de Beauvoir's fairy-tale version of the romantic story, lover and waiting woman assume the active and passive roles first played out by father and daughter.

Rich points out that readers often remember *Jane Eyre* as if it began and ended with the love story, forgetting the overarching narrative of female development.[5] Brontë contributes to the isolation of the love story in the reader's mind by setting it off as if she were beginning anew. She wipes Jane's consciousness clean of past concerns, to make of her simply a woman waiting, in a setting stripped of physical and mental furniture:

> The ground was hard, the air was still, my road lonely. . . . the charm of the hour lay in its approaching dimness. . . . I was . . . in a lane noted for wild roses in summer, for nuts and blackberries in autumn . . . but whose winter delight lay in its utter solitude and leafless repose. If a breath of air stirred, it made no sound here; for there was not a holly, not an evergreen to rustle, and the stripped hawthorn and hazel bushes were as still as the white, worn stones. . . . Far and wide, on each side, there were only fields, where no cattle now browsed . . . in the absolute hush I could hear . . . thin murmurs of life [from the distant village of Hay]. . . . A rude noise broke on these fine ripplings and whisperings . . . a positive tramp, tramp; a metallic clatter, which effaced the soft wave-wanderings. (114–15)

This description elaborates what isn't there: no roses, no nuts, no blackberries, no holly, no evergreen, no leaves on the hawthorn and holly bushes, not even a rustle of sound—and, framing this picture of nothing, vacant fields where no cattle browse. Jane's mind is equally empty of present and past, focused on what is about to happen ("the approaching dimness"). The "absolute hush" is the hush of expectancy, and into the empty center of Jane's life rides, on cue, the man. He brings the distant promise of the world into the foreground, transforming the aerial whisperings of Jane's girlish imagination into the concrete noise of life. Building on a girl's daily experience of the excitement generated by the return of her father from the glamorous outside world, this sequence—of life suspended, followed by life intensified upon the entrance of the hero—encourages female readers to think of their time alone as mere prelude, perhaps even a necessary prelude. If they wait long enough, the right man will enter so that life can begin. This waiting robs women's time alone of meaning, save that of expectation.[6]

Rochester's bizarre behavior toward Jane—compounded of ambiguity, disguise, and deception—imitates a peculiarity of father-daughter interactions. The psychoanalytic account of female development stresses the importance of the father's role in diverting his daughter's erotic impulses, first oriented toward her mother, into heterosexual channels. The taboo on incest, however, prevents a father from following through. As Chodorow says, "The father's role is to shape his daughter's sexuality (without getting too involved in it)." He is "supposed to make himself available (while not making himself available) to his daughter" as her first heterosexual object of desire (*Mothering*, 139, 118). A father walking this tightrope of sexual flirtation is bound to give his daughter contradictory signals, and she is bound to be confused. Rochester enacts the same baffling behavior, again and again signaling his attraction to Jane only to put her off by insisting he means to marry Blanche Ingram—his equal in a social hierarchy that, echoing the oedipal configuration, enthrones the legitimate couple on a level high above Jane's reach. The hidden promise of Rochester's seductive behavior toward Jane fills Jane with the excitement mixed with bewilderment and resentment of a girl encountering again and again a mysterious promise she cannot read, a promise continuously deferred: "To speak truth, sir, I don't understand you at all" (140). "I don't understand enigmas" (199). "[His] discourse was all darkness to me" (141).

In response to Rochester's ambiguous come-ons, Jane alternates between fantasies of desire and strict self-inhibition. The oscillation between hope and guilt, between the illusion of intimacy and the irremediability of distance, puts the female reader identifying with Jane into a familiar bind. Indeed, if the reader were not familiar with the prolongation, over years, of such teasing behavior, the cruelty of Rochester's vacillation between attraction and withdrawal, lasting 180 pages as it does, would undermine his attractiveness.

A girl feels uneasy inveigling her father in part because the attention he gives her seems stolen from her mother. Bertha Mason is Rochester's legal wife, and her physical power and rage make her a satisfyingly ferocious mother avenger. Her presence also keeps the oedipal dream of marrying one's father from coming too true. As Norman Holland and Fredric Jameson point out, we can tolerate watching our primitive desires played out in art only if they are contained within strictly symbolic structures.[7] Otherwise the dread and guilt attached to archaic desires would overwhelm us. As Jane's wedding day approaches, her increasing anxiety and fragmentation reflect a female reader's malaise at the imminence of marriage with the father. On the night before the wedding Jane's fears explode from nightmare into reality as Bertha invades her room to tear up her wedding veil. The next day this symbolic prevention of marriage becomes actual as the discovery of Bertha's existence stops the wedding. Bertha's presence thus prevents oedipal desire from passing the point of safety, ensures its containment within the purely symbolic structure of a white wedding.

Rochester embeds the acknowledgment of his wife's existence in a flattering comparison:

> With a fierce cry . . . the clothed hyena rose up. . . . the maniac bellowed. . . . I recognized that purple face—those bloated features. . . . "That is *my wife*," said [Rochester] . . . and *this* is what I wished to have . . . this young girl. . . . Compare these clear eyes with the red balls yonder—this face with that mask—this form with that bulk."
> (295–96)

"This young girl," or the reader identifying with her, can rest secure with this unambiguous declaration of preference: the desired father considers *her* a fresh pure radiance, his wife a monster. Oedipal fantasy has it both ways: the father figure makes a clear statement of undivided love for his girl; yet the existence of Bertha prohibits his acting it out. Rochester continually refers to Jane as childlike—"a little sunny-faced girl with . . . dimpled cheeks and rosy lips" (260), "this one little English girl" (271)—thus reinforcing the parallel with a father's flattering attentions to his daughter.

How does Brontë manage a reader's oedipal anxiety in the end, when—Bertha dead—Jane returns to marry Rochester? Jane's adventures alone, after the discovery of Bertha, follow the pattern of a child leaving the parental home to establish her own place in the world, her own household. Jane leaves the patriarchal mansion governed by Rochester to find work and establish a family of her own. But unlike a girl who has to leave an adored father behind forever, Jane unexpectedly discovers that her new family (Diane, Mary, and St. John Rivers) are actually blood relations—cousins, or, as she affectionately calls them, "brothers and sisters" (387).

Brontë thus turns the newly established family unit into Jane's original one, so that Jane must leave it to marry an exogamous lover—Rochester after all. By thus manipulating the bloodlines of Jane's kinship chart Brontë effectively disguises what is after all the fulfillment of the oedipal dream: eternal and exclusive union with the father figure.

Illusion in various guises—Rochester's deception and ambiguity, her yearlong separation from him—sustains Jane's love for Rochester at the height of intensity. If, as I maintain, romantic love derives some of its features from father-daughter relations, it is no wonder that many of its excitements are based on illusion. A daughter's erotic love must necessarily remain a fantasy, but the attentions of a father responsible for guiding his daughter's erotic feelings into heterosexual channels continually feed the fantasy. If we think of the features of female romantic love that prolong its intensity—the glamour it gives to a distant or absent lover; the desire that hope and uncertainty impart to waiting for his return or for his call; the attraction of alternating seductive and rejecting moves; the increment of desire that a love triangle adds—all the fevered excitements of elusive love can be seen to have their source in the shadow play of love between father and daughter.

Romantic love is debilitating, then, not only because it encourages women to reproduce the dependency structure of their first heterosexual love, but because it encourages them to find again the excitement of desire in games that manipulate illusion based on a man who is in important ways not there. Chodorow's and Dinnerstein's solution to the damaging asymmetry of child-raising in Western culture—shared parenting—seems to offer one solution. If a father were *there* more, engaged in child-rearing in the same daily way as the mother is now, girls' model of heterosexual relationship would be less founded on idealization, more embedded in concrete daily interactions.

Burning down the House

Jane Eyre provides a satisfying vehicle for the other side of a girl's feelings for her father as well: the anger that must accompany her disappointment in not getting what she wants from him. According to Chodorow's retelling of the female developmental story, a girl turns toward her father for reasons beyond the need to find a heterosexual love object. Feeling hemmed in by the primary relationship with the mother that seems overwhelmingly close, she "looks for a symbol of her own autonomy and independence, and a relationship which will help her get this" (*Mothering*, 124). By allying herself with her father she hopes to share in his power, mobility, and independence—but she is disappointed on all counts. Fathers are more apt to gender-type their daughters than are mothers, according to the studies Chodorow cites; they discourage "masculine" assertiveness and reward their daughters for stereotypical feminine qualities such as coyness, submissiveness, and docility (124, 118–19, 138–39). Brontë's insistent imagery of female containment must appeal to female readers' buried frustrations at bumping up against the walls of parental gender definitions. And Jane's repeated, and repeatedly thwarted, attempts to gain autonomy must call up the anger associated with her female readers' similarly frustrated declarations of independence. Whenever Jane claims the right to her own identity, the patriarchy inevitably puts her in her place. Being locked into the Reeds' Red Room is only the most forcible of her confinements to the gender compartments of the patriarchal family.[8]

If Jane's verbal defiance of patriarchal restrictions presents the reader with an appealingly noble image of herself as brave resistance fighter, Bertha satisfies the reader's anger against patriarchal constraints on a more primitive level. Bertha raging in triumph on the battlements of the burning house, Rochester pinned beneath its falling pillars, must gratify a female reader's repressed rage against her father and the whole family structure that limits female aspiration.

This combination of Jane's verbal protest with Bertha's vivid action is only one example of the way Brontë uses Bertha and Jane to lodge a powerful protest against women's oppression at all levels of her reader's psyche. Bertha, appropriately preverbal (she groans, screams, mutters, and laughs, but never speaks) addresses the quirks of a female unconscious through images of painful incarceration and fiery revenge. Jane appeals to a reader's intellect through a reasoned analysis of how confinement in domestic structures damages women. While Bertha demonstrates, Jane articulates the causes of her madness. Brontë thus manages to appeal to the reader's unconscious fantasies of revenge while analyzing the social oppressions that cause them.[9]

A fairly simple example of their collaboration occurs when Jane makes her famous third-story speech against the confinement of women to domestic tasks. As she finishes elaborating the emotional damage that can result from "too rigid a constraint, too absolute a stagnation," Bertha's mad laughter rings out in confirmation (112–13).

Jane's long enumeration of the ills she would suffer as St. John's wife is a more complex example of how her commentary reflects on Bertha's ordeal. Brontë's hold on the reader's imagination comes, at least in part, from the cumulative effect of varying the same fantasy, now in Jane's experience, now in Bertha's. The dumb show of Bertha establishes the basic fantasy structure: being incarcerated in a patriarchal structure and burning it down in revenge. Jane's impassioned rhetoric—addressed to St. John, who wants her to be his wife—adds a layer of elaboration, a cogent articulation of the oppressions of wifehood implicit in Bertha's images:

> I . . . fancied myself in idea *his wife*. Oh! it would never do! As his curate, his comrade . . . my heart and mind would be free. I should still have my unblighted self to turn to: my natural and unenslaved feelings with which to communicate in moments of loneliness. There would be recesses in my mind which would be only mine, to which he never came; and sentiments growing there fresh and sheltered, which his austerity could never blight . . . but as his wife—at his side always and always restrained, and always checked—forced to keep the fire of my nature continually low, to compel it to burn inwardly and never utter a cry, though the imprisoned flame consumed vital after vital—*this* would be unendurable. (410)

It is as if Bertha's fire had found a voice to explain the suffering that passion turned inward by patriarchal prohibition inflicts on wives. When Jane imagines how her own fire would destroy her if confined by her husband's disapproval, she makes Bertha less a monster, more an emblem of *wife* (the italicized word recalls Rochester's term for Bertha, loaded with all the sarcasm of his bitterness). Jane's picture of physical annexation ("at his side always") and radical constraint ("always restrained, and always checked") similarly glosses Bertha's immobilization, presenting wifehood as the utter loss of freedom, physical and spiritual. Not even Virginia Woolf's Mrs. Dalloway could conjure up a more frightening vision of male dominance invading every room of the soul.

Part of the constriction Jane (and, one supposes, Bertha) feels, comes from the readiness of patriarchal authority both to define female propriety and to punish infractions of it. Just as Rochester banned Bertha for being "intemperate and unchaste," St. John unhesitatingly brands Jane's words "violent and unfeminine" (309, 415), punishing her with a spiritual isolation that is the counterpart of Bertha's solitary confinement. But allowing St. John to impose his definition of female virtue on her—"you are docile, diligent, disinterested, faithful, constant and courageous; very gentle, and very heroic"—makes Jane feel threatened too. Her desires, vague and diffuse before, "assumed a definite form under his shaping hand . . . my iron shroud contracted around me" (406). The metaphor extends the physical constraint of Bertha's prison cell to a deadly spiritual constriction. Jane's repetition of death images implies that both succumbing to patriarchal definitions and braving them imperil her survival as an individual:

> "If I were to marry you, you would kill me. You are killing me now." (415)
>
> All this was torture to me—refined, lingering torture. It kept up a slow fire of indignation, and a trembling trouble of grief, which harassed and crushed me altogether. I felt how—if I were his wife, this good man . . . could soon kill me. (413)

Jane brings out the full emotional weight of pain and indignation implicit in the image of Bertha's "slow fire." Bertha's death borrows meaning retrospectively from Jane's images of violent annihilation. Jane feels not only "banished," but "banned" (414) by St. John—deleted like Bertha from the rolls of patriarchy for transgressing patriarchal limits on female behavior.[10]

By thus building up, through Jane's elaboration of Bertha's primitive images, several layers of fantasy based on the common female experience of containment and repression, Brontë must evoke her reader's resentment at having to live hemmed in by patriarchal strictures and structures. Two interrelated questions arise. If a novel attaches a reader, as Holland says, by reflecting his or her infantile fantasies, does that mean that the novel simply reinforces existing unconscious fantasies, or can awakening the repressed emotion attached to old wounds make it available for investment in the new patterns the novel suggests? Does a reader simply revel in burning down Thornfield, or does destroying the patriarchal household clear a space in the reader's imagination, as in the novel, for the construction of a more egalitarian domestic structure? The second question has to do with what fantasy patterns *Jane Eyre* actually offers readers, what finally attaches them so powerfully to the novel. After the novel's imagery of wifehood as "iron shroud" has focused the reader's anger at the cramp of growing up female in a patriarchal family, does the novel channel that released energy into a vision of alternative living arrangements that would offer women more room for growth? Is reading *Jane Eyre* an imaginative experience that leads to change, or does it simply reinforce old patterns?

Alternative Forms of Community

Jane Eyre does present an alternative to patriarchal living arrangements in Moor House where, after leaving Rochester, Jane builds a family circle based on sisterly solidarity. After inheriting a fortune from her uncle, Jane becomes the mistress of Moor House, which she delights in making comfortable for her cousins, Mary and Diana. Her new family is utterly satisfying to her in its combination of emotional support and intellectual challenge: "What they enjoyed, delighted me; what they approved, I reverenced . . . thought fitted thought; opinion met opinion: we coincided, in short, perfectly" (351–52). Yet dreams of Rochester haunt her, "dreams where, amidst unusual scenes, charged with adventure . . . I still again and again met Mr. Rochester, always at some exciting crisis; and then the sense of being in his arms, hearing his voice, meeting his eye, touching his hand and cheek, loving him, being loved by him—the hope of passing a lifetime at his side, would be renewed, with all its first force and fire" (369). The Moor House episode is marked by Jane's joy in daily tasks—cleaning and refurbishing her home for her loved ones—but the new note of domestic realism cannot compete with the excitements of the old romantic dream. When Rochester calls, Jane returns to him without a backward glance.

A community that offers only respect and self-respect based on productive work and financial independence, along with family warmth, intellectual companionship, and emotional kinship, is not enough; passionate love is. The sequence is the message. To introduce the possibility of a community of women based on shared intellectual pleasures and mutual affection, only to reject it without question for a man, does not so much suggest an alternative as affirm the cultural myth that without a man a woman's life is incomplete. Mary and Diana marry in the end too, reinforcing the message of Jane's final felicity: what makes a woman *really* happy is love and marriage.

In the next to last chapter Jane returns to Rochester a new woman—that is, rich and independent. Since Bertha has burned down Thornfield, Jane and Rochester are free to build a new domestic structure from the ground up. At first they seem emotionally free too. In a bantering review of alternative structures, Rochester suggests—yet again!—that they could be father and daughter to each other, or nurse and patient (439). Jane boasts of her new independence: "I can build a house of my own close up to your door" (438). As an alternative to the hierarchy of patriarchal domesticity, the image of houses side by side embodies a notion of marriage as "parallel lives," in Phyllis Rose's phrase. Together, yet with a margin of separation, husband and wife would be equally autonomous, equally masters of their own houses.

This vision of a separate and equal love is but the creation of a moment's imaginative freedom, though. It is swept away almost immediately by the ideology of love that floods the last chapter.

> I have now been married ten years. I know what it is to live entirely for and with what I love best on earth. I hold myself supremely blest—blest beyond what language can express; because I am my husband's life as fully as he is mine. No woman was ever nearer to her mate than I am: ever more absolutely bone of his bone, and flesh of his flesh. I know no weariness of my Edward's society: he knows none of mine, any more than we each do of the pulsation of the heart that beats in our separate bosoms; consequently, we are ever together. To be together is for us to be at once as free as in solitude, as gay as in company. We talk, I believe, all day long: to talk to each other is but a more animated and an audible thinking. All my confidence is bestowed on him, all his confidence is devoted to me; we are precisely suited in character—perfect concord is the result. (454)

Karen Rowe claims that by the time Jane marries, Brontë has found the fairy-tale paradigm of romantic love wanting and developed in its place a broader concept of romance based on Shakespearean and Miltonic models: "The domestic realism of the reconciliation scene testifies to Jane's mature concept of romance" (89). But Jane's tone here is rhapsodic rather than domestic, reinforcing the fairy-tale message of the happy ending: if you marry the right man, you will live happily ever after. Jane has lived out this static happiness for ten years without a wrinkle in her bliss.

Jane's idyll of romantic fusion merges images of relationship recovered from oedipal and preoedipal times. Out of the frustration of not being able to have the father, oedipal fantasy spins a dream of plenitude. The father figure fills Jane's life, leaving no desire unsatisfied. But the content of this dream of unity—"bone of his bone, and flesh of his flesh"—cannot be traced to the ambivalence and distance between father and daughter; it must come from the remembered symbiosis of a girl's first relationship, with a mother whom the infant does not distinguish from herself. As Freud says in "Female Sexuality," the object of desire changes from mother to father in the oedipal stage, but "except for the change of her love-object, the second phase scarcely adds any new feature to her erotic life"

(225; see also 227). (Janice Radway has shown that popular romances feature a similar grafting of heterosexual motifs onto a preoedipal base. In the plots that prove most gratifying to female readers, the heroine captures a hero who can stand in for both mother and father: the hero's "spectacular masculinity" unexpectedly reveals a soft underside—an "extraordinary tenderness and capacity for gentle nurturance" [147].)

Jane Eyre thus shows how the potentially revolutionary energies of the preoedipal—which in the novels surveyed in chapter 10 lead to new family configurations—can be subsumed into oedipal fantasies that underwrite the patriarchal family. On the other hand, we can see the drawbacks of the preoedipal itself as an ideal. Merged with Rochester, "literally" his vision and his right hand (454), Jane cannot move away to pursue any autonomous activity whatsoever. Even child care must be shelved, Adèle packed off to boarding school, because "my husband needed all my [time and care]" (453).

Pointing to the terms of equality that Jane's economic independence and freedom of choice impose on her marriage to Rochester, Rich insists that the feelings expressed in Jane's celebration of marriage are not "the feelings of romantic love or romantic marriage" ("Temptations," 105). Indeed, as Maurianne Adams also argues, Brontë's acute awareness of social and economic issues makes her resolution more complicated than a simple fairy-tale ending.[11] Jane has acquired a fortune that makes her the economic equal of a Rochester diminished by the destruction of Thornfield; and Rochester's loss of hand and eye leaves no doubt that he needs Jane as much as she needs him. She is Rochester's "guide" as well as his "prop," "leading" him as well as "waiting on" him (451, 448): Brontë articulates precisely the degree of control in Jane's help that distinguishes it from her former service to her "master."[12] The balance of power has shifted so that their relationship no longer recapitulates, on the political surface, the asymmetries of a father-daughter relationship; yet on the personal level Rochester still embodies the patriarchal strength a girl can depend on.

> His form was of the same strong and stalwart contour as ever: his port was still erect, his hair was still raven black. . . . not in one year's space, by any sorrow, could his athletic strength be quelled or his vigorous prime blighted. But in his countenance, I saw a change . . . that reminded me of some wronged and fettered wild beast or bird, dangerous to approach. . . . The caged eagle . . . might look as looked that sightless Samson. (434)

This is not a Philip Wakem, whose crippled helplessness evokes in Maggie Tulliver pitiful images of "wry-necked lambs" (Eliot, *Mill*, 191). An eagle, later "a royal eagle," or a lion (439, 441), Rochester is still commanding, still a king beneath the metamorphoses that but enhance his animal vitality. Human analogues, too, contribute to the impression of virile strength: Rochester is a Samson (434), "a Vulcan . . . brown, broad-shouldered" (389). In perhaps their most telling metaphorical exchange Rochester, comparing himself to the lightning-struck chestnut tree in his garden, hesitates to ask Jane, "a budding woodbine," to twine around him. He is not a ruin, Jane assures him, but a strong tree, "green and vigorous. Plants will grow about your roots . . . they will lean towards you, and wind round you, because your strength offers them so safe a prop" (391). A girl need not learn to stand on her own two feet if she can drape her sweetness around a man's oak-like strength. Brontë's images, appealing directly to the level of unconscious fantasy, repeat a familiar duo of paternal strength and graceful girlhood, belying the reassuring surface fantasy of a new balance of power.

What has become of the fantasy of autonomy and adventure in the wide world that Jane used to hold dear? Brontë projects it onto a male figure. While Jane melts into passionate union, St. John explores the world alone: "resolute, indefatigable pioneer . . . amidst rocks and dangers . . . he labors for the race" (455). *Jane Eyre* ends, it seems, with a confirmation of Freud's assertion that men and women dream differently: "In young women erotic wishes dominate the phantasies almost exclusively, for their ambition is generally comprised in their erotic longings; in young men egoistic and ambitious wishes assert themselves plainly enough alongside their erotic desires" ("Creative Writers," 147). Freud probably accepted only erotic fantasies in women as normal because he defined normal women as passive, and romantic love, as we have seen, gives woman the passive role; women's ambitious fantasies Freud dismissed as "penis envy," consigning their possessors to the pathological condition of "masculinity complex" ("Female Sexuality," 230; "A Case of Homosexuality," 169; "An Example of Psycho-analytic Work," 193). Freud's establishment of a passive norm for female fantasy, like his description/prescription of passivity as the norm for female personality structure, has the cultural effect of limiting possibilities for women.

The ending of *Jane Eyre*, with its strict division between St. John's quest and Jane's love story, reinstates the sex roles that the whole novel has demonstrated to be painfully restrictive. This parceling out of life's possibilities along rigid gender lines in effect mimics the "successful" conclusion of the oedipal struggle, the moment when the libido of the child is structured according to the position of desire appropriate to his or her gender (Rubin, 195–96), the "little woman" oriented toward love and relationship, the "little man" toward mastery of the world. As a mirror of female development, then, *Jane Eyre* reflects the whole discouraging sequence of oedipal conflict and resolution. Jane's insistence on her own integrity, autonomy, and self-definition parallels the demand for autonomy in the early stages of the Oedipus complex, when, according to the feminist account, a girl turns to her father to gain a measure of his autonomy and power. When she finds in her father a mediator of social expectations who "bribes" his daughter with love and tenderness to renounce active and aggressive tendencies, she is persuaded to give up the position of demanding subject and to become the object of her father's love (Deutsch, 251–52; quoted in Chodorow, *Mothering*, 139). Jane Eyre mimics this oedipal resolution, as she relinquishes the demand for autonomy and wide-ranging activity to become what Rochester makes of her, the object of his affections: "Literally I am (what he often called me) the apple of his eye" (454).[13]

To return now to my opening questions: what fantasy structures do girls take away from reading *Jane Eyre*? and what accounts for readers' lifelong passionate attachment to the novel? One cannot ignore the testimony of readers like Rich and Lazarre, who say that *Jane Eyre* gave them alternative ideals of female autonomy and female solidarity. Jane's refusals to be contained within gender categories, in the face of countless pressures and temptations to accept a subordinate role, can inspire her reader with a determination to make the fantasy of defiant autonomy her own.

But I suspect that many readers, including feminists like myself, are attached to *Jane Eyre* because it reflects so vividly our own ambivalence. On the level of lucid and compelling rhetoric, Brontë advocates feminist ideals, arguing against patriarchal institutions that confine and warp women's energies and for an open field for women's ambitions; yet underneath flows unchecked a passionate desire for that most restrictive of all female spaces, the bubble of bliss promised by romantic love. Intellectual conviction is notoriously ineffectual in changing what is deeply felt—not only in Brontë but in her readers as well. A text whose conscious ideals of female autonomy and sexual equality are sabotaged by images of symbiosis with a strong oak of a man probably reflects the contradictions of women who, like Brontë, have grown up in a family structure dominated by a strong father but wish to construct their lives differently.[14] If the text mirrors readers' conflicts between high ideals and unregenerate unconscious desire, however, it does nothing to move readers beyond that impasse, toward change. Instead, the ideologically correct structure of an egalitarian marriage enables readers to enjoy without guilt the old fantasy of having one's patriarch all to oneself.

2

Down the Yellow Brick Road

Unconscious Reading Processes and Change

MY ANALYSIS OF *Jane Eyre* shows novel-reading interlocking with oedipal patterns to reinforce fantasies in which a woman's happiness depends on the attentions of a loving man, so that her own autonomous activities recede to the margins of existence. Might the reverse also be true? That is, could a girl reader caught in the dislocations of the oedipal family turn to fantasies in literature to put the self back in the center of things and find excitement attached to what a girl does for herself rather than to the presence of a man? *Little Women*, *The Wizard of Oz*, and *Heidi* offer fantasies of autonomy that contradict the scripts for proper girlish behavior in families organized by conventional sex roles.[1] Can a girl reader make these images of autonomy her own, integrate them into her store of unconscious fantasies, even if they contradict the family-patterned fantasies already absorbed from early childhood experience?

My speculations on what happens when a girl brought up in a male-centered family reads *Jane Eyre* imply that reading on the unconscious level is profoundly conservative: Brontë's surface advocacy of a change in patriarchal relations is undermined by the imagery of male dominance that addresses a reader's unconscious fantasies of union with a father figure, returning unconscious energy to containment in the structures of desire that reproduce the skewed power relations of the nuclear family. I think we have to admit, with Norman Holland, that the unconscious is at least in part patterned by fantasies that reflect a child's earliest relational experiences in the nuclear family. But the unconscious may be more complicated and contradictory than Holland's theory allows. His notion of a static unconscious, with energy contained within a set number of fantasy structures that do not change throughout life, implies a static reading process in which readers *always* "recreate the text to make it an expression of [their] own personal . . . identity, matching defenses and expectations to the text so as to project [their] fantasies into it" ("Gothic," 231). If we shift from a fixation on unconscious structures to consider unconscious

processes, we can perhaps do justice to the dynamic nature of the unconscious and to the possibility that reading can lead to an unconscious
attachment to *new* fantasy structures. The primary processes that govern
the unconscious—condensation and displacement—work in a fundamentally different way from the secondary processes of the conscious mind. By
imagining how primary processes intersect texts, I set out here a theory of
how the unconscious can both process and integrate into the machinery of
unconscious fantasy the revolutionary messages embedded in the kinetic
and visual imagery of *Little Women, Heidi,* and *The Wizard of Oz.*

Freud distinguished sharply between the "thing-presentation" by means
of which unconscious thinking operates and the "word-presentation" that
characterizes conscious thinking. "The unconscious presentation is the
presentation of the thing alone," whereas "the conscious presentation
comprises the presentation of the thing plus the presentation of the word
belonging to it" ("The Unconscious," 201). In their extended discussion of how the "language of the unconscious" functions, contemporary
French theorists Jean Laplanche and Serge Leclaire similarly conclude
that "at the level of unconscious language there are only images" (161).
Unconscious language "can by no means be assimilated to our 'verbal'
language. The 'words' that compose it are elements drawn from the realm
of the imaginary—notably from visual imagination—but promoted to
the dignity of signifiers. The term *imago* . . . corresponds fairly well . . .
to these elementary terms of unconscious discourse" (162). Analysts
have been basing their practice on this hypothesis since the time of Freud
and Breuer, as Mardi Jon Horwitz remarks: "They simply told patients
to think in visual images rather than words. . . . Even without such specific instructions, the emergence of previously repressed memories or fantasies is often in the form of image representation" (81). In recent research on the brain, the model of mental functioning has changed, but
the distinction between image processing and word processing remains:
"brain researchers have told us that images belong to the right hemisphere of the brain, while speech is controlled by the left hemisphere"
(Ragland-Sullivan, 142). Regardless of the model of the mind that is
current, then, the distinction between word processing and image processing persists; and the sense that the two are radically different continues
to be projected in terms of a topographical division. Though Freud's and
Ragland-Sullivan's statements perhaps oversimplify the complex interaction between various parts of the brain, the simplicity of Freud's division
between "thing-presentation" and "word-presentation" is useful in draw-

ing an initial distinction between conscious and unconscious reading processes.

If the primary processes that govern the unconscious operate by means of concrete representations—"thing-presentation"—they will be more active when a reader is processing descriptions of concrete objects or actions described in physical detail. Secondary processes, primarily verbal and obedient to the rules of logic and language, will be dominant in processing abstract explanations. The objects that recur in children's literature—the bread and cheese that Heidi eats in Alpine meadows, or the yellow brick road down which Dorothy walks resolutely, or the attic room where Jo writes—will trigger primary processes, while the parental homilies on ladylike behavior in *Little Women*, or what Dorothy *says* about her harmless and helpless ways, will be processed primarily on the conscious level. One may object, of course, that there *are* no visual images on the page, only words; thus the lexical items that go into a description of a physical object are not different in kind from the lexical items that make up an abstract speech. But if the reader will process the sentence before last, she or he will see that some signifiers evoke pictures in the mind and some do not. Persons "see" an object like the yellow brick road by means of a mental representation called up by the words, whereas a purely expository sentence evokes no such visual image in the mind.[2]

In some novels that have been popular through many generations of child readers, vivid images of female power in action contradict set speeches that repeat lessons in feminine decorum. For example, the dutiful daughters of *Little Women* respond to their father's exhortations to self-effacement and self-sacrifice with pious resolutions: "Amy sobbed out, 'I *am* a selfish girl! but I'll truly try to be better.' . . . 'I'll try to be what he loves to call me, "a little woman" and not be rough and wild, but do my duty here [at home],' . . . said Jo" (29–30). But the body language of Jo's consistently self-assertive movements invites the reader to identify with a whole range of "masculine" expressiveness and initiative and self-expansion and "wildness" that the gender ideology of the verbal surface outlaws:

Jo put her hands in her pockets and began to whistle. (21)

Jo tossed up her napkin. (27)

Jo choked in her tea and dropped her bread, butter side down, on the carpet, in her haste to get at the treat. (27)

Jo began to dig paths with great energy. (75)

going to the back entry window, [Jo] got out upon the roof of a low porch, swung herself down to the grassy bank, and . . . hailed a passing omnibus. (202)

Perhaps *Little Women* continues its long-lived popularity because its contradictions mirror the internal contradictions of its readers. Girls, whose "self-esteem becomes hostage" to the gender schema of their culture as early as age three (Bem, 355), no doubt feel more comfortable and free from anxiety if they can identify with protagonists who are proper young girls; but the same readers' unconscious desires, repressed because they do not fit cultural stereotypes, find in the novel's kinetic subtext vehicles for their expression. But here I am positing an unconscious different from the repository of patriarchal structural relations implied by Anglo-American Freudian critics like Holland. French theorists imagine instead an unconscious that contains "the repressed of culture" (Cixous, "Castration," 52). To summarize the simultaneous construction of speaking subject and unconscious posited by Lacan (and more fully explicated in the Introduction to this book): when a child enters language, repression establishes the unconscious. That is, the subject is split between a speaking subject—constructed by the positions of language and subject to the cultural values they inscribe—and an unconscious composed of signifiers attached to drive energies that language cannot accommodate. The very constitution of the unconscious thus defines it as that which exceeds linguistic structures and hence escapes cultural constraints.[3]

If a female reader is thus split between an ideologically constructed conscious self and a heterogeneous unconscious, we can begin to understand the appeal of stories like *The Wizard of Oz* and *Little Women*. The part of the reader that genuinely wants to be a good girl—the conscious, socially constructed speaking subject—becomes involved in decoding abstract speeches that enjoin a coherent gender ideology. But underneath, visual and kinetic images offer pictures to the unconscious mind of "what has been forbidden to women . . . anger, together with the open admission of the desire for power and control over one's life (which inevitably means accepting some degree of power and control over other lives)" (Heilbrun, *Writing*, 13).[4] Dorothy in *The Wizard of Oz*, for example, is in terms of straight "word-presentation" a model of feminine docility and perfect goodness: "Dorothy was an innocent, harmless little girl . . . and she had never killed anything in her life" (20). But on the level of concrete action she expresses both power and anger, killing not just one but two witches and thus "freeing" whole countries "from bondage" (154). On the level of conscious self-definition, a young reader can feel secure identi-fying with Dorothy's self-presentation: "I am Dorothy, the Small and Meek. I have come to you for help," she says to the Wizard (120). In direct contrast to this self-portrait of female helplessness, the yellow brick road offers—over and over—a kinetic and spatial equivalent of autonomy to the reader's primary processes: Dorothy walks down the open road competent and self-sufficient, headed toward her own self-chosen goals and carrying everything she needs for survival packed into the basket on her arm. What Dorothy does, as opposed to what she says, appeals to a female unconscious that contains what is left out of family stories of women's lives: power, self-assertion, autonomy.

How do we reconcile this picture of a heterogeneous unconscious with Holland's idea that unconscious energy is contained within family-based (and therefore culture-bound) structures? Hélène Cixous describes the unconscious in what seem to me appropriately contradictory terms: "The unconscious is always cultural," she says, "and when it talks it tells you your old stories"—cultural stories, I think she means, like the tale of female passion swirling about the figure of an elusive man. But the uncon-scious also "consists of the repressed of culture. . . . And it's also always shaped by the forceful return of a libido that doesn't give up that easily, and also by what is strange, what is outside culture, by a language which is a savage tongue" (52). Along with the "old stories" of the culture, then, the unconscious contains voices excluded from the cultural scenarios that dictate gender-specific roles for men and women. Denied cultural expres-sion, these repressed energies are presumably in search of "new stories," vehicles to give them form.

In addition, Cixous makes room in the unconscious for a libido that won't give up, a flow of desire not bound to social structures but free to seek out the new. What Holland's theory leaves out, finally, is the subversive nature of desire. His model of a reader crystallized around "an unchanging inner form or core of continuity" that remains recognizably the same through all its variations ("Unity," 814) prevents his imagining a site of contradictory energy in the reader, a source of desire for something new—even something revolutionary that might overturn the "identity theme." Desire for a kind of living that one has not yet experienced is after all a primary motivation for reading novels in the first place.

Pinchas Noy offers a precise analytical equivalent for Cixous's wandering libido. He claims that the primary processes perform the work of assimilating new experience into the ongoing structures of the self. Noy's theory affords one answer to my opening question: can readers take in fantasy structures from literature and make them their own? Noy claims that infants integrate experience into the building blocks of an ongoing self through condensation and displacement; these primary processes then continue throughout life to integrate new experiences into the self-system. We can assume, then, that material in a form adapted to primary-process thinking will be more easily incorporated into the fantasy structures of the unconscious than material that addresses the secondary processes of the rational mind.

Literary images, when they are effective, do some of the work of condensation for the reader. In condensation a single image compresses many meanings. The image of the yellow brick road, for instance, speaks the language of primary process: "It did not take her long to find the [road] paved with yellow brick. Within a short time she was walking briskly toward the Emerald City, her silver shoes tinkling merrily on the hard, yellow roadbed. The sun shone bright and the birds sang sweet" (Baum, 31). Condensation pulls together pleasurable sensations (bright space, cheerful sounds, pleasurable movement) with a multiplicity of ideas (the attraction of venturing into the unknown, the satisfaction of doing something on one's own) and envelops them in the overriding pleasure of autonomous movement. When the reader encounters that image again, as it reappears over and over in the text, she performs her own condensing operations, fusing "feelings, ideas, memories" (Noy, 175) into a single form that she can then assimilate to give body to her own suppressed yearnings for autonomy and mobility.

In displacement, an emotion connected to one idea is transferred to another idea. Freud emphasizes that energy in the unconscious is mobile, so that the psychic energy invested in one object may be fully removed and committed to another (Laplanche and Pontalis, *Language*, 123). In terms of the reading process, displacement means the total shift of an emotional charge from one situation to another—a process activated by the repetition, with variation, of a particular image.

In *Jane Eyre* the room functions as such a trigger for unconscious displacement: the various rooms in the novel are connected not by the plot, but by the similar emotional charge that invests them. The Red Room into which Jane is locked as a child, the room next to Bertha's where Rochester locks Jane in to tend the injured Mason, and finally the room where Bertha is caged are connected not by logic, but by the emotions that fill them: fear, hysteria, madness, claustrophobia. Jane becomes schizoid with fear in the Red Room haunted by her dead uncle; Bertha is maddened by solitary confinement. Underlying the frenzy of both women is rage at being imprisoned by the "master"—"master John" in Jane's case, the "master" Rochester in Bertha's—for having transgressed the limits of proper female behavior. The reader encounters the Red Room and the den where Bertha rages at a distance of some 250 pages, and within the context of entirely different chains of events; she/he would be hard put to make conscious connections between them. But the repeated image of spatial containment and the recurrence of the hysteria that fills that confining space lead the reader to make unconscious pathways of association between the two rooms, transferring the charge of rage and dread from one imprisoning room to the other. Thus though there is no overt connection between Bertha and Jane, unconscious scanning connects them. By displacing feelings of dread and anger from one room to the other, the reader can integrate the room into the operations of her own unconscious fantasy life, where it may serve as a symbol to contain repressed feelings of rage at her own confinement to the narrow rooms of patriarchal gender structures.[5]

The unconscious can pick up details such as the disparate rooms of *Jane Eyre*—fragments that are not woven into the conscious texture of a novel—because the unconscious lacks the conscious mind's desire for coherence. The conscious mind's drive to make words cohere into meaningful patterns is described by Wolfgang Iser as "consistency-building." A reader selects, from the multitude of items that a novel offers, the details that form a coherent gestalt. Progressing through the text, the reader is forced to take into account other items that bombard this pattern; so the gestalt must be continually reformed (*Act*, 121–29). But always "the reader will be in search of [consistency]" ("Reading," 58), dismissing the details that do not match the overall design. The unconscious operates according to no such imperative. Its vision is "syncretistic," according to Anton Ehrenzweig, capable of grasping "in a single undivided act of comprehension data that to conscious perception would be incompatible" (*Hidden*, 32). It may be that through unconscious scanning readers can pick up fragments repressed from the author's consciousness that turn up as anomalous fragments in the text. Freud says that "everyone possesses in his own unconscious an instrument with which he can interpret the utterances of the unconscious of other people" ("Obsessional Neurosis," 320).[6] A reader might thus connect with subversive elements in the text, transmitted from author's unconscious to reader's unconscious without ever passing through the ideological sieve of their conscious minds. One suspects that this is true of the room symbol in *Jane Eyre*: Brontë wrote the novel at white heat, in three weeks, and her writing process has been described as "trancelike," "almost . . . suspending consciousness" (Gérin, 16). If she did not connect Bertha's plight with Jane's consciously, it would seem that she did so unconsciously. A reader can similarly string the disparate rooms together through unconscious scanning.

It would be difficult to argue that *Heidi* is any way a divided text adapted to the needs of a reader split between an ideological superstructure and a base of subversive unconscious desire. The novel is univocal in celebrating young girls' rights to autonomy, power, and freedom. Nevertheless *Heidi* offers readers' primary processes the opportunity to assimilate vivid images of female autonomy. The frequent meals of fresh milk, bread, and cheese in *Heidi* condense autonomy with nurture. Heidi first eats bread and cheese on the evening of her arrival at her grandfather's house, so the meal is first associated with the egalitarian arrangements of their household. (Heidi contributes as much as her grandfather to their common meal, and he praises her for acting on her own initiative.) Then each day she eats bread and milk and cheese outside, on the Alpine meadows. The unvarying simplicity of this meal seems to condense into comestible form the feelings of joyous autonomy associated with being alone and free in the mountain air; but these pleasures of independence are always grounded in the support of the paternal figure who milks the goats and makes the cheese and bread that sustain Heidi when she is on her own. Because this eating of bread and cheese recurs—seemingly on every third or fourth page—the reader is invited to displace the pleasure and nurturance associated with independence from one meal to another, assimilating through that displacement an oral equivalent of autonomy. In Freud's account of condensation, "the energies which have been displaced along different associative chains accumulate upon the idea which stands at their point of intersection" (Laplanche and Pontalis, *Language*, 83). The powerful attraction of Heidi's mountain meals stems from the condensation of two strains of emotion: the joy associated with Heidi's freedom of movement, and the security associated with the grandfather's different kind of nurturing.

The images of autonomy in *Heidi*, *Little Women*, and *The Wizard of Oz* are fused with vivid bodily movement. For example, Heidi is introduced through an action that dramatizes the overturn of gender rules and indeed of all civilized inhibitions. Walking up the Alm with her aunt on the way to her grandfather's house, Heidi wears "two or three dresses, one over the other, and a big red cotton scarf round her neck . . . her feet were lost in heavy hobnailed shoes" (4). The springy movements of the goats and their goatherd give her a better idea:

> She said not a word, but gazed first at Peter, who jumped about without any difficulty in his bare feet and light trousers, then at the goats with their small, slender legs climbing still more easily over bushes and stones and steep rocks. Suddenly the child sat down on the ground and in great haste pulled off her shoes and stockings; then she stood up again, took off her thick, red scarf, unfastened her Sunday frock, quickly took that off, and began to unhook her everyday dress. . . . there the child stood in her light underclothes with delight, . . . she laid them all in a neat little pile, and, by Peter's side, jumped and climbed after the goats as easily as any in the whole company. (9)

With the hampering clothes go inhibitions on Heidi's mental assertiveness: "Feeling so free and light, Heidi began to talk with Peter, and he had all sorts of questions to answer" (12). Kinetic reminders of this scene of liberation dot the pages of Heidi's sojourn in the mountains. The reader is called upon to displace sensations of assertive action associated with Heidi's autonomy in the mountains from one page to another: "Heidi and the goats skipped and jumped along merrily by his side" (14); "Heidi jumped here and there and shouted for joy" (28); "Heidi in her delight kept running back and forth" (58).

As we have seen, Dorothy walks with a similarly exuberant freedom of movement down the open road. And Jo escapes female containment (the family home) by climbing out a window, shinnying down a tree, and hailing a bus, acting out her determination to make a mark on the public world by getting her story published. These images condense ideas of self-determination with energetic movement. Does the reader take in kinetic images in a different way from visual images? And does the particular quality of kinetic memory give these images, once recalled, a push toward actualization in the life of the reader?

I. A. Richards hypothesizes that our muscles make incipient adjustments to sensual stimuli encountered in reading. If in everyday life perception triggers a muscular response, he says, the shadow of a perception experienced in reading must trigger the shadow of a muscular response. Our muscles prepare for action, even though we do not complete the action while reading (107–13). Our bodies might then repeatedly make the same adjustments when we read and reread the oft-repeated notations of Jo running or Dorothy walking or Heidi leaping from rock to rock.

Mardi Jon Horwitz describes a system of information storage even more primitive than visual memory as "enactive thought." Apparently the body has a memory: infants learn from recording information about their bodily responses to particular events, and when those events recur they can reproduce the original muscular impulses. More germane to my purpose here, children also mimic the muscular responses of other people, remember them, and can later reproduce them (Horwitz, 78). They thus retain "motor knowledge" of others, so to speak, and can express information about others by reproducing their bodily gestures. Identification with others can thus take the form of bodily imitation. Heidi, for example, wordlessly absorbs the movements of Peter and the goats in the passage cited above and then reproduces them. If we are capable of recording and reproducing with our muscles the information gained from watching other people move, then perhaps a reader's repeated muscular responses to Jo's vivid "tomboy" movements or Heidi's skipping or Dorothy's walking inscribe memory traces that carry the sense of autonomous action in kinetic form. Such a bodily memory, whose content is recorded along with motor impulses toward its expression, might give its recall a physical immediacy, even a muscular pressure toward enactment in the life of the reader, that an abstract conception of autonomy could never transmit.

Pinchas Noy's work makes it possible to postulate precise mechanisms for readers' introjection of new fantasy structures. But it is only if we combine Noy's theory with Lacan's and Cixous's notion that the unconscious is the home of desires that cannot find expression within language and social formations that we can imagine how reading might change the reader. Repressed desires for power and assertiveness—desires baffled by cultural stereotypes of feminine passivity—meet the vivid kinetic and visual images of female power in the "thing" subtext of novels. When these images recur, they trigger the displacing and condensing operations that enable the reader to assimilate new fantasy patterns into the unconscious.[7]

Once a reader has found a kinetic or spatial image that meets her need, desire will likely propel her to reread the novel and hence to encounter more opportunities for displacing the emotional charge from one reading of a significant image to the next. Repetition is finally the key to integrating new material. Thus young female readers *can* make fiction's patterns of autonomy their own.

3

The Two Stories
of *Little Women*
Oedipal Prescriptions,
Preoedipal Creativity

LITTLE WOMEN TELLS two different stories: one is linear and developmental, the story of four sisters' struggle to grow from the selfish, willful girls they are in chapter 1 to the unselfish, industrious little women of the ending.[1] This story is governed by the Words of the Father: his letter, read aloud by Marmee, sets the goals for their spiritual journey in chapter 1; and in the next to last chapter he announces their arrival at the developmental goal of "little women" with formal speeches congratulating each in turn. The story is sequential, pegged to stages that follow each other in a progression identified—through numerous allusions—with the moral quest of *Pilgrim's Progress*. We realize from the abstractions of chapter headings taken from Bunyan's tale that, viewed from the perspective of the absent father, the events of the novel make up a spiritual journey toward a clearly defined goal: "I know they will remember all I said to them, that they . . . will do their duty faithfully, fight their bosom enemies bravely, and conquer themselves so beautifully, that when I come back to them I may be fonder and prouder than ever of my little women" (28). The spiritual goal is maturity defined exclusively in terms of gender. Individual differences play no part in this view of development: the girls are lumped together as "they" and expected to attain the uniform identity of "little women" by suppressing "bosom enemies" that turn out to be the enemies of feminine self-denial and humility: vanity, selfishness, envy, pride, and "wildness" (30).

Since Mr. March is absent for most of the novel (he is away at the front, a chaplain serving northern soldiers in the Civil War), his words fall on his daughters' ears with the abstract authority of the Law of the Father, laying down rules for social conformity. His language is that of the symbolic order, conforming his daughters to the shape of the gender niches that await them in a preexisting social order. The end of the father's story, when he congratulates them on having vanquished all the rebellious idiosyncrasies of creative individuality, is the end of the oedipal story: "When the child leaves the Oedipal phase, its libido and gender identity have been organized in conformity with the rules of the culture which is domesticating it" (Rubin, 189).

The other story has the shape not of linear development, but of circular stasis. The circle of love that joins Marmee and her daughters can only be repeated: development is not a relevant concept because this circle already contains plenitude. So time can only bring loss. The desired end of the developmental story—the emergence of the "little women" as "good wives"—seems like death: Meg's marriage makes "a hole in the family" (Alcott, 271), just as Beth's death does.[2] As opposed to the linear unfolding of a quest through time, this story centers on "maternal space," the space filled by the unity of mother and sisters. Even as the disembodied words of the father fall on their obedient ears, the female family physically opposes a different configuration to the father's model of female development within the patriarchal family: "'Now come and hear the letter.' They all drew to the fire, mother in the big chair, with Beth at her feet, Meg and Amy perched on either arm of the chair, and Jo leaning on the back" (28). (In most editions, this circle of bodies materializes in an illustration.) The girls continually return to the "nest" of mother and sisters, an event conveyed to the reader by repeated tactile images of warmth and physical contact.

Although the father's letter occupies the center of chapter 1, that chapter ends with a song. It merges past and present in opposition to the father's direction of time to future goals, and it celebrates the merging of voices in an enveloping harmony that contrasts with the disembodied words of the paternal letter dropping into the void.

> At nine they stopped work, and sang, as usual, before they went to bed. . . . They had always done this from the time they could lisp "Crinkle, crinkle, 'ittle 'tar," and it had become a household custom, for the mother was a born singer. The first sound in the morning was her voice, as she went about the house singing like a lark; and the last sound at night was the same cheery sound, for the girls never grew too old for that familiar lullaby. (32)

The day is not envisioned as a unit in a sequence unrolling toward a future goal, but as a totality rounded by the mother's voice, which starts and ends the day. That voice also takes the girls back to their first lullaby, negating linear development. Time past is the same as time present in terms of the maternal voice that encircles them.

The two stories—the father's linear one, marching in so determinedly straightforward a line that it leaves out all the rich concrete details of the girls' actual lives, and the circular one, composing plenitude from the daily return to the maternal nest—correspond to two family structures. The one is rigid, hierarchical: the father and mother hand down gender directives from on high to obedient children. The other is reciprocal, blurring the differences between parental and filial roles in a mutual give-and-take. Broadly speaking, one family organization corresponds to an oedipal perception of the family, the other recalls preoedipal interactions. Marmee plays the central part in both dramas, reflecting the double image of the mother "beclouded by simultaneous fantasies of omnipotence and impotence" (Keller, 110–11) that haunts both the personal and the cultural unconscious of societies whose child-rearing practices are based on exclusive mothering. On one level of the text—the level of images—she embodies the omnipotence of the mother imagined by a preoedipal child, her presence radiating light and life to her children (163). But when Marmee speaks she is most often the subservient oedipal mother, no longer a glowing subject in her own right but an adjunct to her husband—his mouthpiece, passing on his directives. Not only does she read his letter aloud, but in that role she continues to generate oedipal role prescriptions in a "tone and language eerily identical with" her husband's, as Patricia Spacks has remarked (121).

The two levels of family interaction address the reader in different ways. The Words of the Father (and his wife's echoes) fall from above, disembodied: they engage the reader in processing signifiers toward the social conventions that underlie them. The images that evoke a preoedipal level of communication are tactile, addressing the reader's body in ways that call up memories from an earlier—and potentially antipatriarchal—layer of experience. Multiple tactile verbs convey the attractions of active physical intimacy with the maternal body:

Beth nestled up to her [mother]. (45, 163)

[Beth] nestled close into the loving arms about her, feeling that the hungry longing was satisfied at last. (266)

Amy sat in her mother's lap and told her her trials, receiving consolation and compensation in the shape of approving smiles and fond caresses. (267)

Jo's only answer was to hold her mother close. . . . [Jo] leaned over her [sleeping] sister, softly stroking the wet hair scattered on the pillow. . . . Amy opened her eyes and held out her arms. . . . Neither said a word, but they hugged one another close. (121)

[Beth] cuddled her sister's feet with a motherly air. (151)

These descriptions of physical closeness give the "home-love and happiness" of the female circle (80) a palpable immediacy that makes the dry, disembodied words of the father pale.

While these corporeal images evoke in the reader buried memories of preoedipal contact with a responsive maternal body and thus the desire for that lost connection, *Little Women* also opens a pathway for the transformation of those impulses into a more mature female bonding. The last two passages quoted above show how the sisters "mother" each other in imitation of the mother they admire: Jo passes on the maternal embrace to her sister Amy; Beth cushions her sister's feet "with a motherly air." Meg and Jo consciously "mother" the two younger girls (68); and, reversing the direction of maternal nurture, "Meg and Jo fed their mother like dutiful young storks" (266).[3] If the text appeals through images of bodily closeness and connection to a repressed stratum of preoedipal desire in the reader, it does not offer to bind that desire with a simple image of regained maternal unity. Rather, it demands a conversion of the drive for symbiosis into a desire for female solidarity, for a reciprocity of nurturing. The level of physical imagery introduces an alternative to patriarchal family organization: instead of one woman's being charged with fostering everyone's development while neglecting her own, *Little Women* involves a whole circle of women in nurturing each other's growth.

Similarly, the reliance of the female circle on facial mirroring to convey feelings both recalls a time before speech and suggests the creative evolution of a preoedipal mode toward a higher level of organization.

"We've got father and mother and each other," . . . the four young faces . . . brightened at the cheerful words. (19)

As they gathered about the table, Mrs. March said, "I've got a treat for you after supper." A quick, bright smile went round like a streak of sunshine. (27)

Beth nestled up to her [mother], and the rest turned towards her with brightening faces, as flowers turn toward the sun. (163)

If speech requires the separation of speakers, light flashed from face to face reinforces identity. Here the assurance of unity radiates from the mother's face to the daughters who reflect her, and each girl's face reflects the happiness of the others. In D. W. Winnicott's developmental ac- counts, a child seeks its own identity in what it takes to be a reflection of itself in the mother's face. If the mother is attentive and responsive, she mirrors back to the child positive feelings about its worth; if her face is chronically unresponsive, the child fails to develop feelings of vitality and self-esteem (Winnicott, "Mirror-Role," 111–16).

The drawback of this mirroring relation is that it leads nowhere. There is no leeway for change or growth between mirrors that reflect each other. But the ring of faces that seems to promise only preoedipal stasis turns out to have a developmental dimension in *Little Women*. It liberates Jo's cre- ative potential, in ways best understood through Heinz Kohut's theory of narcissism.[4]

How to Raise a Creative Daughter

The contradiction in family values finds expression in the differential treatment of the two artist daughters, Jo and Amy. The preoedipal values of facial affirmation and loving continuity redouble Jo's creative energies, while gender training in feminine self-abnegation effectively destroys the artist in Amy.

The oedipal family in its function as a training ground for social roles must target narcissism in its daughters, for narcissism is by definition the enemy of feminine self-effacement and self-sacrifice. Heinz Kohut's em- phasis on fostering healthy narcissism provides a counter-ideology. Moth- ers should encourage rather than squelch the grandiose fantasies of their children and applaud exhibitionistic self-displays, he maintains. If the "gleam in the mother's eye" (252) reflects affirmatively the child's self on display, its self-esteem will be affirmed; narcissistic drive energy will re- main intact, available to fuel creative ambitions later in life. A child who is reinforced for showing what it can do will later be able to extend the sense of the "pleasurable confirmation of the value, beauty and lovableness of the self" (253) to its creations and so find the courage to commit its energies to the completion of creative projects.[5]

The circle of mirroring faces in *Little Women* encourages Jo's creativity through a multiple version of "the gleam in the mother's eye," affirming the worth of what Jo does and so encouraging her to invest in further creative projects. "'I don't see how you can write and act such splendid things, Jo. You're a regular Shakespeare!'" is Beth's response to the script of Jo's play (26). Jo's grandiose acting—she plays with equal panache both the magniloquent villain and the all-conquering hero of her own play—receives thunderous applause.

The sisters make Jo the center of a circle of excited praise—"they all clustered about Jo" (211)—when they realize that she is the author of the story she has just read to them anonymously:

> "Who wrote it?" asked Beth, who had caught a glimpse of Jo's face.
>
> [Jo] suddenly sat up, cast away the paper, displaying a flushed countenance, and, with a funny mixture of solemnity and excitement, replied in a loud voice, "Your sister."
>
> "You?" cried Meg, dropping her work.
>
> "It's very good," said Amy.
>
> "I knew it! I knew it! Oh, my Jo, I am so proud!" and Beth began to hug her sister, and exult over this splendid success.
>
> Dear me, how delighted they all were, to be sure! . . . how Beth got excited, and skipped and sung with joy . . . how proud Mrs. March was when she knew it; how Jo laughed, with tears in her eyes, as she declared she might as well be a peacock. (211)

Jo's success resonates in Beth, especially, as if it were Beth's own: she reflects back and so confirms her sister's pride, a model of the empathic response that Kohut makes the central function of parenting. But all the girls' celebratory responses have the effect of Kohut's "gleam in the mother's eye," reflecting back to Jo a joyous affirmation of the self on display. Their jubilation has the effect of reinforcing Jo's grandiosity—"Jo wondered if Miss Burney felt any grander over her *Evelina* than she did over her *Rival Painters*" (211)—and so inciting her to new heights of ambition. The scene ends with Jo determined to support herself and her sisters through her writing.

Amy's grandiose fantasy, like Jo's, is to be a great artist: "to be an artist, and go to Rome, and do fine pictures, and be the best artist in the whole world" (196). Amy's strong narcissistic drives for perfection and fame, combined with a measure of talent and an admirable determination, sustain her for a remarkably long time, given the lack of encouragement in her environment: "she persevered in spite of all obstacles, failures, and discouragements, firmly believing that in time she should do something worthy to be called 'high art'" (*Good Wives*, 272). But Amy is caught up in the father's script of development toward a gender ideal of selflessness and modesty; assaults on her narcissism (framed as "vanity" and "conceit") eventually drive grandiose fantasy into repression and turn narcissistic impulses in the direction of making herself into a beautiful object.

One scene among many will suffice to illustrate the continuous assault on Amy's narcissism:

> "You are getting to be rather conceited, my dear," [replied her mother.] "You have many little gifts and virtues, but there is no need of parading them, for conceit spoils the finest genius. . . . the great charm of all power is modesty.". . .
>
> "I see; it's nice to have accomplishments and be elegant, but not to show off, or get perked up," said Amy thoughtfully. (106)

"Conceit" (as well as "vanity," Amy's besetting sin) is another name for the self-confidence necessary to an artist, who has to be convinced enough of the importance of his or her ideas to inflict them on others: to put one's ideas onto paper or canvas is to project them into "someone else's most private space" (Joan Didion, quoted in Braudy, 109). Similarly, the "selfishness" that Amy is always accused of could be construed, from a perspective that valued creativity, as the determination to conserve her energies for creative self-expression. That is not allowed in a group that values only female altruism: even in the very first chapter, the family forces Amy to spend the money she has been saving for colored pencils on a gift for someone else.

Kohut remarks that "in the girl the exhibitionism of the urethral-phallic phase is soon replaced by exhibitionism concerning her total appearance and by an interrelated exhibitionistic emphasis on morality and drive control" (253). Because gender is not a category of analysis for Kohut, he does not inquire closely into the causes of this developmental glitch. Amy's case can fill in the gap. Amy's self-display is not allowed the expansion that might transform it into a positive creative force because the process of socialization bends narcissism back upon the self. In the passage quoted above, a healthy grandiosity becomes "showing off," art is diminished to feminine "accomplishments," and narcissistic impulses are trained toward an ideal of feminine "elegance." The process of transformation is completed in *Good Wives*, where Amy vows to "become a true gentlewoman in mind and manners," elegant in every particular—"an attractive and accomplished woman, even if she never became a great artist" (272, 328). Having met with disapproval at every turn, Amy's narcissistic ambitions are not wiped out—the conscious aim of parental pressure—but retrained toward the beautification of the self as object.

The speech with which her father crowns Amy's arrival at his gender ideal betrays the hypocrisy of patriarchal gender training, which ostensibly wipes out narcissism only to invite it in at the back door in the guise of feminine vanity:

> I observe that Amy . . . gave Meg her place tonight, and has waited on everyone with patience and good humor. . . . I conclude that she has learned to think of other people more and of herself less, and has decided to try and mould her character as carefully as she moulds her little clay figures. I am glad of this; for though I should be very proud of a graceful statue made by her, I shall be infinitely prouder of a lovable daughter, with a talent for making life beautiful to herself and to others. (295)

Thus a girl can have her narcissism reinforced for making herself an object to adorn others' lives, in the spirit of womanly service to the well-being of others—but not for making something beautiful.[6] While exhibitions of creative ambition are branded "vanity," exhibitions of the self as good girl receive positive mirroring. No wonder, then, that girls divert narcissistic energy from creative ambitions into exhibitions of appearance, morality and drive control (Kohut, 253).

The differential treatment accorded the two artist figures focuses the contradictory ideologies of *Little Women* and surely reflects the ambivalence of Alcott herself. Only by subjecting Amy to the harsh extirpation of a potentially creative egotism can she make retribution for trampling on gender ideology to indulge Jo's grandiosity.

Image-presentation versus Word-presentation

The various kinds of power that writing confers on Jo—powers to escape the prison of gender and to exert her own will effectively on the world—are given material embodiment and kinetic expression. The attic room where Jo writes is a concrete shape that readers can grasp and use to express their own needs for autonomous creativity—a "room of one's own" that anticipates Virginia Woolf's condensation of privacy, self-sufficiency, and creative space.[7] Here Jo sits "crying over the *Heir of Redclyffe*, wrapped up in a comforter on an old three-legged sofa by the sunny window . . . here she loved to retire with half a dozen russets and a nice book, to enjoy the quiet and the society of a pet rat who lived near by" (46). Although Jo is reading—unquestionably a symbolic activity involving linguistic operations of the mind—her pleasure is rendered through oral and tactile images that attach a reader's body: a cozy comforter, a familiar couch, and good things to eat and read. Autonomy has sensual appeal—even preoedipal appeal—when it comes wrapped in the oral and nestling pleasures of Jo's attic room.

Characteristic of Alcott's concrete imagination, Jo's stated ambition— "I shall write books and get rich and famous" (196)—does not remain an abstract declaration but takes a kinetic form that invites the reader's physical identification with the act of writing:

> Jo was very busy in the garret. . . . For two or three hours the sun lay warmly in the high window, showing Jo seated on the old sofa writing busily, with her papers spread out upon a trunk before her, while Scrabble, the pet rat, promenaded. . . . Quite absorbed in her work, Jo scribbled away till the last page was filled, when she signed her name with a flourish, and threw down her pen. . . . Lying back on the sofa, she read the manuscript carefully through, making dashes here and there, and putting in many exclamation points, which looked like little balloons; then she tied it up with a smart, red ribbon, and sat a minute looking at it with a sober, wistful expression which plainly showed how earnest her work had been. (201)

A room of one's own communicates competence through spatial values. That is, a child reader, used to cutting an insignificantly small figure in spaces constructed to adult specifications, can, in an attic room like Jo's, relish the sense of spatial adequacy, of being able to fill the space allotted. In Alcott's text, the sense of a room just big enough for Jo is doubled by the page that she also fills: both spatial containments offer the reader satisfyingly concrete forms for the sense of completion. Jo celebrates her ability to finish what she starts by "sign[ing] her name with a flourish," thereby claiming without ambivalence her right to express herself on paper, and "throwing down her pen." Alcott thus makes what is after all a sedentary process active. We see Jo's text itself in process, gaining the many "dashes" and "exclamation points" that bear witness to the bold strokes of its author's pen. Although Jo's is serious work—the narrator drops her habitually facetious tone to describe Jo's workmanship in sober detail—the many "little balloons" of the exclamation marks borrow color from the "smart, red ribbon" that Jo uses to tie up the manuscript to festoon the story with the celebratory colors of a birthday party.

The chapter continues by celebrating in one vivid kinetic image after another the liberation from the prison of gender that writing enables. Earlier, the sight of the family home had deterred Jo from running away with Laurie, though she was sorely tempted because she "was tired of confinement and care": "'If I was a boy, we'd run away together, and have a capital time; but as I'm a miserable girl, I must be proper, and stop at home'" (282). But writing enables a girl to make a serious contribution to the world beyond the home and so justifies an escape from domesticity that takes the literal form characteristic of Alcott's imagination: "She put on her jacket as noiselessly as possible, and, going to the back entry window, got out upon the roof of a low porch, swung herself down to the grassy bank, and took a roundabout way to the road. Once there, she . . . hailed a passing omnibus, and rolled away to town, looking very merry and mysterious" (201–2). Her errand is to a magazine publisher in town, who subsequently accepts her story.

This daring escape from the ladylike confinement of the house into the world of adventure is only the beginning. The whole chapter seems to endorse a girl's ambition to step outside role prescriptions. Throughout the novel, the attractive vitality of Jo's "tomboy" movements has undermined the overt gender ideology of the text (see chapter 2, above). The subversive energy that has throughout infused Jo's physical assertions of an active self-will is expressed here through running: "Jo darted away, soon leaving hat and comb behind her, and scattering hairpins as she ran . . . with flying hair, bright eyes, ruddy cheeks. . . . 'I wish I was a horse; then I could run for miles in this splendid air, and not lose my breath. It was capital; but see what a guy it's made me'" (207–8). If the horse epitomizes the freedom and power of mobility to Jo, her own running epitomizes vigor and the joy of free movement to the reader—to be gained, as Alcott's text always implies, at the cost of breaking the frozen mold of femininity.

Not only does Jo's run send the accoutrements of womanhood flying (hat, comb, hairpins), but Meg soon arrives to remind both Jo and the reader that such freedom of movement is against the rules:

> Meg, looking particularly ladylike in her state and festival suit, for she had been making calls, . . . regarded her dishevelled sister with

well-bred surprise. . . . "You have been running, Jo; how could you? When will you be stopping such romping ways?" said Meg, reprovingly, as she settled her cuffs and smoothed her hair. . . .

"Never till I'm stiff and old, and have to use a crutch . . . it's hard enough to have you change all of a sudden; let me be a little girl as long as I can." . . . for lately she had felt that Margaret was fast getting to be a woman, and Laurie's secret [of Meg's impending engagement] made her dread the separation which must surely come sometime, and now seemed very near. (208)

The blandness of Meg's model of perfect female propriety, following Jo's strong, joyous action, persuades the reader kinetically to accept Jo's alignment of womanhood with crippled immobility. To become a woman is to lose: Jo's pang of insight into the separation that Meg's marriage will entail adds the idea of emotional loss to the diminution of physical vigor.

The father has the last word on Jo's vigorously enacted protests against gender constraints. In his congratulatory speech to her on his return, he simply smooths out the "boyish" excrescences that have been the signs of her vitality, shaping her to his idea of what a woman should be:

I don't see the "son Jo" whom I left a year ago. . . . I see a young lady who pins her collar straight, laces her boots neatly, and neither whistles, talks slang, nor lies on the rug as she used to do. Her face has grown gentler, and her voice is lower; she doesn't bounce, but moves quietly. . . . I rather miss my wild girl; but if I get a strong, helpful, tender-hearted woman in her place, I shall feel quite satisfied. (294)

The formal symmetry of the speeches the father makes to each daughter in turn matches the uniformity of the "little woman" model to which he reduces each. Governed by the requirement of the social order that individual idiosyncrasy be smoothed out to fit a uniform gender role, the patriarchal narrative imposes on the girls' individual growth a uniform pattern of development. Thus his praise of Jo both obliterates the vigor of physical movement that makes Jo herself and leaves out the main achievement of her year, the writing and publication of her story. The only work that surfaces in the father's account is Meg's "woman's work": "I value the womanly skill which keeps home happy more than white hands or fashionable accomplishments" (293).

The gathering contradictions give the final chapter a confused tone, a forced note of celebration conflicting with a deeper sense of loss. Although this chapter contains the marriage proposal that forms the climax of the romantic sequence in other novels of female development (John Brooke proposes to Meg), the emotional intensity of the proposal is dissipated and derided by Jo's parodic rehearsal of the proposal before it happens (298) and by her comic lamentations after (307).

The novel ends with a frozen tableau whose stasis seems to invalidate the father's notion of developmental progress.

> Father and Mother sat together, quietly re-living the first chapter of the romance which for them began some twenty years ago. Amy was drawing the lovers, who sat apart in a beautiful world of their own, the light of which touched their faces with a grace the little artist could not copy. Beth lay on her sofa, talking cheerily with [Mr. Laurence], who held her little hand as if he felt it possessed the power to lead him along the peaceful way she walked. Jo lounged in her favourite low seat, with the grave, quiet look which best became her; Laurie, leaning on the back of her chair, his chin on a level with her curly head, smiled . . . and nodded at her in the long glass which reflected them both. (310–11)

The narrator's rhetoric presents one message, while the images contradict it; the stasis of each girl (except Amy, the only one not encased in a couple) expresses an extinction of vitality to a reader used to images of dynamic activity. Jo's new sedateness is embraced by a glib narrator who goes over to the side of the fathers, celebrating "the grave, quiet look which best became her" (310); but the reader can only mourn the loss of vigorous movement that has made Jo a model of robust determination. In spite of the narrator's attempts to infuse the separate worlds of the couples with the promise of romance, a reader who is habituated to the shining faces of an unbroken family circle must see in these isolated units the fragmentation of an englobing and nourishing totality.

Only from the perspective of the father's social law can the change to "little women" be construed as developmental progress. The real potential for development seems, in retrospect, to lie in the nurturing power of the circle of female faces and in the complementary plenitude of Jo's private creative space. In spite of the narrator's effort to create in the last line the sense of something wonderful to come ("Laurie, leaning on the back of her chair, his chin on a level with her curly head, smiled . . . and nodded at her in the long glass which reflected them both"), the reigning perspective is one of loss. Like Jo, we are reluctant to look ahead: "'Don't you wish you could take a look forward and see where we shall all be [in three years]?' 'I do,' returned Laurie. 'I think not,' [said Jo], 'for I might see something sad'" (310). Indeed in the next developmental stage, represented by *Good Wives* (*Little Women*, part 2), Amy gives up art altogether and marries Laurie; and Jo, like her mother before her, is inspired to a ladylike extinction of self-expression by her (future) husband's moralistic censure: she burns all her published stories.

What messages does a girl reader take away from this novel's contradictions? If *Little Women* speaks to all levels of a girl reader—to her who tries to be a good girl in conformity with the wisdom of parental figures as well as to her who wants something different—surely the images speak louder than the words. The father's gender storyline may dominate the novel's structure, giving it a clear beginning and end that appeal to a reader's conscious desire for coherence. But scattered representations of autonomy and creativity as concrete action and concrete space speak directly to a reader's unconscious. According to the theory articulated in chapter 2, above the repeated kinetic images that express Jo's exuberant ambition and independence—running, climbing, writing a story and setting off into the world to get it published—engage the primary processes whose function is to assimilate new experiences into the ongoing structures of the self. The vivid visual and kinetic imagery of the subtext should thus enable girl readers to take in and make their own Alcott's model of creative autonomy. And bodily images of a family organized along the lines of preverbal communication—"nestling" bodies, reflective faces—call upon preoedipal memories to evoke an alternative to the distances and hierarchies of the patriarchal family.

4 Revolutionary Languages in *The Awakening*

THE AWAKENING, written for mature readers and featuring the awakening of a woman's sensuality, seems light years away from the coming-of-age drama of *Little Women*, yet it makes a similarly divided appeal to the reader. While the dominant narrative voice adheres to the conventions of realism, other voices interrupt its flow and destroy its coherence.[1] Most notably, a rhythmic, alliterative language associated with the voice of the sea conveys desires for a sensual merging of identities that exceeds the logic of realistic discourse. *The Awakening* thus offers the reader, as does *Little Women*, a ground for preoedipal responses to language that interfere with the unified identity of reader usually constructed by realistic texts. Julia Kristeva's analysis of semiotic breaks in language— moments when impulses associated with preoedipal drives surge into a language based on their repression—provides a framework for understanding what happens when the reader engages the heterogeneous discourses of *The Awakening*.

Chopin and Kristeva share an optimism about the human capacity to change—as well as a faith in unconscious impulses to initiate change. Even the dynamics of Edna's final transformation—obscure without some help from Kristeva—can be clarified by an alignment with Kristeva's concept of rejection. And a Kristevan explanation of the revolution that occurs in Edna's thinking when she confronts the concrete reality of childbirth can in turn illuminate the changes triggered in the reader by encounters with bodily processes usually repressed from narratives of love and marriage.

Other Voices from Other Scenes

My rather unorthodox reading of *The Awakening* rests on the French feminist construction of female sexuality and the female unconscious as areas outside the discourse of Western culture. Writers like Hélène Cixous speak of a female unconscious that is heterogeneous to male language and culture. Were the specific contents of that female unconscious to escape the repression successfully practiced on it for centuries and enter women's writing, the explosion of authentic difference into expression would destroy the coherence of phallocentric culture (Cixous, "Medusa," 879, 885, 887). Likewise, Cixous, Luce Irigaray, and Annie Leclerc claim that female sexuality necessarily eludes a discourse constructed on the basis of a male libidinal economy. Lacan agrees: "It is . . . elsewhere that [woman] upholds the question of her own *jouissance*" ("Phallic Phase," 121).

In *The Awakening* Chopin suggests the "elsewhere" of female sexuality both spatially and discursively. She locates her protagonist's sensual awakening in the sea and in other spaces outside patriarchal territory, notably Madame Antoine's island hut. The sea offers Edna a polymorphous, preoedipal sensuality that contradicts her culture's circumscription of female sexuality within the roles defined by myths of romantic love and motherhood. As an uncharted, unlimited expanse stretching beyond the completely articulated social world that surrounds and confines Edna, the sea provides the "nonsocial space" opposed to the city and its laws that Tony Tanner finds in many novels of adultery, an "outside, where the socially displaced individual . . . may attempt to find or practice a greater freedom" (23). But Tanner's topographical model does not exhaust the uses of the sea in *The Awakening*: as a point of reference outside social discourse it reminds Edna of alternative possibilities within. The sea elicits responses from a psychic realm heterogeneous to Edna's consciousness, calling up from unconscious memory a corresponding image of free natural space and provoking indistinct impulses that baffle thought but propel Edna toward change.

To convey the sense of areas outside social discourse Chopin uses languages that diverge from the dominant narrative voice, which for the most part adheres to the realistic convention of transcribing events in apparently clear, transparent language. Vague and amorphous in the case of Edna's unconscious, sensual and poetic in the case of the sea, these voices blur the clear categories of realistic discourse, unsettling a reader's habits of mind and throwing her or him into process along with Edna.[2]

Whether or not one embraces the French feminist contention that there is an outside where female difference exists, "not bounded by any system or any structure" (Féral, 91), depends on where one stands: namely, whether one occupies a male position (defined not so much by sexual difference as by integration into the social system) or a female position (understood in the political sense of an exile from power). The differing views on female sexuality from these two standpoints, one inside and one outside the social consensus, are represented by the competing stories that Dr. Mandelet and Edna tell at a dinner party. The two stories construct the subject of *The Awakening*—that is, a woman's attempt to establish a free sexual life—through opposing paradigms. In a context of male stories of war and hunting told by all the patriarchal figures of Edna's life—father, husband, doctor—Dr. Mandelet tells the "old story" of "a woman's love, seeking strange, new channels, only to return to its legitimate source" (70). In response, Edna tells about a woman disappearing into the sea with her lover. The doctor's narrative presents the patriarchal definition of female sexuality: the instinctual flood of female erotic energy only appears to take an erratic course; inevitably, it must return to the "legitimate" channels constructed by patriarchal engineers, because it has nowhere else to go. From the vantage point of someone planted firmly within the social world, there is no outside. Assured of ultimate control, the patriarchal figure can afford to be tolerant, knowing that female sexuality is always safely enclosed within male-determined boundaries.

The doctor's paradigm reverberates because we have seen in Edna's husband a consummate practitioner of its patience, tolerance, and control. When Edna first swims out to sea, seemingly beyond gender boundaries—"far out, where no woman had swum before" (28)—Mr. Pontellier's paternal watchfulness reduces her encounter with death and boundlessness to child's play: "'You were not so very far, my dear; I was watching you'" (29). And he similarly extends an overarching domestic structure to cover her move into a house of her own, again converting what seems to Edna a venture into new, free space into a mere extension of the patriarchal establishment. He makes the "pigeon-house" into which she moves with all her belongings seem to be nothing more than a playhouse in the parental backyard by adroitly inserting an announcement into the newspaper that all furniture is being moved out of the couple's household to make way for alterations: "There was to be an addition—a small snuggery"(93). This discursive reappropriation of Edna's pigeon-house converts it into a mere annex to the husband's mansion, at least in the world of social reality constructed by the newspaper's social pages.

According to the patriarchal perspective, the social *is* the only reality. There is finally no extrasocial space in Edna's world, no free female movement that is not already foreseen and forestalled by patriarchal plans: her sexual freedom is as much an illusion as her freedom of movement in the sea and her freedom to construct a house of her own. Critics who adopt this view of reality take Edna's drowning to be Chopin's acknowledgment of limitations, "a reversal of the Romantic dream of the unlimited outward expansion of the self," in Otis Wheeler's words (128). Suzanne Wolkenfeld similarly concludes that "ultimately Chopin places Edna's suicide as a defeat and a regression, rooted in . . . a romantic incapacity to accommodate herself to the limitations of reality" (220).[3]

But there is room for a more positive interpretation of Edna's final disappearance into the sea, one suggested by the story Edna tells in response to the doctor's.

> The [doctor's] story did not seem especially to impress Edna. She had one of her own to tell, of a woman who paddled away with her lover one night in a pirogue and never came back. They were lost amid the Baratarian Islands, and no one ever heard of them or found trace of them from that day to this. It was a pure invention. She said that Madame Antoine had related it to her. That, also, was an invention. Perhaps it was a dream she had had. But every glowing word seemed real to those who listened. They could feel the hot breath of the Southern night; they could hear the long sweep of the pirogue through the glistening moonlit water, the beating of birds' wings, rising startled from among the reeds in the salt-water pools; they could see the faces of the lovers, pale, close together, rapt in oblivious forgetfulness, drifting into the unknown. (70)

Rejecting the "impress" of the doctor's narrative pattern and thus of its gender design, Edna tells "a story of her own," in which female sexuality refuses enclosure. Her attribution of the tale to Madame Antoine emphasizes Edna's refusal of patriarchal precedents: Madame Antoine is chief storyteller of an island oral tradition untouched by mainland culture. Edna also takes Madame Antoine's sensual language as a model. Madame Antoine had cast a sensual spell over Edna and Robert as they listened to her story, so that they "heard" the "whispering voices of dead men and the click of muffled gold" (39); now Edna makes her listeners "hear," "see," even "feel the hot breath of the Southern night."[4] Edna's discourse models the sensual language Chopin invents for the voice of the sea, a language that plays upon the reader's senses while withholding a final meaning. The open ending of Edna's tale is a synecdoche of *The Awakening*'s inconclusive conclusion: the lovers sailing into an "unknown" sea beyond existing systems of representation models Edna's disappearance into an equally uncharted and unlimited sea. Edna's tale then teaches us to read

Chopin's lack of closure as a narrative endorsement of a female sensuality that exceeds the limits of patriarchal discourse.

According to this reading, *The Awakening* tells the story of Edna's growth from an identity circumscribed by her position within patrilinear networks toward a diffuse sensuality that exceeds not only social roles but the enclosure of a differentiated identity. Introduced in the opening pages as the object of her husband's patriarchal vision—as "his wife," "Mrs. Pontellier," "a valuable piece of personal property" (4; Treichler, "Construction," 240)—Edna gradually replaces this positional identity with a sensuality developed outside social structures—through swimming, extramarital sex, and the exploration of her body by herself, for herself, in the matriarchal space of Madame Antoine's island hut. When Edna walks into the sea at the end, we can read her act as a choice of the unbounded sensuality she has discovered in communion with the sea over the constricting roles of wife, mother, and distant object of romantic desire. Chopin thus releases female sensuality not just from the bonds of marriage (Edna is unfaithful to her husband), but from enclosure within romantic love (Edna has sex with Alcée Arobin, "who was absolutely nothing to her" (77), rather than with Robert, the man she loves), and finally from containment in heterosexual, indeed human, structures. Edna's connection with the sea proves more fulfilling than her relationship to any of the men.[5]

Such a reading depends on accepting both the sea and the unconscious source of Edna's awakening sensual impulses as areas heterogeneous to the established discourse and on foregrounding the affinity between the two. The sights and sounds of the sea stimulate Edna's unconscious processes in a way that changes her sensibility over time.[6]

Chopin places the unconscious beyond thought and language by giving it a specific locus ("a vast cavern wherein discords wailed," 88) and an alternative language. Anticipating Lacanian and Kristevan models of the split self, Edna seems to be divided between a role-defined social self and an undercurrent of amorphous, undefined impulses. Chopin presents this split as positive, at least in one respect: it enables Edna to change. The notion of a split subject elaborated by Julia Kristeva in *Revolution in Poetic Language* is optimistic because it posits the individual as the site of a dialectic that can lead to change. The drive energy not assimilated into the linguistic structures of the speaking subject remains a source of disruptive impulses that can assail the social definition of identity, destroying its apparent unity and coherence and throwing the self into process. "Contradictory impulses," or "discords," from Edna's unconscious invade her from time to time like autonomous utterances, "extraneous, independent of volition," to disrupt her settled life as wife and mother (14, 88).

In one passage it is the sounds of the sea that activate these disquieting impulses: "the everlasting voice of the sea . . . broke like a mournful lullaby upon the night. An indescribable oppression, which seemed to generate in some unfamiliar part of her consciousness, filled her whole being with a vague anguish. It was like a shadow, like a mist passing across her soul's summer day. It was strange and unfamiliar" (8). To adumbrate the amorphous shapes of a territory beyond language, Chopin adopts a language of abstraction that withdraws meaning into a cloud of generalization. The images do not serve to clarify Edna's feelings but only reiterate their shadowy indefiniteness, "like a shadow, like a mist passing." Vague and contradictory, the language that describes the shifting impulses of Edna's emerging inner world forces the reader to tolerate what has not yet been formulated: we inhabit an indeterminate linguistic territory between the "pas cela" (not that) and the "pas encore" (not yet) (Kristeva, *Polylogues*, 498). Paula Treichler, in an admirably lucid interpretation of Chopin's vagueness, argues that in the verbal territory of Edna's awakening Chopin's "global and nonspecific" language embodies "a kind of verbal groping which duplicates Edna's dim, and at this point tentative, perception of the events that are coming to occupy her consciousness" (241). The text's fuzziness confounds the clear categories of the reader's thought, thwarting the capacity to decipher sentences according to known linguistic codes and throwing the reader into a state similar to Edna's, forced to tolerate the ambiguous and indeterminate expression of a realm outside social discourse that opens up possibilities without clearly defining anything.

On another occasion, gazing at the sea stimulates unconscious memory to produce a vision of female freedom and mobility impossible within the patriarchal enclosure:

> "Of whom—of what are you thinking?" asked Adèle. . . . "Nothing," returned Mrs. Pontellier. . . . "I was really not conscious of thinking of anything . . . but the sight of the water stretching so far away . . . made me think—without any connection that I can trace—of a summer day in Kentucky, of a meadow that seemed as big as the ocean. . . . I felt as if I must walk on forever, without coming to the end of it. . . . I was running away from prayers, from the Presbyterian service, read in a spirit of gloom by my father. . . . I was just a little unthinking child . . . following a misleading impulse. . . . sometimes

I feel this summer as if I were walking through the green meadow again; idly, aimlessly, unthinking and unguided." (17–18)

The gap in the social world represented by the Gulf—aptly named— corresponds to a gap in Edna's conscious thought ("I was thinking of nothing") through which she plunges to explore images beneath. This process anticipates Freud's method of free association (*The Interpretation of Dreams* was not published till 1900, a year after *The Awakening*).[7] The sight of the sea stretching free calls up from unconscious memory an answering image of unrestricted natural space. Chopin thus prefigures Cixous's female unconscious, an area beyond language and hence beyond cultural constraints, a repository of the alternative possibilities repressed from culture ("Medusa," 880). Only in the buried inner world can Edna find a model of free female exploration and discovery, governed by spontaneous impulse rather than by patriarchal directive—a model she follows through the rest of the novel (by walking around New Orleans, for example) in defiance of the passive, bounded quiescence of women in her role-defined society.

When Edna in the end commits herself definitively to the sea's fluidity, the images of the meadow that used to be enclosed in her mind are loosed into the surrounding sea: "There was the hum of bees, and the musky odor of pinks filled the air" (114). Her socially defined separate identity having disappeared, all that is left is the confluence of the two areas heterogeneous to social discourse: the fluid space of the sea and the equally amorphous inner world. The images of fertility suggest that Edna, like the lovers of her story, expands into a natural realm of sensual vitality. Chopin's refusal of closure, like Edna's in her storytelling, is a refusal of enclosure, an affirmation of a sensual life that goes "on and on" (113), beyond the bounds constructed by patriarchal scripts for women's sexuality.

The sea's recurring refrain, quoted below, has throughout the novel conflated the inner world with the depths of the sea, so we should not be surprised to see them fused at the end. Swimming already represents a partial blurring of the boundary between self and other: Edna "knows" the sea by feeling it all around her body, moving when she moves, rather than by confronting it across the space that usually separates the knower from the known, the speaking subject from the objects of speech. Chopin attempts to translate this sensual way of knowing, this substitution of direct physical contact for the distances of language, into a discourse that erases the distance between self and other:

> The voice of the sea is seductive; never ceasing, whispering, clamoring, murmuring, inviting the soul to wander for a spell in abysses of solitude; to lose itself in mazes of inward contemplation. The voice of the sea speaks to the soul. The touch of the sea is sensuous, enfolding the body in its soft, close embrace. (15)[8]

The soul might logically find "abysses of solitude" in the depths of the ocean, but "mazes of inward contemplation" belong to the inner world; indeed, the first glimpse of Edna's consciousness has shown her "lost in some inward maze of contemplation" (5). This breakdown of the distinction between self and world belongs to a preoedipal sense of fusion—what Freud calls "the oceanic feeling" of merging with the environment (originally the mother) (*Civilization*, 12).

Kristeva's discussion of the semiotic in language shows how such an eclipse of logical divisions between inside and outside, self and world, makes way for an influx of drive energy into the text that is expressed by the predominance of rhythm and alliteration. The ascendance of sound patterns over syntax in turn awakens answering preoedipal capacities for merging in the reader.[9] Kristeva insists that in order to understand language, we have to look to its production, including the formation of the speaking subject: before entry into language there is no unified subjectivity, but rather a *chora*, an amorphous receptacle for the drives. This primitive organization is in flux because the drives are contradictory, continually eradicating and replacing each other. At this stage the infant responds to the sounds of words with instinctual energy rather than deciphering their meaning, and it "speaks" its needs directly into the mother's body (*Revolution*, 25–30). Entry into language requires the repression of the motile and contradictory *chora* in order to consolidate a unified position for the speaker, the "I" constructed by speech systems. From now on, the speaking subject will need to connect words to what they signify rather than responding with bodily rhythms to how they sound. But the connection between language and the drives is never completely severed: the *chora* continues as a kind of undercurrent to language, motivating it and threatening to disrupt it through an infusion of instinctual energy. The release of drive energy into symbolic structures can dislocate grammatical and syntactical elements by making rhythm and sound the organizing principles of speech.

According to Kristeva, when we read a passage like the one in which the voice of the sea "speaks," a passage governed by alliteration and rhythmic repetition, we respond with answering physical rhythms in a return to earlier responses to the sound value rather than the meaning of words. Reading such a passage can bring the underlying fluidity of the reader's *chora* to the fore, reminding the reader of his or her own heterogeneity and so destroying the illusion constructed by the singular positions of language that the self is a stable, homogeneous unity. The consciousness of a discrete identity shattered, the reader is given over for a time to the "other" side, to the flux of drive energy left out of symbolic constructions of the self: "Words come to mind, but they are fuzzy, signifying nothing, more throbbing than meaning, and their stream goes to our breasts, genitals, and iridescent skin" ("Novel," 163).

Chopin of course did not have access to Kristeva's analysis, but the notion of the semiotic only extends Chopin's strategy of appealing to the reader's body through onomatopoeia. The passage is structured by the rhythmic repetition, with variation, of the central phrase, "The voice of the sea is," and by the alliteration of *m*'s and *s*'s. The reader identifies the repeated *s* sounds with the sibilance of the ocean foam's ebb and flow and responds to the regular rhythm of the sentences as if to the regularity of waves breaking. As in onomatopoeia generally, the words seem to devolve from their function as signifiers and begin to approach the thing signified. The reader has the unnerving impression of the thing itself coming to inhabit the word, of the sea itself speaking—and in words that do not represent, but *are* what they say. Of course, the words never lose their signifying function altogether: "murmuring" is still a sign that represents the sound of murmuring. But onomatopoeia "works on the bar between signifier and signified and tends to erase it, [as] an anarchic outcry against the . . . socializing positions of language" (Kristeva, "Novel," 178).[10] Making the same kind of physical response he or she would make to the rhythms of the sea itself, the reader has the illusion of circumventing the abstractions of representation to approach the concrete bodily communication the ocean offers Edna.

Onomatopoeia has the effect of drawing us back across the threshold of language, to a period before the line between signifier and signified was clearly drawn. Children make holophrastic utterances like "woof" for "dog" after they have grasped the idea that a particular noise identifies a particular thing but before they have understood the arbitrary nature of the connection. At that stage language is still grounded in the body, in instinctual impulses (*La révolution*, 222). Kristeva, following Jakobson, claims that *m*-sounds originally expressed incorporative drives addressed to the mother's body; *s* and *z* recall the noises of suckling (*La révolution*,

243, 244, 247). If words retain their early connection with instinctual impulses through their sounds, as Kristeva claims, then a passage organized by the alliteration of *m*'s and *s*'s calls upon specific drives in the reader—incorporation, suckling—appropriate to the sea's invitation to engulfment. That is, the *m*- and *s*-sounds awaken the cluster of drives originally organized by dependency on the mother's body, recalling a time when the reader's self seemed indistinct from the other (mother). The specific sounds thus enhance the content of the sea's invitation to the soul to "lose itself" in a return to maternal fusion, "enfolded" in the sea's "soft, close embrace."

The Body in the Plot

Chopin also disrupts the consciousness of the reader by interjecting reminders of bodily processes into the narrative. The conventions of the nineteenth-century novel that she inherited limit female sensuality to the romantic plot: sexual energy is channeled into emotional intensity and directed exclusively toward a man (see chapter 1, above). The reader can recognize the first stage of a familiar line of increasing emotional intensity as the banter between Edna and Robert signals a growing attraction. When Edna and Robert escape the social territory overseen by Edna's husband by sailing away to the Chênière Caminada, then moving yet further into alien space by taking shelter in Madame Antoine's matriarchal household, the reader expects their increasing intimacy to culminate in a declaration of love. But the escape from patriarchal ground unexpectedly includes an escape from patriarchal literary designs. Robert remains outside the bedroom, while Edna discovers her body by herself, for herself: "She stretched her strong limbs. . . . She ran her fingers through her hair. . . . She looked at her round arms . . . and rubbed them one after the other, observing closely, as if it were something she saw for the first time, the fine, firm quality and texture of her flesh" (37). Female sensuality finds autonomous satisfaction. Rather than awakening to a lover's kiss, Edna finds fulfillment in a sensual sleep: "She slept lightly at first . . . she half heard . . . Tonie's slow, Acadian drawl, Robert's quick, soft, smooth French. She understood French imperfectly . . . and the voices were only part of the other drowsy, muffled sounds lulling her senses" (37). From the ground of sleep, altogether outside discursive practices, a corporeal perspective on language emerges. Diverted from the expressive function of lovers' discourse, language becomes "semiotic," in Kristeva's terms, playing over Edna's solitary body and "lulling her senses" rather than signifying anything.

The reader's romantic expectations are even more scandalized at the end of the novel when the long separation of the lovers ends, as it should, in passionate reunion—only to be interrupted by a scene of childbirth. Expecting the closure of a final embrace, the reader gets instead the pain of giving birth as Edna leaves Robert to attend Adèle Ratignolle in childbed. Again, the female body disrupts the narrative pattern.

Thus at key turns of a familiar sequence Chopin substitutes for peak moments what is normally repressed from fictional representations—a woman's experience of her own body, apart from romantic engagements. A discursive sequence that fails to fulfill the expectations it generates leads the reader to question not just the representation of reality in the novel, but the representation of reality in the reader's own head (Belsey, 32–33). Because the narrative patterns that shape events in cultural representations of reality become the structures through which we read our own experience, disruptions of a sequence like the romantic one of separation and reunion can throw into doubt not only fictional conventions, but the imaginative conventions that pattern life for the reader as well.[11]

In "The Novel as Polylogue" Kristeva lists a number of disruptive sensual phenomena—all things "that no one talks about"—whose intrusions tear apart the symbolic fabric: "Questions about sexuality, irregularity in a poem, sounds in a foreign language, eroticism that is forbidden, impossible" (161). In Kristeva's list, as in Chopin's text, eruptions of the semiotic in language function like sexual matters that exceed cultural mores: both intrusions shatter the authority of the dominant discourse by reminding the reader of what that discourse leaves out. Then, as Kristeva vividly describes her own reaction to heterogeneous processes encountered either in reading or in social practice, "the symbolic covering (constituted by acquired knowledge, the discourse of others, and communal shelter) cracks, and something that I call instinctual drive . . . rides up to destroy any guarantees, any beliefs, any protection. . . . An aimless drifting ensues . . . rejecting what is established and opening up an infinite abyss where there are no more words" ("Novel," 162–63). The symbolic order is broken, and with it the identity of speaking subject constructed by that order.

Revolution in Poetic Language gives a more comprehensive, if less dramatic, account of this process. Using Hegel's "negativity" as a point of departure, Kristeva posits that a discovery of some material process that the dominant system of meaning has left unnamed shatters the subject's faith in that system to represent reality. The drive of "rejection," or expulsion, dis-poses the subject from the cultural frame of meaning and dissolves the subjectivity embedded in it. For a time, there is *no* speaking subject, but only the flux of heterogeneous drive energies. Kristeva gets the idea of an expulsion, or rejection, drive from Freud's "Negation," where he describes one of the two original drive energies of an infant as the desire "to eject from itself everything that is bad" (237). According to Kristeva, this drive energy (never subsumed into cultural systems of representation) remains available to us to "spit out," or expel, what no longer fits, what causes discomfort—including outworn signifying systems.

The same energy of rejection also enables one to build a new signifying structure around the newly discovered heterogeneous material process. The capacity to expel, to separate matter from the self, provided the original bridge to language: it initially enabled the child to conceptualize objects as separate from the self that the child had originally considered to be part of the self and so established the precondition for language. The story of Freud's grandson that Lacan borrows to show the entry into language can serve here as paradigm: the little boy separates from the mother by throwing away a spool that represents her, enacting rejection; that separation puts him in a position to make statements about her, which he then proceeds to do: "fort . . . da" (loosely translated, "she is away; she will come back") (*Four Fundamental Concepts*, 62). Separation is the condition of representation.

Throughout life, the energy of rejection is available not only to throw out old signifying systems that no longer fit but also to separate off a new object and construct a new symbolic frame of meaning around it. Therefore, we can change—radically. We can "reinvent the real and resymbolize it" (*Revolution*, 155) and thereby reinvent a new subjectivity grounded in the new, broader-based representation of reality (113, 119, 122–23, 147–64).

By throwing into relief what familiar narrative patterns leave out, *The Awakening*'s evocation of the repressed physical shatters the totalizing coherence of realistic discourse that usually holds the reader in a single unified position. The reader loses his or her bearings; and—if she or he is sufficiently flexible, that is, contradictory—the reader's split-off drive energies may engage the denied physical processes of the female body, building a new signifying system around them and repositioning a new reading identity in relation to them. We can finally only speculate about the specific effects of textual disruption on *The Awakening*'s reader, but Edna models one response to the encounter with a physical process left out of cultural representations. Her confrontation with the pain of childbirth, a physical fact omitted by her culture's spiritualized ideology of motherhood, throws her into a process of instinctual revulsion, rejection, and silence that in the end leads to an articulation of an entirely new paradigm of motherhood. She thus models the whole process of rejection triggered in the reader by a comparable encounter with the repressed female body.

After watching Adèle's torment in giving birth, Edna is awash with repugnance. She kisses Adèle goodbye "stunned and speechless," dislodged from the structure of shared meanings that enabled her to speak and understand. Thus she does not grasp, at least in the way Adèle intends, the meaning of her parting words: "'Think of the children, Edna. Oh think of the children! Remember them!'"(109) Edna can no longer hear Adèle's directive to think like a mother—that is, to subordinate her own desires for sexual self-expression and personal growth to her children's welfare. She has just experienced the destruction of that paradigm of maternal self-sacrifice as she watched Adèle herself, the ideal of protective and self-denying motherhood, dissolve into the physical pain of maternity. On the way home Edna cannot formulate any complete verbal sequence in response to the doctor's concern, stammering in non sequiturs and fragments that always come back to the children—but not the children envisioned in Adèle's maternal thinking: "'I'm not going to be forced into doing anything. . . . I want to be let alone. Nobody has any right—except children perhaps—and even then it seems to me—or it did seem—' She felt that her speech was voicing the incoherency of her thoughts, and stopped abruptly" (109). The old symbolic structures and the self grounded in them overwhelmed by revulsion and rejection, Edna is in transition between signifying systems, unable to formulate a position from which to speak. A final silence confirms the disappearance of Edna as speaking subject, as Chopin, too, is stubbornly silent about what Edna thinks during her final nightlong vigil: "She stretched herself out [on the sofa], never uttering a word. She did not sleep. . . . She was still awake in the morning" (111).

Not until the next day do we discover the content of Edna's final awakening, when she reassembles as speaking subject to frame her experience in a completely new terminology, overthrowing the ideology of love and motherhood.

"Today it is Arobin; tomorrow it will be some one else." . . . There
was no human being whom she wanted near her except Robert; and
she even realized that the day would come when he, too, and the
thought of him would melt out of her existence, leaving her alone.
The children appeared before her like antagonists who had overcome
her; who had overpowered and sought to drag her into the soul's
slavery for the rest of her days. But she knew a way to elude them.
(113)

The hard fact of childbirth has torn away the veil of romantic illusion,
revealing love as a "biological trap," in Otis Wheeler's phrase (128). Up
until now Edna has been in thrall to romantic ideology, periodically seized
by longing for an always absent beloved, as in the dinner party scene:
"seeming to issue from some vast cavern wherein discords wailed . . .
there came over her the acute longing which always summoned into her
spiritual vision the presence of the beloved one, overpowering her at once
with a sense of the unattainable" (88). This invasion from the unconscious produces the cultural pattern of love in generic form, pared down
to its essential feature: the figure of an unattainable beloved (see chapter
1, above). All Edna's love experiences have been conventional in this
respect: the three objects of her adolescent dreams were inaccessible, and
she did not fall in love with Robert until after his departure for Mexico.

But the concrete process of childbirth, which has made visible the inevitable link between love and childbirth, has apparently wiped out all such
abstractions and idealizations. The notion that one man, and one man
only, can make her life happy and meaningful is erased in favor of the
interchangeability of lovers—"Today it is Arobin, tomorrow. . . some one
else." And the phrase "melt out of her existence" acknowledges that her
version of Robert is only a projection of her romantic imagination, like
the three objects of her adolescent desire who earlier "melted impercepti-
bly out of existence, . . . went the way of dream" (19). Love leads not to
the undying spiritual unity of Edna's daydreams about Robert, but to the
physical anguish of bearing children and the weary work of caring for
them day in, day out. She does indeed "think of the children," but not in
the terms of Adèle's self-sacrificing maternal discourse. The words take on
a different meaning within the new maternal discourse of enslavement to
children.

Readers have criticized Chopin for the inconsistency of her character-
ization at this point. George Spangler finds Edna's "sudden concern for
her children" "perplexing" (187), Jules Chametzky feels Chopin's presen-

tation of Edna's feelings for her children is "muddled" (200), and George Arms complains that "while the motivation from the children has been amply anticipated, its final realization produces something of a shift. . . . the children, used in this way, somewhat flaw the novel" (179). (One suspects that these critics' discomfiture may arise as much from the text's demolition of the cultural myths of motherhood as from the infelicities of Chopin's plotting.) To criticize Edna for inconsistency is to embrace the realistic norm of character as unified, logically consistent, fully present. But Edna's development has never proceeded with the internal consistency of a realistic character, true even in the midst of change to certain fundamental traits; she has been propelled by "contradictory impulses" throughout (Chopin, 14). As in Kristeva's model, change springs from a repository of free energy whose impulses are at odds with the fixity of culturally established categories. Useless to complain of inconsistency, then: Edna *is* inconsistency, and that makes it possible for her to think beyond the conventions.

The pessimism of Edna's final vision should not blind us to what is new and constructive in the process of rejection it completes. She is able literally to change her mind, to reject the iron hold of romantic love over her imagination and to articulate an original paradigm of motherhood as enslavement that overturns her culture's ideology of mothers as selfless (and bodiless) angels—"mother-women . . . who idolized their children, worshipped their husbands, and esteemed it a holy privilege to efface themselves as individuals and grow wings as ministering angels" (Chopin, 10). The process of confronting the ideology of motherhood with the concrete processes it leaves out qualifies, then, as "an affirmative negativity," a "productive dissolution" (Kristeva, *Revolution*, 113), that "does not destroy, but originates new organizations, and in that sense affirms" (109).

The intrusion of childbirth on a familiar sequence of lovers' separation and reunion may have a similarly violent effect on the reader, causing a rejection of the conventions of romantic love that exclude material reality and opening the reader up to the possibility of a new symbolic structure based on the heterogeneous physical processes now thrust upon his or her attention.

A text like *The Awakening* is doubly revolutionary. On the one hand, its semiotic language and its intrusions of physical experience break down the unified self-concept of the reader by appealing to a dimension usually repressed from realistic texts: the body. Already, this revolution in self-understanding goes beyond the personal, for the discrete, unified identity of the individual citizen is the basis of bourgeois democratic ideology. By forcing the reader to experience his or her heterogeneity, a text like *The Awakening* can break down the ideology that constructs the reader in the image of the status quo, opening up new possibilities and thus transforming the reader into the only kind of subject capable "of bringing about new social relations," a "subject in process" (*Revolution*, 105).

In addition, *The Awakening* lives up to Kristeva's definition of a practice text, "which is always social" (*Revolution*, 195). What she calls an "experience text" may be revolutionary in exposing a reader's heterogeneity without going beyond the personal and subjective, but the contradictions in a "practice text" correspond to contradictions in the reader's historical situation (196): what triggers rejection are material processes extant in the reader's social reality, but left out of cultural representations. The force of expulsion/rejection is directed into the social sphere, running up against the political structures in which the reader once felt secure, dismantling them and leaving her or him in flux, open to the play of contradictions in the historical situation. The reader "passes into the process of social change that moves through him" (*Revolution*, 205).

Specifically, on encountering childbirth as the inevitable consequence of sexual relations, the reader of *The Awakening* experiences the contradiction between the ideology of democratic individualism that promises the full development of everyone's potential, unimpeded by external limitations, and the concrete reality of women's biological and social imprisonment within childbearing and child-rearing structures. A woman cannot develop all her capacities fully and freely when the expression of her sexuality leads inevitably to motherhood and the subordination of all her varied abilities to the care of children. As Priscilla Allen says, women cannot aspire to the American dream of individual development so long as they live in "a society so at the mercy of biology, despite its vaunted technology . . . that it keeps over half its members in chains" (237).[12] By disrupting the compensatory bliss of lovers' union, the childbirth scene also subverts the romantic ideology that keeps women from noticing their exclusion from the promises of democratic individualism. And it dispels, through the intrusion of maternity's painful physical reality, the ideal of fulfillment through a spiritualized motherhood. All the ideological frameworks that protect the stable identity of the reader shattered, the reader is thrown into confusion—but also into the possibility of representing the neglected material process, childbirth, and erecting a new signifying structure around it. Chopin's novel thus releases the reader's rejection impulses from the repression of ideological structures into the revolutionary undercurrent of her time: namely, the feminist protest against women's subjection to biological imperatives and consequent imprisonment in the home.[13]

But Kristeva cautions against the binding of rejection drives into any fixed ideology, revolutionary or otherwise. The erection of a new and revolutionary symbolic system is only a temporary stasis, to be assaulted in its turn by the recognition of material processes left out of *its* representations. For the revolutionary function of a text is not to give rejection impulses a program to absorb and so block their force, but to "set the drive charge in motion" towards the social outside, so that it may be "invested in the process of transformation of nature and society" (*Revolution*, 176). A continuous challenge to the abstractions of the symbolic register by contradictory material processes ensures the continuous productivity of rejection (negativity). "Thus heterogeneity is not sublimated but is instead opened up within the symbolic that it puts in process/on trial" (*Revolution*, 191). Indeed, *The Awakening* does not end by offering the reader a place of static identification with Edna's brave new vision. Instead it wipes out all the positions of its own discourse to suggest a new dimension of reality, in which Edna neither sinks nor swims but enters the sea changes of an ongoing metamorphosis. The novel's refusal to stay within the limits of its own discourse qualifies *The Awakening* as a revolutionary text in Kristeva's terms, invested in "process over identification, rejection over desire, heterogeneity over signifier, struggle over structure" (*Revolution*, 179).

As the reader has throughout had trouble finding rest in identification with Edna, because she is always changing—and in ways that elude realist conventions of character development—so now the reader loses Edna to fluidity altogether, as Edna walks into the sea and her consciousness disappears from the text.

Cynthia Griffin Wolff describes Edna's final merger with the sea as a "regressive" attempt to attain an oral dream of fusion (217–18). Marianne Hirsch claims that the structure of *The Awakening* is one of "total circularity," returning in the last paragraph to images from Edna's girlhood—family and meadow—and repeating in Edna's final swim her original vision of freedom and fusion with the sea ("Spiritual *Bildung*," 44).

What may be circular in terms of Edna's life, however, is open-ended in terms of fictional discourse, leading outward rather than back. Dipping into the preoedipal "fusion, fluidity, continuity, mutuality, and lack of differentiation" (Hirsch, 27) that releases Edna from ego boundaries seems at the same time to have freed Chopin from narrative convention.[14] The last paragraph subjects all narrative categories to dissolution, including the position of reader.

> Edna heard her father's voice and her sister Margaret's. She heard the barking of an old dog that was chained to the sycamore tree. The spurs of the cavalry officer clanged as he walked across the porch. There was the hum of bees, and the musky odor of pinks filled the air. (114)

When Edna "hears" her family's voices and the dog barking in this final passage, a familiar convention enables the reader to understand that these sounds occur in memory. The sound of spurs clanking is a bit harder to locate, since the subject "she" has disappeared from the sentence. The ontological status of the last sentence is totally ambiguous. Edna's consciousness has disappeared from the text—indeed, we have reason to believe, from life. Do the hum of bees and the odor of pinks then literally fill the air? The locution "there was" insists on presence, and "the hum of bees" and "the odor of pinks" appeal to the senses of hearing and smell that witness what is indisputably *there*—but we are at sea, not just figuratively but literally, far beyond the reach of the most pervasive odor of flowers. Like the listeners to Edna's tale, we are left with intense sensual impressions but no character to enclose them. The existence of an image without a context, or a thought without a mind to think it, throws into doubt a novel reader's fundamental assumption that a particular character thinks thoughts, smells flowers, hears dogs. The semiotic language of the voice of the sea has intermittently called up the fluidity of the reader's infantile sensual self; now the disappearance of the character the reader has been identifying with makes the reader lose the clear outline of enveloped personality that has been confirming assumptions about the reader's own existence as a circumscribed being. The dissolution of all the fixed positions of narrative discourse—narrator, character, reader—enacts through language the fusions and diffusions that the voice of the sea has promised throughout. As Edna moves into a fluidity beyond patriarchal discourse, so do we.

5 Housekeeping
The Impossible Poetry
of the Preoedipal

LIKE *THE AWAKENING*, *Housekeeping* deals with the problem of a disappearing subject. But Edna fades into the preoedipal embrace of the sea only at the end, and the confusions and diffusions of the preoedipal are otherwise contained in interruptions from the voice of a sea safely marked off from the social territory and social discourse it adjoins; Ruth, the narrator of *Housekeeping*, inhabits the diffuse waters of the preoedipal throughout, so that merging is built into the perspective of the novel. Having lost her mother to suicide at an early age, Ruth remains locked in a symbiotic union with someone who is not there. Consequently her narrative pushes up against the limits of the linguistic contract in several ways. First, the narrator often fails to distinguish between self and other, so that the distance between the speaking subject and her objects necessary to language itself is always endangered. Second, her loyalty to the dead takes the form of making death the touchstone of reality. Against death's concrete reality, the physical things of the world that are ordinarily taken to be the containers of being are exposed as meretricious, empty: "Everything that falls upon the eye is apparition, a sheet dropped over the world's true workings. The nerves and the brain are tricked. . . . only the darkness could be perfect and permanent" (116). Ruth's epistemology thus reverses the fundamental dichotomy between being and nothingness that underpins Western cultural constructions of reality, continually ascribing existence to the dead and robbing what is visibly *there* of being.

Desire follows the same trajectory as meaning, drawn after the disappearing mother into the void: "Memory is the sense of loss and loss pulls us after it" (194). Merged with a dead mother, Ruth both feels "incompletely, minimally existent" (104) and longs for complete entry into the nothingness that is for her the final reality: "It is better to have nothing. . . . Come unhouse me of this flesh, and pry this house apart. It was no shelter now, it only kept me here alone, and I would rather be with them [the dead]" (159). The discourse this desire produces tends toward dissolution: Ruth gradually wipes out her own position, trying the limits of a narrative frame that depends on her presence as the subject of enunciation.

The central question of this chapter is: what becomes of the reader who identifies with a narrator who first merges with her objects, then denies her own being, and disappears?

Dissolving the Temporal and Spatial Parameters of Narrative

The narrator's opening words promise a conventional *Bildungsroman*: "My name is Ruth" (3). Enclosing the self in a single name promises containment, belying the diffusions of identity to come. This seeming circumscription of the self is buttressed by the insertion of the speaker into a family network, where other clearly differentiated identities surround and support her own: "I grew up with my younger sister, Lucille, under the care of my grandmother, Mrs. Sylvia Foster, and when she died, of her sisters-in-law, Misses Lily and Nona Foster, and when they fled, of her daughter, Mrs. Sylvia Fisher" (3). "I grew up" further alerts the reader to expect the conventions of a *Bildungsroman*, as does the family setting of this growing up. Each family member is formally named and so placed in a network of social relations governed by the Name of the Father. The next sentence consolidates this promise of conventional solidity by lodging the family in a particular house and binding them to the patriarchal order through a founding father: "Through all these generations of elders we lived in one house, my grandmother's house, built for her by her husband, Edmund Foster, an employee of the railroad" (3). Following the narrative conventions of realism, *Housekeeping* smooths the reader's entry into a circuit of identification with a narrator who seems to offer a stable locus of identity, firmly positioned in a social network.[1]

But this is not in fact a *Bildungsroman* in the usual sense: it is rather a novel of reverse *Bildung*. That is, the images Ruth uses to express her sense of existence describe a decline down the developmental path established by Lacan and Kristeva. The separate position of speaking subject that opens the novel with the firm assurance of self-containment—"My name is Ruth"—loses its clarity and definition as Ruth merges in a symbiotic union first with her sister, then her aunt; images of shattering mirrors signal her refusal of the separate unified position of the mirror stage. Then Ruth moves (on the level of imagery) into a fetal position within her aunt's body. Toward the end she reconstructs an image of her self before it was corrupted by conception: "I (and that slenderest word is too gross for the rare thing I was then) walked forever through reachless oblivion, in the mood of one smelling night-blooming flowers, and suddenly—My ravishers left their traces in me, male and female" (214–15). The final pages of the novel complete the trek backward toward the purity before conception with a discursive celebration of nonbeing, as the narrator piles up variations on the theme of her being "nowhere . . . nowhere . . . nowhere" (218–19). This discursive reversal of the process of ego formation undoes both the conception of the self as a closed structure and the fixed position of the subject who is generating the present discourse, eroding the principal supports of the symbolic order.

The movement backwards toward oblivion is not so obvious as my description makes it seem. On the narrative surface, dialogue and action proceed (for the most part) from characters who occupy conventionally delimited positions; but on the level of the underlying imagery, blurrings and dislocations of the "I," fluid transgressions of identity boundaries, and mirror images that appropriate the reality of the persons they reflect, disrupt all the certainties of the symbolic order. The same could be said of the tension between the text's seeming adherence to temporal and spatial conventions and the undermining distortions of time and space that reflect a preoedipal view of the world. Events do follow events in a semblance of temporal sequence—else the story could not be told—and the characters inhabit some space (at least until the final pages, when Ruth and Sylvie emphatically occupy *no* space). But the initially firm spatial and temporal contours of Ruth's world become increasingly blurred, paralleling her slide toward nondifferentiation.

Ruth appears to anchor her personal history in a temporal context by locating it, autobiography-fashion, in the march of generations toward the event of her birth. But in fact the generations merge, and they dwell in a time that has nothing to do with progression toward a goal. Linear time is only a distant memory, presented in the moment of its demise: the moment of Ruth's grandfather's death. His drowning in the lake is paradigmatic for the fate of everything that belongs to the clearly delimited structures of a masculine order—including the house he built, doomed to be inundated periodically by the flooding waters of the lake. With the disappearance of her grandfather into the lake, Ruth reports, her grandmother and her three daughters "were cut free from the troublesome possibility of success, recognition, advancement. They had no reason to look forward, nothing to regret. Their lives spun off the tilting world like thread off a spindle, breakfast time, suppertime, lilac time, apple time" (13). Losing their link with the goals of the public world—"success, recognition"—the now exclusively female characters also lose the sense of time as "advancement" along a line. Replacing the masculine notion of "time as project . . . time as departure, progression, and arrival" (Kristeva, "Women's Time," 34) is a "women's time" attuned to diurnal and seasonal cycles ("breakfast time, suppertime, lilac time, apple time"). The metaphor that assimilates the earth to a spinning wheel gestures past normative divisions—night and day—to the spatial production of time through the earth's turning, so that time is presented as continuous motion.

This encircling time indeed subverts the generational sequence that Robinson borrows from the realist novel. The movement from Ruth's mother's childhood to her own is not, after all, a movement forward. Rather, Ruth occupies the same maternal enclosure as her mother did: she is brought up in the same house by the same woman in the same time frame (five years). "For five years my grandmother cared for us very well. She cared for us like someone reliving a long day in a dream, . . . baffled by an awareness that this present had passed already" (24). Ruth's childhood recycles the events of her mother's childhood.

If we look at the spatial dimension of *Housekeeping*, we see the same picture of a conventional structure undermined by the dissolving impulse of the preoedipal. Robinson describes the town and the lake where Ruth grew up in painstaking detail, as if to ground us in the familiar world of the symbolic order, where names delineate clearly demarcated geographical spaces. But the name of the town *is* the name of the lake: Fingerbone. So when one speaks of the town, one may be invoking the lake. "One is always aware of the lake in Fingerbone" (9) thus appears to be a tautology (of course one is always aware of the lake if one is in it). The physical world immediately mirrors this discursive conflation by violating the physical law that only one entity can occupy a given space at a given time: the lake in fact inundates the town.

> The terrain on which the town itself is built is relatively level, having once belonged to the lake. It seems there was a time when the dimensions of things modified themselves, leaving a number of puzzling margins, as between the mountains as they must have been and the mountains as they are now, or between the lake as it once was and the lake as it is now. Sometimes in the spring the old lake will return. One will open a cellar door to wading boots floating tallowy soles up, . . . the stairway gone from sight after the second step. The earth will brim . . . the grass will stand in chill water to its tips. (5)

The clear structures of patriarchal society—the house, the town—are thus at the mercy of invading waters that eliminate all partitions and divisions. Even the solidity of the ground beneath one's feet melts away as lake water unexpectedly emerges where earth should be: "when the ground is plowed in the spring . . . what exhales from the furrows but that same sharp, watery smell" (9). The metamorphosis of earth into water has implications for one's physical safety, for the "delicate infrastructure" of lake water frozen into the ground collapses into fluidity every spring: "such delicate improvisations fail . . . we foundered as often as we stepped" (93). If the full and firm physical world described in realist novels reaffirms the solidity of our assumptions not just about the way space and ground are articulated but also about our place in relation to that familiar universe, a novel that erodes basic certainties about the way the physical world surrounds and supports our bodies must involve the reader kinetically, bodily, in uncertainty.

The water's dissolution of all distinctions is echoed on the discursive level by the metonymy that governs the elements of the physical world: no element remains reliably itself, but rather air, water, earth exchange properties. Thus "air brims," "the wind is watery" (9), "earth brims" (5), and the water of the lake impossibly exhibits the geological strata that belong to earth:

> At the foundation is the old lake, which is smothered and nameless and altogether black. Then there is Fingerbone, the lake of charts and photographs, which is permeated by sunlight and sustains green life and innumerable fish. . . . And above that, the lake that rises in the spring and turns the grass dark. . . . And above that the water suspended in sunlight, sharp as the breath of an animal, which brims inside this circle of mountains. (9)

"All our human boundaries are overrun," as Ruth says in another context (115). The distinct lines between things that enable us to read the world are elided. Where is the border between "water permeated by sunlight" and "water suspended in sunlight"? Does water suspended in sunlight qualify as water or as air? Ruth describes her world as one of "puzzling margins," referring to the disconcerting way that mountains and lake shift and change places. The landmarks of the discursive world are equally mobile, replacing the clear dividing lines between things with "puzzling margins" where elements blend.

The shifting parameters of Ruth's world create a context for shifting identities. Coming unmoored from its location in a temporal continuum, identity becomes mobile, too, sliding from generation to generation. "When I look at Ruthie, I see Helen, too," Ruth's Aunt Sylvie says; and Sylvie, located in the present, takes the place of Helen (Ruth's mother) in the past contained in memory: "Sylvie began to blur the memory of my mother, and then to displace it. Soon it was Sylvie who would look up startled, regarding me from a vantage of memory in which she had no place" (53). This temporal merging is discursively reflected in a break with the convention of first-person narrative, which limits what the narrator can know of the past to what others report to her. Ruth delivers the feelings of her grandmother about her marriage and her child-rearing as if Ruth herself had felt what her grandmother felt, lived through her experiences. This overlap in point of view reflects the interpenetration of identity along a temporal axis.[2]

Identities slide along a spatial axis, as well. Proximity becomes identity as Ruth merges with Sylvie on the trip across the lake to one of Sylvie's "secret places."

> I lay down on my side in the bottom of the boat. . . . Sylvie climbed in and settled herself with a foot on either side of me. . . . I lay like a seed in a husk. . . . I toyed with the thought that we might capsize. It was the order of the world, after all, that water should pry through the seams of husks. . . . It was the order of the world that the shell should fall away and that I, the nub, the sleeping germ, should swell and expand. . . . Say that . . . I drank water into all my pores . . . and given that it is in the nature of water to fill and force to repletion and bursting, my skull would bulge preposterously and my back would hunch against the sky and my vastness would press my cheek hard and immovably against my knee. (162)

Ruth grows—but, here as elsewhere, not in the usual direction. In a metaphorical rejection of the normative order of development toward independent human being she becomes ever more gigantesquely embryonic. Although Roberta Rubenstein contends that this scene ends in rebirth (*Boundaries*, 221–22), Ruth herself discourages that speculation. Separation is not in "the order of the world," according to Ruth: "my first birth had hardly deserved the name [of parturition], and why should I hope for more from the second?" (162). This is in fact a scene of birth *manqué*, ending with Ruth still fused—unborn, drowsed in a warm and wet fluidity encompassed by Sylvie's body: "I slept between Sylvie's feet, and under the reach of her arms, and sometimes one of us spoke, and sometimes one of us answered. There was a pool of water under the hollow of my side, and it was almost warm" (164). No conversation can be reported, for the complete merger implied by the metaphor of bodily fusion definitively cancels out the separate positions necessary for language: the differentiated pronominal positions, "she" and "I," are replaced by a single designation, "one of us." Indeed that signifier echoes the metaphor of pregnancy: the singular "one" cannot be articulated without a simultaneous incorporation into the dual unit, "of us."

For similar reasons, names fail in this scene:

> The faceless shape in front of me could as well be Helen herself as Sylvie. I spoke to her by the name Sylvie, and she did not answer. Then how was one to know? . . .
> "Sylvie!" I said.
> She did not reply. . . .
> "Helen," I whispered, but she did not reply. (167)

A system of linguistic signifiers depends on the speaker's assuming the fixed position of "I" in order to be able to make statements about others confined to similarly fixed positions designated by stable names. Names fail when the "I" becomes indistinguishable from its objects and the objects themselves slide into one another.

This passage makes a mockery of the opening narrative promise that characters will be enclosed in the safely singular positions of the symbolic and linked by the Name of the Father. Sylvie and Ruth no longer belong to the fixed geometries of patronymic charts, but abide in a maternal circle of identities where Sylvie may well be Helen, Ruth embodies Helen, and Ruth slides into Sylvie.

In Ruth's developmental progress backward toward the purity of nonbeing before conception, this image of embryonic development is central. From this point on she is committed to a dual identity with Sylvie: she returns a vagabond in Sylvie's image, enfolded in her greatcoat (the insignia of Sylvie's transient status) and riding the rails; later the two pursue Sylvie's transient way of life together. In a rhetorical reverberation of this merging, Ruth increasingly slides into dual forms that better reflect her uncertain sense of where she ends and another begins: "We—in recollection I feel no reluctance to speak of Lucille and myself almost as a single consciousness" (98); "Sylvie and I—I think that night we were almost a single person" (209); "We are the same" (144); "We are drifters" (213).

When identities fold into each other, the difference between signifiers that generates meaning comes under increasing pressure. Names and pronouns fail, and the separate position of the narrator who produces the discourse is threatened. Ruth's trajectory back toward nondifferentiation is reflected by the movement of the text to dissolve the bases of its own existence.

Shattering Mirrors, Mirroring Faces

When *Housekeeping* thus erodes the supports of the symbolic order—the autonomy of the speaking subject, the distinctions between things—the rift in the symbolic texture opens the way for an infusion of images from the imaginary.[3] I use Lacan's term "imaginary" for the preoedipal because *Housekeeping* pulls the reader into a preoedipal confusion of self and other through mirror images; Lacan likewise uses mirrors to express the reflections and doublings of identity in the imaginary. The central scene of Ruth's move into identification with Sylvie, above, is embellished with images of shattering mirrors and intermirroring faces.

Ruth's meditation on a shattering mirror-image during the boat ride with Sylvie affirms her refusal to move forward, developmentally, into a separate identity.

> It would be terrible to stand outside in the dark and watch a woman in a lighted room studying her face in a window, and to throw a stone at her, shattering the glass, and then to watch the window knit itself up again and the bright bits of lip and throat and hair piece themselves seamlessly into the unknown, indifferent woman. It would be terrible to see a shattered mirror heal to show a dreaming woman tucking up her hair. (163)

According to Lacan, a child first gets the idea of a coherent identity by catching a glimpse of itself in a mirror. It takes on the unity of its body image, saying in effect: I am the image in the mirror, I am whole. Lacan stresses that this recognition of a unified self is a misrecognition. The perceiving consciousness is *not* all of a piece like the delimited shape in the mirror, but shifting, contradictory, fragmented. In the passage above, it is the shattered window that knits up after it is broken, not the woman herself; the process is repeated, as if for emphasis, in the image of a shattered mirror that "heals" into a seamless whole and then shows the image of a whole woman. Unity is not the property of the woman's body; rather, wholeness inheres in the reflecting mirror—exactly where Lacan locates the "reality" of coherence. By leaving coherence where Lacan says it inheres—in the mirror—Ruth rejects the saving illusion of an integrated self that in Kristeva's developmental schema prepares the way for the projection of subjectivity into the equally self-contained (and equally alienated) signifier, "I" (Kristeva, *Revolution*, 44). Ruth prefers to stay on this side of the mirror, finding self-definition not in a mirror that would reflect her as a single demarcated shape, but in the mirroring face of the other that blurs identities.

Sylvie and Ruth will have none of the developmental logic that decrees that once you have found your identity in a mirror, you have to move on, displace it onto the letter "I." Rather, each finds herself in the mirror of the other: "More than once [Sylvie] stooped to look in my face. . . . It was as if she were studying her own face in a mirror" (160). Ruth and Sylvie thus remain fixed in the developmental stage that D. W. Winnicott places even before Lacan's mirror stage: "The precursor of the mirror is the mother's face . . . ordinarily, what the baby sees [in the mother's face] is himself or herself. . . . the mother is looking at the baby and what she looks like is related to what she sees there" ("Mirror-Role," 111–12). Ruth's regress thus moves from a shattering of mirror-stage illusions back toward the more primitive phase of seeing the self reflected in the (m)other's face.

Housekeeping follows this imaginary logic to disturbing extremes:

> Anyone that leans to look into a pool is the woman in the pool, anyone who looks into our eyes is the image in our eyes, and these things are true without argument, and so our thoughts reflect what passes before them. . . . the faceless shape in front of me could as well be Helen herself as Sylvie. I spoke to her by the name Sylvie, and she did not answer. Then how was one to know? And if she were Helen in my sight, how could she not be Helen in fact? (167)

If one finds oneself in the reflection of the other's look, then one *is* the image one sees in the other's eye. By extension, one *is* the image reflected in the mind of the other. By this logic, the female shape in front of Ruth depends for definition on Ruth's image of it. If she thinks it is Sylvie, it *is* Sylvie; if she constructs it as Helen, it *is* Helen. In a psychic world where each exists only by virtue of the other's recognition, there is no stable entity to answer to a name, for a name presumes a constant identity. Here, identity shifts with the other's shifting attention.

This insubstantiality is of a piece with Ruth's view of the world. Where nothingness is the only reality, being is evanescent, insubstantial: "my grandmother, [dying], had entered into some other element upon which our lives floated as weightless, intangible, immiscible, and inseparable as reflections in water" (41). The desire that arises out of this epistemology is a kind of death drive—a desire to resolve back into the nothingness that is the underlying reality. In the concluding pages Ruth moves through the reflections of the imaginary into nothingness by locating her image in the mind of the other (her sister, Lucille) and then obliterating that other.

Ruth's final meditation begins with a seeming restoration of the house, together with a housekeeper devoted to keeping order. Ruth never actually sees the house after she and Sylvie set fire to it and move into a vagrant life, but she imagines it from the distance of the moving train: "Someone is living there. Someone has pruned the apple trees and . . . restrung the clotheslines and patched the shed roof. . . . I imagine it is Lucille, fiercely neat, stalemating the forces of ruin. I imagine doilies, high and stiff, and a bright new pantry curtain" (216). This restoration of household order is the logical outcome of an alternative developmental track adumbrated in *Housekeeping*, the one chosen by Lucille, Ruth's sister. Lucille tried in vain to take Ruth with her along the normative path of female development, "nudging, pushing, coaxing, as if she could supply the will I lacked, to pull myself into some seemly shape and slip across the wide frontiers into that other world" of social order and convention (123). But they parted ways when Lucille moved out of "Sylvie's house," her scornful appellation for a home where leaves, squirrels, crickets, sparrows indoors and sofas on the lawn erased the line between inside and outside, natural and domestic orders (99). Seeking apparently a more socially approved form of housekeeping, Lucille moved into the house of the home economics teacher. Thereafter Ruth and Lucille are separated by the gap between the imaginary and the symbolic: in their last meeting Lucille "talked and talked," but Ruth, submerged in dreams of a dual identity with Sylvie, "could not hear a word she said" (174–75).

In Ruth's vision of Lucille's housekeeping, Lucille seems to have reached the goal of female maturity marked out for "little women" on traditional developmental charts. In the role of good housekeeper she restores the clear dividing lines of patriarchal order, repairing roof and lines and setting up partitions everywhere, "high and stiff." But in fact there is no ground in the fluid world of *Housekeeping* to support such a solid and well-ordered establishment, any more than there is a position for a sister who has passed beyond the mergings and dualities of the preoedipal into the gender role definitions of the oedipal. Revealed as a figment of Ruth's imagination, Lucille and her house melt away: "I imagine it is Lucille . . . but I know Lucille is not there" (216–17).

But knowing that Lucille is not there does not preclude Ruth's grounding her own existence in Lucille's mind.

> Lucille . . . has, in my mind, waited there in a fury of righteousness, cleansing and polishing, all these years. . . . Sometimes she dreams that we come walking up the road in our billowing raincoats, hunched against the cold, talking together in words that she cannot quite understand. And when we look up and speak to her the words are smothered, and their intervals swelled, and their cadences distended, like sounds in water. . . . Perhaps she is in the kitchen, snuggling pretty daughters in her lap, and perhaps . . . they look at the black window to find out what their mother seems to see there, and they see their own faces and a face so like their mother's, so rapt and full of tender watching, that only Lucille could think the face was mine. If Lucille is there, Sylvie and I have stood outside her window a thousand times. (217–18)

In the realm of the imaginary the symbolic order fails. Sunk in the medium of the preoedipal, the discrete units of words blur, "distended," and the intervals between them are obliterated, filled with connective waters.

What takes the place of words is faces: Ruth exists because Lucille's daughters see her face in the window. We are in the realm of the imaginary, where the ontological argument runs: "You see me, therefore I exist." If one learns to seek one's identity in the mirrors of others' faces, one may avoid the alienation concomitant with projecting oneself into the "I" of the symbolic, but at the cost of great confusion. This confusion Robinson's sentence captures. The girls turn to look at the window because they see their mother, Lucille, gazing at something there: "they see their own faces and a face so like their mother's, so rapt and full of tender watching, that only Lucille could think the face was mine" (218). It is impossible to tell from this sentence whether Lucille's daughters see the reflected image of their mother's face (which we know to be facing the window) or Ruth's face looking in from outside. If Ruth's face is there, the girls ought to see it beside the reflection of their mother's. But Robinson's statement captures the essence of imaginary identification through its refusal to choose between one and two. The project of trying to capture a reflection of one's own existence in the mirror of the other's face leads precisely to this fluctuation between one and two. One confuses what one sees in the other's face with what the other is looking at (one's own face) (Winnicott, "Mirror-Role," 112). Probably one does not definitively equate the other's face with one's own, but rather vacillates between a conviction of sameness and a recognition of difference, finding rest neither in differentiation nor in union. Robinson's sentence reactivates this uncertainty by depriving us of a distinction between one and two. As the sentence slides away from the ground rule of the symbolic, that only one entity can occupy one position at a time, it supplies in its place the principle of imaginary identification: homeomorphism. The face that is (possibly) looking in from outside is *like* the face that is (possibly) reflected in the glass. It thus dramatizes the confusion of imaginary dualities, which establish identity by homeomorphism ("We are the same," 144), but do not distinguish clearly the one from the other.

The last sentence, "If Lucille is there, Sylvie and I have stood outside her window a thousand times," makes Ruth's and Sylvie's presence contingent on Lucille's being there to dream them up. The reader, whose hold on reality has been severely taxed during the reading of *Housekeeping* by this kind of shift in the locus of being from reality to reflection, now loses his or her grasp on the narrator altogether, as even the reflecting surface of the other's mind is wiped out: "but I know Lucille is not there" (217). The passage exaggerates the circularity of imaginary identification, exposing the precarious nature of an existence founded on the shaky grounds of the other's imagination: if the other is not there to mirror one, one is not there either.

My argument proceeds now, in the spirit of the imaginary, by means of a homeomorphism. Ruth's difficulty in believing that she exists can be understood as the predicament of a child who lost her mother during a time when she depended on the maternal face to reflect and so confirm her existence. She is left looking for self-affirmation in a face that isn't there. Hence she often feels "invisible"—and therefore, with mirror-stage logic, "incompletely and minimally existent" (104). By the end of the novel the reader is in a similar position, searching in vain for a reassuring reflection of self-contained identity in a narrator who keeps dissipating into darkness.

Imaginary Identifications and the Reader

While Lacan speaks of imaginary operations as originating in a stage that developmentally precedes language, he does not mean to imply that once the subject enters the symbolic, she or he ceases to function in the realm of the imaginary. Rather, he presents the imaginary as intertwined with the symbolic. We may assume that the act of reading, like any other activity of a human being, calls on both symbolic and imaginary capacities of the reader. Critics like Belsey and Coward and Ellis have described the reader's entry into a fictional text through the position carved out for the reader by realist texts, a unitary position that reinforces the reader's symbolic construction as a "transcendent and non-contradictory being" (Belsey, 78); I argue that readers also enter first-person texts by way of an identification with the narrator that corresponds to the mirroring processes of the imaginary. The very term "identification" recognizes an implicit parallel between the projection of the self into the fictional world and mirror-phase operations.

Because human beings first grasp the concept of a unified self through identification with an other human shape, they "forever after anticipate their own images in the images of others, a phenomenon Lacan refers to as a sense of 'thrownness'" (Ragland-Sullivan, 25). The capacity to project oneself into the shape of the protagonist and house one's consciousness there for the length of the reading probably stems from that original investment of the self in the other's form. Not only the capacity, but the desire: having initially established the unity of one's ego "in a fictional direction" (Lacan, "Mirror-Stage," 2), we can assume one continues in a fictional direction, scanning the text as one scans the world for the equivalent of a mirror image on which to "throw" the turbulent movements of one's consciousness in order to get back a unified self-image.

In a movement parallel to Ruth's regress down the steps of the imaginary, I want to follow the implications for reading of two distinct stages of imaginary identification. The first phase corresponds to Lacan's mirror stage: a reader finds in the unifying vision of the singular "I" in the text a reassurance of his or her own coherent, framed identity. The second corresponds to the more primitive sense of existence that a baby receives from seeing itself reflected in its mother's face: a reader is continuously reassured about the stability of his or her own existence by the constant presence, the continuity of being, of the "I" who is telling the story—that "I" in which the reader has for the time invested his or her consciousness. Now what happens when that "I" is withdrawn?

In a first-person narrative the containment of the narrator within the narrow confines of the "I" seems to offer an unambiguously singular position visually as well as verbally—an analogue to the Lacanian mirror image of self-containment. Further, a first-person narrative is unified by the single point of view from which it is told. With opposing perspectives closed off by this enclosure in a single consciousness, a reader can rest secure within a unified and noncontradictory vision: "each apparently present episode is contained in a single, intelligible, and all-embracing vision of what from the point of view of the subject of enunciation is past and completed" (Belsey, 78).

Looking to the "I" in *Housekeeping* for a mirror image of the self as a unified being, the reader finds neither unity nor, finally, being. Counting on the narrative "I" for delivery on its opening promise of singularity— "My name is Ruth"—the reader encounters an increasingly indeterminate "we" as Ruth first merges with Lucille, then burrows ever further into a dual identity with Sylvie. When the reader looks to the narrator for that assurance of a unified vision with which a first-person narrative usually shores up the reader's sense of his or her own coherence, the reader is referred, dizzyingly, to the mind of the other as the medium of the narrator's vision:

> If Lucille is there, Sylvie and I have stood outside her window a thousand times, and we have thrown the side door open when she was upstairs changing beds, and we have brought in leaves, and flung the curtains and tipped the bud vase, and somehow left the house again before she could run downstairs, leaving behind us a strong smell of lake water. (218)

"*If* Lucille is there"—but we know Lucille is not there. By inscribing itself within the mind of someone who does not exist, Ruth's autobiography self-destructs. The text draws the reader into the baffling circularity of imaginary identification: looking for the equivalent of a mirror image—a framed, demarcated position that will verify and validate his/her own "thrown" identity—the reader finds the narrator's identity thrown in its turn onto the mirror of the other's mind. And the other's mind is then rubbed out. Thus the reader not only reads about Ruth's self-elusiveness, but experiences in his/her own person the precarious nature of a self in passage through the positions of the imaginary.

Even deeper than the question that Lacan claims the specular ego is always asking of the other—"Who am I?"[4]—lies another question, un-asked and unanswered because formulating it would threaten to disintegrate the nucleus of the ego: "*Where* am I?" Even acknowledging the validity of the question threatens to expose the alterity at the foundation of the ego, the original false identification of the self with the whole body-image reflected in the mirror. In the passage cited above, in which Ruth imagines the fragmentation of a woman's body only to see her mirror image knit up into a whole again, Ruth locates cohesion not in the woman's actuality but in the reflective glass. The text thus comes perilously close to exposing the misapprehension that grounds the reader's sense of a unified self: it reverses the direction of the original transfer of wholeness from the mirror to the self, threatening to destabilize the reader's certainty about exactly where the unity of the self is located. *Housekeeping* continues to exert pressure on the reader's mirror-stage certainties by constantly shifting the locus of reality from things and persons to their reflections in ponds, mirrors, and the minds of others. The novel ends with the dreaded answer to the question, "Where am I?" "Nowhere."

In the last paragraph Ruth repeats that answer with a vengeance:

> Or imagine Lucille in Boston, at a table in a restaurant. . . . Sylvie and I do not flounce in through the door, smoothing the skirts of our oversized coats and combing our hair back with our fingers. We do not sit down at the table next to hers and empty our pockets in a small damp heap in the middle of the table, and sort out the gum wrappers and ticket stubs, and add up the coins and dollar bills, and laugh and add them up again. My mother, likewise, is not there, and my grandmother in her house slippers with her pigtail wagging, and my grandfather, with his hair combed flat against his brow, does not examine the menu with studious interest. We are nowhere in Boston. However Lucille may look, she will never find us there, or any track or sign. We pause nowhere in Boston, even to admire a store window, and the perimeters of our wandering are nowhere. No one watching this woman smear her initials in the steam on her water glass . . . could know how her thoughts are thronged by our absence, or know how she does not watch, does not listen, does not wait, does not hope, and always for me and Sylvie. (218–19)

What does the annihilation of the narrator beneath this barrage of verbal negation do to the reader? It puts the reader in the position of Ruth, gazing for affirmation into an empty mirror. The disappearance of the reflecting other is of course what *Housekeeping* is about: when Ruth looks into the mirroring face of the mother, there is nothing. If Ruth's difficulty in believing in her own existence comes from looking for an affirmation of who she is in a maternal face that is not there, does the reader suffer a parallel ontological doubt when placed in a parallel situation, searching in vain for a reassuring reflection of identity in a narrator who is emphatically *not there*?

To answer this question, I want to reconstruct the condition of a reader responding to *any* first-person narrative. When "I," the reader, look into the text and see an other "I" there, I must on some level assume identity. That "I" in the text seems to replicate my "I" and therefore to signify me; yet at the same time the "I" in the text represents a different person.[5] Reader identification then recreates the ambiguous condition of the first identification with the mother. That is, the baby may sometimes believe unequivocally what Winnicott says it believes: "I look in my mother's face and what I see there is myself." But as it grows more aware of difference, it must oscillate between the ontological positions "I am you" and "you are you." If reading fiction returns us to this questionable identificatory mode, where one half-believes the other is the same, yet half-perceives the other's difference, it may also return us to the ontologically vulnerable position of the infant. Winnicott specifies that an infant's basic faith in its existence depends on the maternal gaze giving back an image of aliveness: in cases where the mother is too depressed or preoccupied to mirror back an image of vitality to the baby, "the baby receives inadequate mirroring and has trouble, later in life, believing in its own existence" ("Mirror-Role," 111–16). As the mirroring narrator of *Housekeeping* disappears from the reader's purview, the lack of reflection may return the reader to the primitive ontological dread voiced by one of Winnicott's patients: "Wouldn't it be awful if the child looked into the mirror and saw nothing!" (116). The constantly receding and finally self-eliding figure of the "I" in *Housekeeping* may thus bring the reader to the question implicit in this expression of ontological anxiety: "If there is no one in the mirror of the text, then where am I?"

Housekeeping does not keep an awareness of specular interdependency relegated to the safe distance of the characters' experience. The text makes the reader experience his/her own dependency on the mirror reflection of the other by gradually withdrawing all the props to his or her ego. First the reader looks and cannot find a mirror image, clearly delineated, because the "I" blurs into a "we"; the reader looks again, and there is nothing. The reader's progress (or regress) down the gamut of supports usually provided for readers by narrative discourse thus parallels Ruth's devolution from the initially unified position of the symbolic ("My name is Ruth") through all the declensions of the imaginary. The reader is forced to feel in his/her own person the precariousness of an existence dependent finally on a reflecting other.

Making the Symbolic Signify Nothing

The logic of Ruth's conviction that death is the only reality should lead her to take her own life and so rejoin her dead family; but her suicide is purely discursive. On the level of the plot she becomes a "transient," embodying her oft-repeated definition of the living as mere evanescent gleams on the surface of that enduring reality, death (41). "Transient" is a synonym for "ephemeral" in any dictionary; but the lexicon of *Housekeeping* ultimately makes transients entirely immaterial by assimilating them to the dead: "their lives as drifters were like pacings and broodings and skirmishings among ghosts" (179). As a transient, then, Ruth occupies no position in the social order. In terms of the cultural symbolic, she is "nowhere."[6]

From that nonposition in the plot line she can rub out the narrative "I." The denial of being in the final paragraph—"we are nowhere," "we are not"—elaborates the impossible proposition "I am not." "I am not" (or, in Ruth's habitually dual form, "we are not") is a statement that cannot be made, because the words "I am not" imply the existence of the I who speaks them: "Thought . . . can include no negation that is not already an affirmation, always already positing the indestructible presence of the unitary subject: 'I'" (Kristeva, *Revolution*, 119). Robinson winds the mechanism of language up in internal contradiction until it breaks down altogether, leaving the page blank. Or, seen from another angle, she eliminates the speaking subject who generates the discourse, so that the discourse must perish.

But, as Kristeva maintains, the dissolution of the symbolic is not destructive merely. It produces a new signifying system constructed on the basis of what the old one repressed: in this case, death (*Revolution*, 109; "Identity," 134–35). The absence of being is beyond a language whose function is to represent what *does* exist. By forcing language to accommodate something that cannot be articulated in its terms—the invisible, the nonexistent—Robinson creates a new discourse. If we take the text as a narrative generated by Ruth's drive to rejoin her dead mother in not-being, we can see her desire for death operating discursively in passages that bring nonexistence vividly into language.

> If I could see my mother, it would not have to be her eyes, her hair. . . . There was no more the stoop of her high shoulders. The lake had taken that, I knew. It was so very long since the dark had swum her hair, and there was nothing more to dream of. . . . She was a music I no longer heard, that rang in my mind, itself and nothing else, lost to all sense, but not perished, not perished. (160)[7]

Throughout the novel, metaphors of sensual immediacy make tangible what isn't there: "this sense of a presence unperceived . . . a sense of imminent presence, a palpable displacement, the movement in the air before the wind comes" (121–22).

I submit that the same desire to make language signify death, or non-being, "which no signifier could ever contain" (Kristeva, *Revolution*, 50), turns the rules of symbolic discourse upside down to make the final paragraph celebrate Ruth's (and Sylvie's) nonexistence. Because of the very impossibility of denying the subject who speaks, the modifier "not" becomes attached to the verb, leaving the subjects standing in unassailable presence.[8]

> Sylvie and I do not flounce in through the door, smoothing the skirts of our oversized coats and combing our hair back with our fingers. We do not sit down at the table next to hers and empty our pockets in a small damp heap in the middle of the table, and sort out the gum wrappers and ticket stubs, and add up the coins and dollar bills, and laugh and add them up again. My mother, likewise, is not there, and my grandmother in her house slippers with her pigtail wagging, and my grandfather, with his hair combed flat against his brow, does not examine the menu with studious interest. We are nowhere in Boston. (218)

We see double: in spite of the "not" we continue, because of the sequential nature of reading, to see unfold a vivid picture of what the characters "do not" do. The wealth of specific detail that we are used, in a realist text, to take as a token of reality, here describes nonbeing—and so precisely and concretely that we are compelled to see it in all its living detail. The exuberance of the language conveys the narrator's feeling of triumph. On the level of the individual, Ruth arrives at the only place she could ever occupy, a nonspace that joins her to the absent dead who have throughout been most vitally present to her. Her discourse, propelled by the same drive toward death, successfully manipulates the ground rule of the symbolic—the resistance of the subject to negation—to force language to positivize negation, to realize absence.

As Lacan's terminology implies, the symbolic encompasses not just language but the order to which linguistic structures belong: the cultural structures of knowledge that form what we take to be reality. The impossibility of negating being in language corresponds to a larger repression of death and nonexistence from cultural constructions of reality. Western signifying systems exclude death by relegating it to the other end of a bipolar opposition between life and death. When Ruth sees death witnessing against the hollowness of life's apparitions from the interstices of the visible, her vision dis-covers the reality hidden by the assumption of a specular culture that what you see is all there is. As Ruth's perception implies, death is in fact indissolubly knit up with life processes, growing beneath the surface of every flower, tree, face whose visible surface a specular culture identifies as the whole reality. By inserting nonexistence, impossibly, into language, Robinson challenges not only language, but conventional structures of meaning, "tracing a space within a society's cognitive frame."[9]

In at least three ways, then, *Housekeeping*'s subversion of symbolic structures opens up a new space for writing. The dissolution of the singular speaking subject in a merger with her loved ones dis-covers the other way of seeing, natural to mother-child relations but usually hidden beneath the symbolic order's insistence on the individual as a separate, closed entity. Objects and places seem to interpenetrate and time seems to circle when identity is in perpetual transition between self and other. Removing the wraps of the symbolic enables Robinson to articulate the language of facial reflection that always goes on, unacknowledged, beneath spoken conversations that pretend to tell the whole story. And threatening the linchpin of symbolic systems, the link between signifier and signified, by forcing language to articulate death—pure absence, "the signifier without a signified" (Cixous, "La fiction," 231, cited in Jackson, 69)—generates an impossible poetry whose metaphors make emptiness palpable, concrete.

2 Writing toward Change

6 Toward a More Creative Autonomy

To the Lighthouse, Violet Clay, Bodily Harm, "How I Came to Write Fiction," and *On Not Being Able to Paint*

ISSUES OF AUTONOMY are central to artist novels written by women. Stories of artists' lives—at least those told by middle-class white women—tend to polarize a woman's possibilities: a woman can carve out for herself the autonomous space necessary for creating works of art; or she can relax into a sensual and emotional intimacy—not both. The female artist figures I explore in this chapter are representative of the type: Lily in *To the Lighthouse*, Mlle. Reisz in *The Awakening*, Rennie in *Bodily Harm*, and the title character of *Violet Clay* defend themselves against emotional involvement, as if autonomy were possible only through a total denial of intimacy.

They may thus be cutting themselves off from an interpersonal realm (and a corresponding inner realm) rich in creative possibilities. The work of Evelyn Fox Keller and Joanna Field (pseudonym of Marion Milner) suggests that a more flexible autonomy, one that allows an artist to retreat from time to time to an indeterminate area between self and other, may be more fruitful for art than an insistence on maintaining the self separate. D. W. Winnicott's theories (especially as elaborated by Ruth Perry) suggest that if one can relax into an ambiguous space where the distinction between self and other loses its clarity, one can more easily recognize and accept creative impulses from the unconscious. An experience like sexual passion, which throws boundary definition into question (Kernberg, 94–101), may allow an artist to recreate the intersubjective dimension of experience that once stretched between herself and her mother—an area where the child felt safe to play in imaginary worlds. A loss of ego boundaries necessarily affects one's thinking, dissolving customary mental divisions and triggering the kind of unstructured mental flux that Ernst Kris and Brewster Ghiselin claim is the prerequisite for creating something new. My later chapters on *The Waterfall, The Golden Notebook,* and *The Color Purple* consider the effects of an enabling sexual relationship on the female protagonists' art. Joanna Field's work, reviewed later in this chapter, suggests that an artist can also recover the capacity to slide into the ambiguous area between self and other through a continual give-and-take with her own created works—which are by definition part self, part other.

This chapter explores the psychological origins of these two different conceptions of autonomy. What psychological structures you think are necessary to creative work depends on your view of what is important in psychosexual development. Kohut and Winnicott tend to ignore the oedipal period, extending processes usually associated with the preoedipal to the whole continuum of development. That is, they envision individual growth as a sustained interpersonal dynamic between parent and child. This emphasis on the intersubjective dimension of development gives rise to a definition of autonomy that allows for some fluidity in the boundary between self and other, some incorporation of the other in at least the early stages of creative work.

The concept of autonomy as absolute self-containment and absolute self-reliance that governs most female artist novels is a product of the oedipal stage, a period when girls feel the pressures of gender training in a male-dominant society. Faced with the demand that they accept the subordinate female role embodied by their mothers, girls can either accept that role and continue to identify with the mother who has nurtured them through preoedipal times; or they can strike out towards autonomy and the power to define the self differently. But then they risk the loss of the mother's love. That either-or split, engraved in the unconscious of women writers, results in the dichotomy that rules most female artist fantasies: a woman has to choose between a nurturing and sensual love and the autonomy requisite for art.

Other feminist critics have explored the cultural forces that pressure women to choose between autonomous work and love.[1] To adopt a psychoanalytic perspective, as I do here, is not so much to replace the analysis of cultural influences as to broaden it to include the traces left on a daughter's unconscious by family relations that are, after all, the principal conduits between cultural ideology and the individual unconscious. Cultural ideology is most subtle and insidious when it comes in the form of interpersonal relations in the family; those patterns of relationship become embedded in unconscious fantasy as patterns of desire that govern what women want and hence their life choices.

The Creative Potential of Transitional Space:
A Developmental Model

Evelyn Fox Keller has redefined autonomy in ways that seem especially fruitful for creative work. To the dominant cultural definition of autonomy as "a radical independence from others" (97), she opposes a flexible autonomy that

> leaves unchallenged a "potential space" between self and other—the "neutral area of experience" that, as Winnicott describes it, allows the temporary suspension of boundaries between "me" and "not-me" required for all empathic experience—experience that allows for the creative leap between knower and known. It acknowledges the ebb and flow between subject and object as the prerequisite for both love and knowledge. (99)

The notion that relaxation into an ambiguous space between self and other can foster creativity rests on a view of human growth that emphasizes the interpersonal dimension of child development. Winnicott and Heinz Kohut (and Nancy Chodorow in some of her later work—for example, "Gender, Relation") focus on the way maternal attentiveness, love, and identification foster a child's growth. When one looks at development through their eyes, one sees a picture of growth as a dynamic between self and other.

In the beginning, says Winnicott, "there is no such thing as an infant . . . meaning, of course, that whenever one finds an infant one finds maternal care, and without maternal care there would be no infant." A baby's manifest helplessness makes the notion that "the infant and the maternal care together form a unit" ("Parent-Infant," 39) accessible even to minds habituated to the idea of people as separate entities. But Winnicott takes unity as the basis of selfhood a step further when he envisions the self coming into its own, claiming its sensations for itself, only within the space created by the mother's presence.

> It is only when alone (that is to say, in the presence of someone) that the infant can discover his own personal life. When alone in the sense that I am using the term, . . . the infant is able . . . to become unintegrated, to flounder, to be in a state in which there is no orientation, to exist for a time without being either a reactor to an external impingement or an active person with a direction or interest or movement. The stage is set for an id experience. In the course of time there

arrives a sensation or an impulse. In this setting the sensation or impulse will feel real and be truly a personal experience. ("Capacity," 34)

That is, the most basic self-realization, the most primitive recognition of one's sensations as one's own, occurs in a shared setting. If one's initial self-perception is centered by the presence of an other, the presence of an other can continue in adult life to give one access to impulses from the unconscious and to allow one to claim them as one's own. Kohut argues along parallel lines: a child recognizes its achievements as its own and as good when they are reflected back by a parent's affirmation. Only then can they be integrated into the child's ongoing self-concept. "A sense of self evolves through relationships that validate what we can do for ourselves," as Jessica Benjamin puts it (94).

If a child's developing selfhood is a joint project, an artist's creative self may similarly thrive in an intersubjective dimension. At least for some artists, as Ruth Perry writes, "the most propitious conditions for writing, for playing with versions of reality, might include the presence of another—someone who bears a complicated relationship to that initial presence in which the self came into being."[2] Trying to recapture the enabling space between mother and child through an adult relationship must necessarily engender complications and conflicts, some of which I deal with in the chapters that analyze the relation between sexuality and creativity in *The Waterfall*, *The Golden Notebook*, and *The Color Purple*. Here I offer, by way of paradigm, George Eliot's autobiographical account of how the relationship with George Henry Lewes gave birth to her novels.

Writing a novel had long been a dream of Eliot's; but up until the age of thirty-eight, when she began her liaison with Lewes, she had not ventured beyond writing essays and translations. Lewes encouraged her to try her hand at fiction, but Eliot "deferred it, . . . after my usual fashion." Then,

> one morning, as I was lying in bed, thinking what should be the subject of my first story, my thoughts merged themselves into a dreamy doze, and I imagined myself writing a story the title of which was—"The Sad Fortunes of the Reverend Amos Barton." . . . I was soon awake again, and told [George]. He said, "O what a capital title!" and from that time I had settled in my mind that this should be my first story. (Eliot, "Fiction," 407)

I present Eliot's story as a kind of parable that dramatizes the possibilities for adult creativity that emerge from Winnicott's theories: if infantile receptivity to impulses from the id depends on the presence of a loving other, the presence of a loving other later in life can again grant access to unconscious intuitions and enable one to claim them as one's own. Eliot's "dreamy doze" next to Lewes seems to recapture the indeterminacy of the space between mother and child, a space where trust in the mother's protective presence frees the child from the adaptive demands of reality, so that the child can play—that is, "slip back and forth from fantasy to reality, constructing, demolishing, and reconstructing worlds" (Perry, 4). Because Eliot can afford, in the transitional space guaranteed by Lewes's presence, "to flounder," "to become unintegrated," "to let go of her orientation to reality" (Winnicott, "Capacity," 34) her consciousness can open up to "unrealistic" images from a realm beyond conscious purpose.

Eliot is able to claim the vision of herself as author, to integrate it into her ongoing sense of self—"I had settled in my mind that this should be my first story"—in part because Lewes, like the empathic mother described by Kohut, mirrors it back to her with unqualified enthusiasm: "O what a capital title!" And Lewes continues to play the facilitating mother throughout the anecdote, smoothing the transition from dream to actuality: "It may be a failure—it may be that you are unable to write fiction. Or perhaps, it may be just good enough to warrant your trying again. . . . You may write a chef-d'oeuvre at once—there's no telling" (Eliot, 407). By making every eventuality part of a world known and accepted in advance, Lewes marks out a safe ground for experimentation that is free of the dread of failure (and of success).

Winnicott ties the transitional zone, where the boundaries between reality and illusion blur, to a stage when the child is in transition between being merged with the mother and perceiving her as a separate entity. Reclaiming this intermediate area of experience as an adult should then be facilitated by a parallel eclipse of the line between self and other. Sexual intimacy, Otto Kernberg says, gives a person the sense of crossing the boundaries between self and other and entering the terrain of the other's subjectivity (94–101). Sex can thus provide access to a realm where the self is not clearly differentiated from the nonself. Although Eliot's Victorian reticence prevents our knowing whether the "dreamy doze" was a postcoital reverie, certainly the location of her epiphany—in bed beside Lewes—suggests a sexual space. Phyllis Rose, at any rate, "sees the story of George Eliot's 'birth' as a moving testimony to the connection there may be between creativity and sexuality" (*Parallel*, 212); and U. C. Knoepflmacher finds it likely "that George Eliot herself connects her latent creativity to her sexual intimacy with Lewes" (107).[3]

Because Eliot's account, self-contained in the short essay "How I Came to Write Fiction," isolates this moment of erotic creativity from the complex social context that surrounded it (and no doubt impinged on her creative processes), it can serve as a paradigm for the recovery of transitional space through sex. In the next three chapters I explore how the fantasy of love inspiring creativity plays out in the here and now of patriarchal sexual politics. In *The Waterfall* and *The Golden Notebook* the artist-protagonists work their way out of various kinds of inhibiting containments, emotional and artistic, in part through writing, in part through sexual relationship. But the complications of loving within patriarchal structures—the subordination of female to male fantasy within a male-dominated imaginary, the dependency patterns of romantic love—so weight down these heterosexual relationships that they cannot continue, at least in the form of ongoing intimacy. In *The Color Purple* the lovers fare better, each creating for the other a maternal space where it is safe to explore both sexuality and creativity. Celie's and Shug's love escapes the contamination of patriarchal dominance patterns partly because both are women and partly because the author's optimism makes creativity a natural extension of erotic relationship.

In order to show how unusual is these novels' blend of art and love, this chapter explores the governing principle of most female artist fantasies (at least those written by white middle-class heterosexual women): the artist-protagonist must choose between intimacy and the autonomy necessary to artistic achievement. Lily, Violet Clay, and Rennie are representative of their type, living by a defensive autonomy that closes out the possibility of emotional connection.

In an artist novel, however, narrative momentum comes from the drive to create a work of art. As if in tacit acknowledgment that some entry into indeterminacy is necessary to create art that catches the life of its subject and communicates it to the viewer, each of these novels of artistic self-containment concludes with a moment when its protagonist abandons her insistence on separation in order to regain a measure of fluidity between self and other—not through sexuality, which remains outside the polarities that structure these novels, but through a diffuse identification with a woman who also becomes the subject of her painting. Not accidentally, to my way of thinking, this final leap into empathy coincides with the completion of a successful work of art.

The Fantasy of Austere Autonomy

Why is the fantasy of erotic love nurturing creativity so rare among female artist novels, at least among those by white middle-class heterosexual women? If developmental processes were simply those I have outlined above, it would seem natural to include relationship with an other at least in the early stages of creative work. But in fact something impedes the idyll of development conceived as a harmonious weaving of identity between self and other, and that same thing impedes women writers who have grown up in traditional nuclear families from incorporating into their fictions the fantasy of erotic energy generating creative projects. By focusing on the ways that maternal attention and love nurture growth, Winnicott and Kohut empower mothers and validate preoedipal relations; but they tend to overlook the power relations of patriarchy within which child development takes place. In other words, they overlook the complications of the oedipal stage, when the power structure of the family comes into focus for the child. Perhaps there is no need for an oedipal stage: Gayle Rubin and other feminists have argued that it is the sex-gender system of patriarchy that is responsible for the damaging convolutions of oedipal development. If the larger society were not constructed on the principle of male dominance, there would be no need to shape girls to roles of subordination, dependency, and service; and there would be no need to devalue the mother in order to teach boys to treat women as inferiors. Indeed, as I argue in part 3, families with a different power structure do allow a child to go on developing, past what is assumed to be the oedipal threshold, in unbroken continuity with the mother.

But as long as children are brought up in a male-dominant system, the resolution of oedipal conflicts will continue to disfigure boys and girls, lopping off some of their capacities in order to overdevelop others. What I want to argue here is that a daughter enters the oedipal stage closely identified with the mother who has nurtured her; in her dawning awareness of family power relations, she perceives that the mother who earlier seemed omnipotent is in fact limited to a subordinate and self-denying role within the family structure. The daughter in this situation can either continue to identify with her mother and accept the devalued female role she represents. Or she can cut herself off sharply from her mother in a bid for autonomy and self-development; but that entails risking the loss of the mother's nurturing love. It is not just emotional intimacy that is at stake, but sensuality too. A girl forms the first impression of her sensual body at the hands of her mother—a sensuality that, in those unstructured times, diffusely englobes the body of the other along with her own. Escaping the female role by severing the link with her mother involves cutting herself off from the preoedipal ground of her sensuality as well as from the source of nurturing love.

As Jane Flax says, "The split between nurturance and autonomy is carried by all of us as one of those archaic residues within the unconscious" ("Conflict," 186).[4] The early wrenching choice between autonomy and love leaves its imprint in the either-or choices of artist novels. In some cases the protagonist herself oscillates between the two extremes of sensuality and autonomy as if between two distinct selves. Or the same dichotomy is embodied in two polarized characters who represent, on the one hand, the self-containment that preserves the self for art but precludes intimacy and, on the other, the dedication of all a woman's energies to the task of maintaining interpersonal relations. *Violet Clay* illustrates the first configuration, *To the Lighthouse* and *The Awakening* the second.

Violet Clay, in Gail Godwin's novel by that name, operates as if she believes that there is a fixed amount of psychic energy: what is invested in erotic experience must be withdrawn from art, and vice versa. Thus, when she marries, she sinks into a sensuality that precludes painting:

> [My husband] kept expecting me to dash out on the deck with easel and paints and capture the fall foliage. But I had gone all funny and languorous. There was something delicious and sensual about my abdication. . . . There was something sexy about . . . having been forced . . . to lie down in the sweet juices of traditional womanhood and abandon the hubris of an edgy, lonely struggle. I didn't touch a paintbrush those first months of captivity. What for? The colors of satisfaction oozed out of my very pores. I posed for myself in front of the mirror, turning this way and that, thinking: I am now a wife. I lapsed, I gave myself up to my senses, to Womanhood. (42–43)

The logic of bipolar opposition requires an equally abrupt break with sexuality and all its consequences when Violet decides to move into her role as artist. Launching her career in New York City requires, first, that she leave her husband; second, it coincides with a miscarriage that wipes out her whole (potential) family. The underlying assumption that the supply of energy is constant—a psychological version, or perversion, of the physical law of conservation of energy—precludes the possibility that erotic activity might generate *more* energy for art, as in the George Eliot anecdote.

The same all-or-nothing principle underlies the distribution of scarce resources in Virginia Woolf's *To the Lighthouse*. Either one can be Mrs. Ramsay, pouring all one's energies into sustaining personal relations; or one can be Lily, hoarding all one's energies for art. The images that express their very different responses to the demand for sympathy that Mr. Ramsay makes on each of them crystallize the contrast between them.

> There he stood, demanding sympathy. . . . Mrs. Ramsay . . . seemed . . . at once to pour erect into the air a rain of energy, a column of spray . . . as if all her energies were being fused into force . . . and into this delicious fecundity, this fountain and spray of life, the fatal sterility of the male plunged itself. . . . He must have sympathy. . . . James felt all her strength flaring up to be drunk and quenched by the . . . arid scimitar of the male. (59)

This feat of giving has sexual overtones: afterward, "there throbbed through her, like the pulse in a spring which has expanded to its full width and now gently ceases to beat, the rapture of successful creation" (61). But in the underlying calculus of energy expended, energy transferred, there is no room for the conception of an erotic activity that would engender *more* creative energy. Mrs. Ramsay has emptied herself by pouring out into the world that "fountain" of compassion. While Mr. Ramsay trots off "filled, . . . renewed, restored" (60), Mrs. Ramsay is left hollow: "there was scarcely a shell of herself left for her to know herself by" (60).

When Mr. Ramsay, having lost his wife, turns for sympathy to the artist Lily, she responds by shoring up the walls of the self to keep all her resources safe and dry within:

> this was one of those moments when an enormous need urged him . . . to approach any woman, to force them . . . to give him what he wanted: sympathy. . . . She should have floated off instantly upon some wave of sympathetic expansion: the pressure on her was tremendous. But she remained stuck. . . . He sighed profoundly. He sighed significantly. All Lily wished was that this enormous flood of grief, this insatiable hunger for sympathy, this demand that she should surrender herself up to him entirely, . . . should leave her, should be diverted . . . before it swept her down in its flow. . . . His immense self-pity, his demand for sympathy poured and spread itself in pools at her feet, and all she did, miserable sinner that she was, was to draw her skirts a little closer round her ankles, lest she should get wet. (225–28)

Drawing in her skirts outlines the boundaries of the self—a gesture of self-enclosure that enables Lily to avoid Mrs. Ramsay's self-diffusion into a wellspring of compassion. But the water imagery also reminds us of what this insistence on self-containment closes out. Earlier, Lily had expressed a desire "for becoming, like waters poured into one jar, inextricably the same, one with the object one adored [Mrs. Ramsay]" (79): the water imagery continues to carry the theme of a possible merger between self and other. Mr. Ramsay's histrionic self-display and his treatment of all women as sponges meant to absorb his emotional outpourings makes the reader applaud Lily's resistance to the demand that she "behave like a woman"; but the water imagery reminds us of what Lily loses in this transaction. The price of holding herself aloof is the loss of an opportunity to participate imaginatively in an other's subjective world—together with the loss of empathic vision that might have enriched her paintings.[5]

A similar opposition of extremes governs Edna's choices in *The Awakening*. She can be either Mlle. Reisz or Madame Ratignolle—pursue either the self-containment necessary to art, at the cost of isolation from human connections, or the full-bodied sensuality and warmth of a "mother-woman" (Chopin, 8) embedded in family relations and limited by convention. At this arbitrary condensation of the whole range of female possibilities into two polar extremes, the reader may feel restive: there must be other possible combinations, she may think, for a woman like Edna who aspires to both the autonomy of the artist and the sensuality of the woman. The stubbornness of this either-or pattern, its resistance to compromise, suggests the arbitrary quality of an unconscious structuring principle.

The radical opposition between the mother-woman and the artist-self reflects not a single decision—not a moment's choice between mother and autonomy—but a long developmental process of defining the self in opposition to the female norm and the mother who embodies it. What I am describing here is akin to the process of negative identity formation that Chodorow ascribes to boys: a definition of the self as "not-mother." Chodorow explains that a father's distance from the business of child-rearing makes personal identification with him difficult; in order to align himself with a masculine role definition that is somewhat distant and abstract, a boy defines himself *against* what is closest—his mother. In the process of denying his primary identification with his mother he also denies "relation and connection," seen as feminine attributes (*Mothering*, 174; see also 175–77). Although Chodorow acknowledges the conflict and ambivalence in a girl's relation to her mother, she implies that a girl maintains her sense of diffuse continuity with her mother even through the oedipal turn to her father; she makes that turn "while looking back at her mother . . . every step of the way" (126). "A girl's internal oedipal situation is multilayered. Her relationship of dependence, attachment, and symbiosis to her mother continues, and her oedipal (triangular, sexualized) attachments to her mother and then her father are simply added" (129; see also 109–10, 125–29). I suggest that Chodorow's description of two different paths toward individuation is more useful if we drop her gender determinism and think of the developmental track Chodorow designates for the male as a possibility open to girls, too—a possibility that the devalued role of the mother in patriarchal family relations (and the maternal depression and low self-esteem that often result) turns into a probability.[6]

Certainly female fiction and autobiography is full of daughters who, like Chodorow's male children, define themselves through denial of the mother in them. Martha Quest in Doris Lessing's *Children of Violence* series is representative. As Lynn Sukenick says, "It is against her mother's vapidity that Martha Quest forms her character; her self-respect is fashioned out of her sense of difference from the woman who hovers uselessly in the margins of her life. . . . Both Martha and her friends wage a battle against the pressing image of the older, lifeless, unfulfilled women around them" (518). This definition of the self through hostile opposition to the mother is so familiar to white middle-class women that they have labeled it as a specific pathology: "matrophobia—the fear not of one's mother but of becoming one's mother":[7]

> Matrophobia can be seen as a womanly splitting of the self, in the desire to become purged once and for all of our mothers' bondage, to become individuated and free. The mother stands for the victim in ourselves, the unfree woman, the martyr. Our personalities seem dangerously to blur and overlap with our mothers'; and, in a desperate attempt to know where mother ends and daughter begins, we perform radical surgery. (Rich, *Of Woman Born*, 238)

Radical surgery, indeed. Defining oneself as not-mother means denying in oneself everything associated with the mother, including capacities and needs for fusion, empathy, intimacy. The mother is embedded in human relations, indeed is defined by them. So the daughter defines herself as exempt from the need for relationship and from the demands of others:

hence the radical opposition in artist novels between the mother-woman embedded in human relations and the artist-self who stands alone.

In Margaret Atwood's *Bodily Harm* the journalist Rennie actually voices the matrophobic ground of her defensive autonomy: "I didn't want to be trapped, like my mother. . . . I didn't want to be like her in any way: I didn't want to have a family, or be anyone's mother, ever. . . . I didn't want to cope. I didn't want to deteriorate" (57); "Griswold [codeword for her mother's traditional life] . . . is merely something Rennie defines herself against" (23). Reacting to her mother's entrapment in the nets of family, Rennie defends against emotional connection. She prides herself on the cool detachment of her relationship with Jake. His habit of circumscribing women as the objects of his designer's vision meets her need to keep the line between self and other clearly drawn: he reflects back to her, continually, an image of her self set off and demarcated by the outline of her body. She enforces the distance between herself and others through various devices that turn the other into the object of her controlling eye: she picks a man on the street and "does him over" with an imaginary brush; she reduces men's bodies to part-objects—the policeman's legs (18), Jake's fingers (24), the doctor's hands (35). All are ploys to avoid taking in the other as a whole, ploys to escape the demands implicit in an acknowledgment of the other's subjectivity.

When she is thrown into a jail cell with Lora in the confusion of a Caribbean revolution, Rennie protects herself against the fellow feelings that might be evoked by their common plight by defining Lora in opposition to herself: "*Women like you* [that is, fallen women] . . . it's a pigeonhole, she's in it; it fits" (253). A self-respecting woman cannot be expected to sympathize with a woman who trades sex for favors; walling off the other into a separate category absolves Rennie of the demand for empathy. When Lora is beaten by their jailers and thrown back into the cell limp and unconscious, the importunity of her silent claim on Rennie's sympathy evokes a last-ditch gesture of boundary delineation: "Rennie picks her way carefully around the outline of Lora" (262).

But this is Rennie's final effort to keep the line between self and other clearly demarcated. A flashback to her childhood enables her to incorporate the maternal heritage of connection. She remembers her senile grandmother coming into the kitchen:

> I can't find my hands, she says. She holds out her arms to Rennie, helplessly, her hands hanging loose at the ends of them. Rennie cannot bear to be touched by those groping hands, which seem to her

like the hands of a blind person, a half-wit, a leper. She puts her own hands behind her and backs away. . . .

Rennie's mother comes in through the kitchen door. . . . I can't find my hands, says her grandmother. Rennie's mother looks with patience and disgust at Rennie. . . . Here they are. Right where you put them. She takes hold of the grandmother's dangling hands, clasping them in her own. (262–63)

The joined hands of the two women represent both the continuity between mother and daughter and the conventional gender role of woman embedded in family relations—the two aspects of the maternal relation that Rennie has abandoned in order to define herself differently. The notion of continuity is rendered through a blurring of bodily limits, too: when Rennie's mother says, "Here they are," does she refer to the hands she extends to the grandmother or to the grandmother's hands that she reaches out to touch? In any case, the hands cannot be located outside the linking handclasp that makes them real. Reintegrating the maternal gift of connection enables Rennie to overcome her need to mark off an autonomous space. She "pulls Lora's head and shoulders onto her lap." She uses her mother's gesture as power: "She's holding Lora's left hand . . . she has to pull her through"—and she pulls her back, into life (263).[8]

Recovering empathy transforms Rennie's writing. Before, Rennie had used her writing skills to denigrate women through a flippant reportage of their fads and fashions; distancing them through ridicule enabled her to deny female solidarity. In the end she resolves to write about Lora's ordeal, becoming "a subversive . . . a reporter" (265) who, in witnessing against what she now perceives to be the systematic social abuse of women, acknowledges her own share in that victimization.

The progress of Rennie's autonomy from an exaggerated emphasis on detachment and separation to a final integration of the maternal capacity for emotional connection describes an arc generic to the female novel of artistic autonomy. Up until the end, Violet and Lily also gird themselves against the incursions and diffusions of personal relations. But in the final pages a collapse of ego boundaries enables each to enter into the feelings of the person she is painting; and finding her way into that intersubjective dimension enables each, for the first time, to complete a painting that satisfies her. Rachel Blau DuPlessis and Susan Gubar have argued that it is important to daughter-artists to reestablish connection with their mothers.[9] Though my argument parallels theirs, I claim that female artists need to recover for their creative use not so much continuity with the mother herself as the psychic ground where the distinctions between self and other, between inner and outer reality, blur or disappear.

Like Rennie, Violet Clay fights to preserve an autonomy that imitates the male model of total self-sufficiency and denial of all dependency relations. Violet in fact enacts the male myth of the artist described by Maurice Beebe: "the typical (male) artist-novel requires that the hero . . . reject the claims of love and life, of god, home, and country, until nothing is left but his . . . consecration as artist" (6). Imitating her writer-uncle's pattern of the artist as exile, Violet withdraws from all human contact to an isolated cabin in the mountains (formerly her uncle's), to dedicate herself to painting. But that seclusion produces only the works of self-involvement—endlessly repetitive sketches for a picture self-reflexively entitled "Violet in Blue." Not surprisingly, in view of the solipsism of their creation, the sketches "didn't communicate anything" (325).

It is, finally, relationship that enables Violet to paint something that *does* communicate. Only when she constructs an empathic space between herself and her model, Sam, can she create a work that both captures something of her subject and communicates it to the viewer. Sam reflects Violet's own ideal of self-sufficiency: "completely self-contained" (329), she is "self-sufficient in a beholden-to-nobody way, able to build [her] own cozy quarters . . . and go [her] own way and raise [her] own child . . . without a man" (336). Paradoxically, Violet gains a new autonomy by relinquishing her defense of boundaries: identifying with Sam gives her a clearer vision of the autonomy she wants for herself. If Sam thus reflects back to Violet an image of her own ideal, the mirroring is reciprocal: "I gave her something in return. . . . I held the mirror for her. . . . As she spread out the pieces of her adult life and looked at them for the first time in the company of a friend and saw what kind of picture they added up to, a confident pride grew in her" (351).

Violet thus provides the empathic mirroring that enables Sam to acknowledge the worth of her own achievements and integrate them into her self-image. Assuming this maternal function puts Violet in a new position. She does not so much lose the border between herself and her model as enter a new dimension of perception: "It is the quality of light I remember most intensely about that morning when it all started to happen, and how Sam's body seems to float in it. . . . She appears to be crafted out of the light, so continuously and harmoniously do the parts of her body mesh with its contours. And yet I need her outline, too. . . . The linear plane of her individuality must be there so the light will have a special form to keep afloat" (348). This multiple perception of her subject as both melting into the circumambient air and clearly delineated as a unique individual form signals a recovery of the continuum between merging and differentiation that a child traverses with its mother. Violet's access to this new fluidity of perception enables her to catch the light and shape of her subject in a way that communicates a vision of female possibilities to her viewers (364–65).

The ending of *To the Lighthouse* presents a similar epiphany, with Lily overcoming her resistance to empathy through the process of painting itself. It is Lily's personal vision that renders Mrs. Ramsay, with her child, as a purple triangle; yet that idiosyncratic shape also replicates Mrs. Ramsay's own image of her central self as a "wedge-shaped core of darkness" (95). Similarly, as Susan Gubar points out, the single stroke that completes Lily's painting by "moving the tree more to the middle" (128) repeats Mrs. Ramsay's personal identification with trees (97, 169, 177).[10] In contrast to her resistance to empathy-on-demand in the scene with Mr. Ramsay, Lily's reproduction of Mrs. Ramsay in the self-images of Mrs. Ramsay's most private reveries is evidence of a leap of imaginative empathy worthy of the mother figure herself. It can be argued that the painting itself furnishes the transitional ground where identities meet and merge: the painting is filled with Mrs. Ramsay's presence, but it is Lily who recreates her. The art work itself recaptures the diffuse blending of self and mother.[11]

Lily's decision to invest empathy in a creative identification with a strong woman rather than in shoring up the self-esteem of a man can be read as an affirmation of Adrienne Rich's prescription for female creativity: "It is the lesbian in us who is creative, for the dutiful daughter of the fathers is a hack" ("Lesbian," 201). The term "lesbian" in this context does not, Rich says, invoke "the fact that two women might go to bed together," but signifies "the woman who refuses to obey, who has said 'no' to the fathers" in order to "choose herself" (200, 202). Lily refuses Mr. Ramsay—and, as Jane Marcus says, "the text exults in Lily's refusal" (228)—in order to find better uses for her merging impulses, outside the gender requirement that women must sympathize always with men. In a system of social relations where saying yes to the fathers results in Mrs. Ramsay's infusion of erotic and creative energies into the project of sustaining others' emotional well-being, "the rapture of successful creation" produces not a work of art, but the rehabilitation of her husband's self-esteem. It is not surprising that women writers living in such a system move toward a woman-identified resolution rather than toward enclosure in the romantic couple. In Rennie's and Violet's stories, as in Lily's, choosing "a primary intensity between women" (Rich, "Lesbian," 200) means choosing one's creative self: that is, allying oneself with a woman who embodies female energy engenders a work of art that expresses the creative merger of self and other.[12]

Creative Ways of Thinking

Joanna Field's *On Not Being Able to Paint* completes the picture begun in these novels of the impediments to an artist's work imposed by "an autonomy too rigidly and too statically conceived" (Keller, 98). *On Not Being Able to Paint* is a book-long account of Field's struggles to overcome her psychological need to preserve the boundary between the "me" and the "not-me" intact. Like the artist novels surveyed above, Field's account follows a trajectory of hope: through the practice of drawing itself, she develops the capacity to merge with the subjects of her representation.

Field's projection of the necessary boundary between self and other onto the visual field initially limits the range of her perception and hence the range of her experimentation. She tries to practice perceptual flexibility after she reads in one of her art books that "a line seems a poor thing from the visual point of view, as the boundaries [of objects] are not always clearly defined, but are continually merging into the surrounding mass and losing themselves, to be caught up again later on and defined once more" (Speed, 50, quoted in Field, 15). But although she accepts this indeterminacy intellectually and actually forces herself to see how the edges of two jugs "seemed almost to ripple now that they were freed from this grimly practical business of enclosing an object and keeping it in its place" (16), "the effort needed in order to see the edges of objects as they really looked stirred a dim fear, a fear of what might happen if one let go one's mental hold on the outline which kept everything separate and in its place" (16). Field understands that this perceptual resistance reflects a deeper psychological defense: "this idea of there being no fixed outline, no boundary between one state and another, also introduced the idea of no boundary between one self and another self, it brought in the idea of one personality merged with another" (24). Field's experience supports Keller's contention that ways of knowing support emotional needs (Keller, 80–92). Field's excessively delineated view of reality corresponds to a defensive insistence on keeping the boundaries of the self fixed and firm.

But psychological need opposes creative need: Field's need to keep the line between self and other strictly defined blocks the reciprocal relation, the "dialogic interchange" between inner and outer worlds that she finds is crucial to creating art that is "alive." Placing the creative act even more decisively within the psychological dimension of merging, she asserts that recognition of the object becomes complete, becomes vivid, only when it springs from a mental sympathy so total that it is felt as a physical merging: "For the making of any drawing, if it was at all satisfying, seemed to be accomplished by a spreading of the imaginative body in wide awareness. . . . In drawing that tree, the spread of the branches and leaves gives an awareness of my shoulders and arms and fingers and I feel its roots in my feet" (106–7). The metaphors of physical union point to the basis of this enabling vision in early illusions of bodily fusion with the mother. If one's identity is founded on a decisive split from the mother and a correspondingly violent repudiation of one's original oneness with her—as in the psychology of the artist figures described above—then one's identity requires a vigilant defense of ego boundaries, a vigorous insistence on separation: one cannot let go of that basic definition of "me" as "not-her" to relax into a blurred identification with the other. When Lily mentally pulls her skirts about her to outline self-containment and Rennie paces off a border around Lora's body, they are falling back, in moments of stress, on a primitive delineation of body-ego to reassure themselves of the reliable boundedness of their bodies, of their physical separation from the world (Chodorow, "Gender," 6). We can only guess at the effect on their creative processes. But Field *tells* us how her need for sharp boundaries gets in the way of a creative merger.

The feedback from her own finished works informs her that it is only when she can relinquish "the emotional need to imprison objects rigidly within themselves" (16) that she can create drawings that have some vitality. The sketch in which she catches the fluidity and "play" of the two jugs' edges, for instance, is interesting for its movement and tension. Similarly with color: she finds in looking over some landscape paintings that "the only glimmer of interest came where there was a transition of colour; for instance, where the yellow lichen on a barn roof had tempted me into letting the yellows and reds merge, so that you could not say exactly where one colour began and another ended" (22). But her need for clarity of outline tempts her to keep colors within borders, "fixed and flat and bound" like the countries on a map (24).

Even while Field's journal entries make visible the presence of some primitive self in charge of survival who fears the plunge into nondifferentiation, her openness to feedback from her drawings enables her to re-mother herself. That is, she finds in the interchange with them a simula-crum of the original fluidity between mother and child. Field traces her boundary difficulties back to an inadequate mirroring relation with her mother. "The relationship of oneself to the external world [was] basically and originally a relationship of one person to another . . . in the beginning one's mother is, literally, the whole world" (116). Since her mother often failed to notice or understand or reflect the meaning of the child's "small gestures," Field's relation to her original world was one of alienation rather than one of continuity and reciprocity. Her sketches offer a medium more reflective than the unresponsive maternal matrix:

> One could reclaim some of the lost land of one's experience, find in the medium, in its pliability yet irreducible otherness, the "other" that had inevitably had to fail one at times in one's first efforts at realising togetherness. Granted that it was a very primitive together-ness, one that allowed the other only a very small amount of identity of its own, yet it did seem able to serve as the essential basis for a more mature form in which both other and self have an equal claim to the recognition of needs and individuality. (118)

Interaction with one's own creations, in other words, prepares one for a dialogic interchange with parts of the external world that are less pliant, less accommodating. Field's creative process is a primitive version of the dialogue she would like to engage in with the external world:

> I would draw a little, at random, spots, shadings, or lines, then feel what these suggest, . . . let the line call forth an answer from the thought. . . . It was an interplay . . . of an inner image and the . . . line actually outside on the paper. And it was when these two interplayed, each taking the lead in turn in a quick interchange or dialogue rela-tion, that the drawings had appeared. (72–73)

The journal by means of which Field reflects on the obstacles that block her creativity—whose entries form the text of *On Not Being Able to Paint*—also represents a creative practice that helps her to overcome her resistance to the "ebb and flow" between self and object. It entails a flexible interchange between thought and external reality—that is, the bit of the external world that is her journal. Taking in what is there, on the page, then catching her first response to it and writing it down, she allows something new to emerge in a dialogic evolution.

Because both journal and drawings are dramatizations of her inner world, interaction with them blurs the boundaries between inner and outer reality, persuading Field through long experience that it is safe to cross over into a territory where it is not clear where the self ends and the other begins. She becomes increasingly comfortable in a zone intermediate between inner and outer realities. This is the creative zone, according to Winnicott, a transitional area retained from childhood where the question, Is it real or is it imaginary? is not even asked ("Transitional Objects," 13–14). It is precisely in this intersection between inner and outer worlds that Field locates the capacity to catch the life of her subjects. Or, in the metaphors of bodily merging that she uses to describe this transitional area, it is here that she can "spread the imaginative body to take the form of what she looked at" (55).

Field's example suggests that an artist—even one whose defensive autonomy requires an excessively demarcated vision of the world—can recover the fertile ground between self and other by practicing a kind of fluid interaction with the work of art itself. In the encounter with the created object that is both a product of one's imagination and actually there, in the external world, the artist recovers the position of a child relative to its transitional objects. To a young child lost in play, the teddy bear or doll is located simultaneously in the world of imagination and in external reality. Winnicott calls the imaginative experience of the baby in this neutral area "primary creativity" ("Transitional Objects," 11): and it can be argued, as Jerome Oremland does, that more sophisticated versions of creativity rest on this ground. Oremland's remarks on Michelangelo's creativity describe the two sides of Joanna Field's efforts to turn transitional experience into art: the receptivity that allows an artist to become "one with other," with the object of his or her representation, enables the complementary active phase of making something that is "part him and part not him" (429).[13]

Dwelling in this intermediate zone is not without its anxieties, as Field's self-study abundantly illustrates. Because a work in progress is not altogether—not yet—an entity with a separate existence, commerce with it engenders the fear that one is interacting with a figment of one's own fantasy world, that one has in fact lost the essential boundary between inner and outer worlds that is society's touchstone for sanity (17). But if one can, like Field, ride out the fears of madness that the temporary abandonment of distinctions engenders, one can recoup many of the encouragements to creativity that lie in the transitional area between baby and mother. The object, by reflecting one's feats of imagination, can function in the same way as the mother's face, mirroring what one has done positively and channeling gratified narcissistic impulses toward further creative acts (see chapter 3, above, on Kohut's theory of narcissism). Yet it is enough "other," once it is thrown onto the page or the canvas, to suggest new directions, to move the project forward.

Field's experience feeds directly into Evelyn Fox Keller's effort to redefine autonomy. Keller argues that a rigidly demarcated and defended autonomy—like that Woolf attributes to Lily, Godwin to Violet, and Atwood to Rennie—"precludes the creative ambiguity without which neither love nor play, nor even certain kinds of knowledge, can survive" (98). Keller's redefinition of autonomy leaves room for a relaxation into the ambiguous space between self and other that is rich in creative possibilities.

Like Field, Keller argues for empathy as a valid way of knowing—a bold move given her position as a scientist, since she thus challenges the central legitimating principle of scientific inquiry: objectivity. She suggests that the absolute distinction between subject and object is a false one, that we can approach an authentic knowledge of the other only by admitting "the very real indeterminacy in the relation of subject and object" and by meeting the object of our study (or art) in a shifting field between merging and differentiation. The developmental paradigm on which Keller's notion of "dynamic objectivity" rests can help us answer an objection that may occur to anyone who reads that the precondition for capturing the essential lines of an object is to merge with it. Doesn't the act of identification preclude a view of the object in its own right? If one is always throwing oneself into the object, surrounding it with a halo of one's own preoccupations and needs, doesn't that cloud one's vision of the object in itself?

Keller's (and Field's) redefinition of objectivity rests on the notion that development is not so much a straight line from primary identification to separation as a continuum of relational modes from merging with the mother to seeing her as a person in her own right. It is this vision of the mother as subject, together with the self as subject, that is the true aim of differentiation.[14] It can be argued that recapturing this fluidity, this alternation "between 'being with' and 'being distinct,'" as Jessica Benjamin puts it (82), enables one to see the object from a number of different angles and so form a global comprehension of it. Field in fact speaks of alternating modes of perception: she moves from a narrow focus on the object that isolates the essential rhythms of its lines from the nimbus of personal associations, to "the wide embracing kind of concentration that gives its own identity to the particular nature of the other" (84). Here Field makes language embrace the shifting relations with the object that are originally part of the mother-child continuum: the recognition of the other depends on accepting one's emotional continuity with it but using that continuity to perceive its individual distinctiveness. Or, in Field's words, it is through "the wide embracing spread of one's own identity" that one "apprehends [the object's] unique reality" (85).

To approach again the fundamental issue of this study: can people change? The stubbornness of the either-or pattern in artist novels by white middle-class women seems to support the Freudian notion that unconscious patterns absorbed from early family configurations impose their arbitrary patterns on us, limiting the range of our imagination. But Field's example supports the counter-idea of Marx that one's daily practice, one's work experience, determines consciousness. "Thought arises out of social practice. . . . In their practices, people respond to a reality that appears to them as given, as presenting certain demands," as Sara Ruddick puts it (341).

Painting itself demands a reciprocal alternation between inner and outer worlds, described by Lily in *To the Lighthouse* as dipping now into the paints, now into the past (256), now into what she sees, now into memory (237–38). This rhythmical interchange between inner and outer realities blurs the defining line between self and world. Losing the clear contours of her social definition, "her name and personality and appearance," Lily also loses track of the distinction between self and painting: "as she lost consciousness of outer things . . . her mind kept throwing up from its depths, scenes, and names, and sayings, and memories and ideas, like a fountain spurting over that . . . white space, while she modelled it with greens and blues" (238). It is painting itself, then, that blurs the border between what is outside (the canvas) and what is inside (the streams of memory that seem to splash across it). And it is this immersion in a transitional activity that prepares Lily for the final empathic vision of Mrs. Ramsay that enables her to complete her portrait. Violet Clay, too, finds through identification with her model the transitional space needed to paint her first successful painting. So even the fictional characters who seem most rigidly bent on defending ego boundaries find their way into an intersubjective dimension through the daily practice of art itself. Similarly, through creating things that are part other, part self, Field gradually replaces the defensive posture of separation based on the gap between self and mother with a stance that is more receptive to the "ebb and flow" between subject and object.

Sexuality as a Bridge to Transitional Space

If a creative discipline is one way of exercising flexibility in self-definition, sexuality is another. Adults long practiced in the painful struggle of keeping subjective reality separate from external reality may need some special solvent of the border between self and other, inner and outer worlds, to jog the mind out of the determinacy of self-enclosure. The next three chapters, on *The Waterfall*, *The Golden Notebook*, and *The Color Purple*, show female artists changing over time, and changing the form of their art, through relationships that are both sexual and creative.

Otto Kernberg's description of the relaxation of ego boundaries in sex provides a theoretical framework for understanding how sexuality can lead to a recovery of transitional space. Kernberg describes sexual passion as "a basic experience of simultaneous, multiple forms of transcendence beyond the boundaries of the self" (99). In mature sexual love—which includes empathy for the loved one—a lover simultaneously transcends the borders of the self into the psychological field of the other and maintains a sense of the self as discrete (95). Sexual love seems, then, to recapture the paradoxical ground between self and mother, where one is neither totally fused nor totally separate.

What occurs on an emotional and psychological level must necessarily affect mental processes. The breakdown of the usual lines of distinction between self and other can trigger a parallel collapse of the mental dividers that keep categories discrete, releasing their contents into a potentially fruitful jumble. Thus in *The Golden Notebook* Anna's erotic merger with Saul precipitates a collapse of the mental divisions that held the various segments of her experience separate: ideas, identities, images previously divided off from each other in sterile containment "were all together" (635), jostling and colliding. Mergings that are both sexual and imaginative thus provide Anna with the opportunity for the interplay of contradictory ideas that has been called the condition of creative thinking (Rothenberg, 313; Winner, 29–31; Koestler, 110). Anna in fact does manage to think and write in a new way: the breakdown of boundaries between self and other enables her to catch the feelings of other people in vivid descriptions that make them seem alive to the reader. Similarly, in

The Waterfall the fluidity of a sexual relationship enables Jane to break out of both her emotional isolation and the artistic containment of poetic convention.

In *The Color Purple*, awakening to sexuality *is* awakening to creativity. Celie and Shug provide for each other a safe maternal space in which both sexuality and creativity can be fully explored and expressed. The lack of a clear dividing line between erotic and creative energies extends to the whole community in *The Color Purple*: the complex erotic connections between the various members of the community encourage the creativity of each.

But Alice Walker escapes the dichotomy between love and art in part because she grew up in a different family structure from the white women writers discussed above. African American family traditions tend to value the mother for her strength and give her control over important areas of life; so daughters do not feel the need to break sharply with their mothers. Walker's artist fantasy is consequently not governed by the need to choose between autonomy with dignity and nurturing love, but rather encompasses creativity and sexuality in a single vision.

7 Talking Back to Jane Eyre

Female Sexuality and the Intertext of Love in *The Waterfall*

JANE GRAY, the protagonist of *The Waterfall*, moves from a position of frozen isolation to a more flexible and productive autonomy through a combination of the strategies used by George Eliot and Joanna Field to recover the fertile indeterminate field between self and other. Like them she suffers the emotional consequences of having a radically unresponsive mother. She initially reproduces the arid gap between herself and her first world by constructing an alienated position both in her love life and in her creative life. In both worlds she waits in a void. As the woman-in-love she waits for an absent lover, her attention abstracted from the concrete world around her to concentrate on "her hopeless, hopeless need for absent James" (169). As poet she waits in a similarly abstract space, sitting motionless, staring at the white walls of her bare room, awaiting an inspiration expected to come, like the idealized lover of romantic fantasy, from beyond the commonplaces of daily life.

Like George Eliot, she establishes a sexual relationship with a lover who remothers her. Her relationship with her cousin Lucy's husband James—confined because of its illicit nature and because of Jane's recent childbirth to one house, virtually to one room, one bed, where she depends on him for her identity as completely as an infant on its mother—is heavily laden with preoedipal overtones.[1] And the recursive journal-like method of writing and rewriting her sexual experience with James resembles the journal that Joanna Field used to record her own development over time. But Jane Gray adds a new dimension to this dialogue with her written work: she inserts into her own text passages from the novels that have become part of her through a girlhood spent in ardent reading—novels by Austen, Hardy, Brontë, Eliot, and others—texts that she uses alternately to reflect her own romantic situation and to establish a position on love that differs from theirs. This ongoing dialogue throws her own position into motion, so that she shifts from the abstract stasis of her initial identification with "those fictitious heroines [who] haunt me" (161) through a number of tentative philosophical positions on love established in relationship to theirs. This dialectic of sameness and difference mimics a process of healthy differentiation from parental figures that are at some level part of the self. And indeed Jane has to a large extent substituted the patterns of love in nineteenth-century novels for the hollow pieties on family love uttered by her own mother, a woman so defended against real connection that she blanches when a family member threatens to touch her (58).

Jane Gray's narrative thus engages the issue of change broached in part 1. To the question, Can reading change the reader? Jane's text returns an emphatic yes. An impassioned reader, Jane Gray has assimilated the plots of literature to such a degree that she now feels the need to launch a conscious written struggle against their overwhelming influence on her patterns of desire. The problem of change shifts in *The Waterfall* from the question whether fictional patterns can replace family patterns in the unconscious to the question whether women can work their way out of the myths embedded by reading (and, by extension, other cultural media)— myths that pattern female desire according to the script of romance. Writing out the various versions of her love affair with James is in part an attempt to catch the distortions and omissions that, unwilled, skew her vision of her own experience to fit the lovely shapes of literature. But Jane also adds something of her own to the intertext on love that she inherits: the voice of active female sexual desire and the sensations of a female body.

Jane's relation to the texts of love that have inscribed their designs on her unconscious fantasy life is complex. On the one hand, inserting herself into a literary structure holds Jane's self-concept static, the complex flow of actual feelings reified into a single stance. Her frequent citation of a tag from *Jane Eyre*—"Reader, I loved him" (87)—implies that her very feelings are frozen into the shapes of literary convention. But the dialogues through which Jane actively engages her literary mentors throw the emotional certainties to which she clings into flux. The complexity of her dialogue with *Jane Eyre* and *The Mill on the Floss*, especially, acknowledges the difficulty of displacing the authority of literary (and, by extension, cultural) paradigms. Like parental imagos, "those fictitious heroines [who] haunt me" (161) cannot be simply dismissed but must be argued with, seen through, contradicted, loved, and finally modified into usable figures that can be understood and lived with. Jane's writing (and her experience) is finally her own just because she does not try to extirpate others' fantasies from her mind, but uses their ideas to evolve her own position on love.

Competing Scripts of Love: Romantic Abstraction versus Bodies Touching

Jane's projection of her obsession with James onto the figure of Tennyson's Mariana focuses the pathology of the romantic script (see chapter 1, above). Because it is the man's actions that bring the woman happiness, his actions rather than her own are the focus of attention. When he isn't there, nothing happens:

> As she sat there, waiting for him, waiting for the telephone to ring, waiting for the sound of his car, she thought that it had perhaps been for this that she had emptied her existence, for this dreadful, lovely, insatiable anguish, for these intolerable hopes. . . . She vainly believed, with the arrogance of all lovers, that she was the only woman who had waited as she waited. . . . She would say to herself: is it more likely that he will come if other cars go along the road, or if the road is empty till his arrival? . . . Madness, she would say to herself . . . she felt herself helpless, ill with longing, quite unable to do anything about her state. . . . she waited. Mariana at the moated grange: he will not come, she said. (139, 141)

Mariana is a figure from Shakespeare's *Measure for Measure*—the woman that Angelo has affianced but refused to marry—whose lonely exile Tennyson imagines in "Mariana." The obsessive quality of her waiting is communicated by Tennyson's refrain.

> She only said, "My life is dreary,
>   He cometh not," she said;
> She said, "I am aweary, aweary,
>   I would that I were dead!"

Repeated seven times, this refrain captures the monotony of obsession. Obsession is stasis: in the poem, time moves (shadows move, the clock ticks, morning changes to evening and evening to midnight), but Mariana can only repeat "without hope of change" (l. 29).

Jane similarly spends the void created by James's trip to Spain in a temporal space abstracted from concrete reality: "in that calendar I saw the abstraction of time delivered to my eyes" (165). Every morning she counts up the hours until his return and moves the red clip on the calendar to the next day—but doing it first thing in the morning "left me with nothing to do for the rest of the day" (164). Time exists only to trace the limits of waiting, but that framework frames nothing—nothing but Jane's "hopeless, hopeless need for absent James" (169).

The waiting woman lives on fantasy because, all her attention concentrated on what isn't there, she is cut off from connection with the concrete world around her. Her senses trained on James's approach, Jane can perceive in her environment only distant rumors of what is to come:

> her ears strained so for the telephone that she could hear it in the clink of a teaspoon, in the baby's sighs, in the creaking cartilage of her own neck as she moved her head. From an upstairs window she could sometimes see the reflection of an approaching car cast around the curve of the corner against the windows of the houses on the street opposite—the first possible intimation, this, of arrival. (139)

If one is a woman waiting, one has little use for one's own perceptions: the concrete world of present experience is meaningless but for the gleams and portents of the lover's approach.

Jane is able to maintain the purity of this abstract position in part because she is cut off from her body and so from the sensations that are our conduits to the material world: "I didn't like anything to happen to my body. . . . my mind was . . . unwilling to accept the events of my body" (108). One cannot blame this extreme alienation from her body solely on a girlhood of ardent reading. Her mother's panic at the touch of her husband's hand (58) suggests the more psychoanalytically respectable explanation that Jane's frigidity stems from early identification with a mother who feared bodily contact. But her tendency to channel sexual intensity into words was certainly reinforced by Brontë's and Eliot's displacement of passion from physical contact onto the prolonged intensity of lovers' conversations.

Thus Jane Eyre at the climax of her union with Rochester makes conversation the site of passionate connection: "We talk, I believe, all day long: to talk to each other is but a more animated and an audible thinking" (454).[2] Even when she describes a kiss, Jane's own physical responses are missing: "He kissed me repeatedly"; "I received . . . an embrace and a kiss. It seemed natural, it seemed genial to be so well-loved, so caressed by him" (258, 260). Where a description of Jane's answering sensations might have been, there is nothing. In her aspiration to match the intensity of Jane Eyre's love, a young reader need never link passion to physical sensation; she can grow up, as Jane Gray evidently has, with a definition of passionate love that excludes the body altogether. Words remain the focus of desire. Thus Jane, "addicted to words, . . . my only passion" (91), could fall in love with her first husband, Malcolm, because when she first saw him he was singing a Campion sonnet. So out of touch with actuality and in love with the literary forms of "love at first sight" (91) was Jane that she confused love for the poem with love for the speaker and so married him, "forgetting that the words were not his, [and] that words and inevitable rhymes move me inhumanly" (92). Her body, locked out of this poetic compact, naturally "refused to accept him, it refused the act, it developed hysterical seizures, it shut up in panic, it grew rigid with alarm" (115).

Joanne Frye has argued that Jane's accepting the role of woman-as-body in the sexual drama of *The Waterfall* puts her in the position of sex object and so inserts her into the cultural scenario of feminine dependency: "To be female is to be defined biologically, to be passive and dependent, to be sexual at the expense of autonomy" (154). Here again is the split between sexuality and autonomy: a woman cannot have both. I argue, rather, that the sexual experience that gradually enables Jane to credit her own sensations is a corrective to the abstractions of romantic love. By putting her back in touch with her own immediate sensations, sex reopens the channel to all the varied concrete experiences of everyday life and so enables Jane to move from the static abstraction of the woman-in-love to a self-in-process who changes in response to the "many-qualitied, changing material processes" of concrete life (Hartsock, 235). The nature of Jane's art changes, too: whereas initially her ideal of poetry was "a poem as round and hard as a stone" (69), the experience of intersubjective flux with James alters the form of her writing to a fluid prose that shifts tone and meaning from chapter to chapter and replaces "the end-stopped phrases of my solitude" with a narrative that, at the end of her chronicle, overflows closure in an affirmation of ongoing possibilities for change.

My interpretation differs from Frye's primarily in that she assumes that the role of woman-as-body makes Jane into a sexual object, whereas I maintain that Jane learns to feel and describe bodily sensations from within, as sexual subject. Frye fastens on the opening third-person narrative in which Jane tells of falling in love with James as "a classic association of femaleness with body with passivity and dependence" (151). Certainly the opening narrative contains declarations of passivity and dependence: "If I were drowning I couldn't reach out a hand to save myself" (7); "'I'll wait for you. . . . And in the end, then, will you rescue me?'" (38). But so complex is this text, so contradictory its mirror of the inextricable interweaving of bodily reality and cultural ideology in a woman's experience of love, that the opening section also contains the germs of a new language that counters the abstractions of the romantic scenario by foregrounding immediate sensual experience.

This language opposes an epistemology based on touch to the specular discourse of Western culture. Words like "hot," "cold," "wet," "dry," recur continuously, conveying physical sensations received through the sense of touch rather than vision. This body language begins well before James's advent: Jane's feelings of being "in touch" start with childbirth, not with her awakening to a lover. Frye views Jane's labor and childbirth as "singularly passive," a preparation for the passivity of her role in the love story to come (150). I contend that the maternal body is not passive but active— not only literally, in terms of producing a baby, but discursively: maternal metaphors govern the love story. When James makes "his willing blind suicidal dive into the deep waters" of Jane's bed (Drabble, 37), he enters a world already defined by the fluid ego boundaries between mother and infant.

The Waterfall opens with Jane in childbirth. Maternity, according to Rich and Chodorow, erases distinctions: "In early pregnancy the stirring of the fetus felt like ghostly tremors of my own body, later like the movements of a being imprisoned in me; but both sensations were my sensations, contributing to my own sense of physical and psychic space" (Rich, *Of Woman*, 63). Living in a woman's body blurs the boundaries between self and other through a number of such equivocal experiences: "menstruation, coitus, pregnancy, childbirth and lactation all involve some challenge to the boundaries of her body ego. Is her blood or her milk me or not-me? Is her baby me or not-me?" (Chodorow, "Family Structure," 59). A discourse based on a female libidinal economy would then include a fundamental loss of distinction between self and other. Indeed, in the aftermath of childbirth Jane enters a world where the line between inside and outside disappears: the dark blue walls of the bedroom blend with the blue of the night sky (9) and "everything . . . could but fall gently into its own place, as the snow fell" (14). The distinction between self and world falls, too: "Everything was soft and still; the whole night, and Jane's nature with it, seemed to be subdued in a vast warm lull, an expectancy, a hesitation, a suspension and remission of trial" (9).

In place of the intervals that govern speech we are in a world where everything touches everything else. Even the air is palpable, "heavy and warm and damp" (9), "dense with smoke . . . and the warm thick smell of milk and wool" (32), so that instead of providing the distances that separate speakers, the room envelops people in a medium with a density approaching that of water: "the room softly surrounded her"; "this warm room held them together" (11)—womblike. Following the logic of this private world where everything touches, James—who is relieving his wife Lucy to watch over Jane's recovery—speaks words impossible in the symbolic order governed by the Law of the Father, where a man and his wife's female relatives inhabit separate categories: " 'I want to be in that bed. The only place in the room is in that bed' " (33).

The bed, where mother and newborn nestle together, *is* the center of this preoedipal world—or, as James says in terms of the collapsed topography of this room, "the *only* place in the room." If, as Michelle Montrelay and Luce Irigaray have said, men privilege sight as the mode of connection with female bodies—a mode that both separates them from the too-intense contact of touch and smell and gives them mastery over the female object governed by their vision—James gives up the distances of a male erotic to enter a relational space governed by infant-mother contiguity.[3] Nor can he convert the bed to a sexual realm: Jane is protected by the six-week ban on intercourse following childbirth. Rather, James accepts the terms of maternal intimacy, an intimacy based on the coextension of reclining bodies: "She lay there, . . . so close that her every breath disturbed him, so close that he was acquainted with all the pains of her still unrecovered body" (40). Knowledge comes through proximity, through physical responses to the rhythms of another's breath, another's body. Jane, ever the anxious interpreter, scans the degrees of James's proximity with the meticulousness of a medieval scholar analyzing the subtleties of a text:

> He turned to her, about to clasp her, and then, . . . he checked himself . . . and reached out for her hand. It was as though she had seen his desire and his hesitation, the one the shadow of the other, both expressed in an instant. . . . The unlikely . . . quality of their proximity, the ways in which they knew and did not know each other, seemed to her to possess a significance that she could hardly bear; such hesitant distance in so small a space, such lengthy knowledge and such ignorance. (35–36)

To know becomes, in this concrete space, to touch: "she touched him, through the limp shirt, laying her hand on his averted shoulder: he was hot to touch, his skin burned her through the thin cotton" (35).

Later, when Jane has shifted out of the third-person narrative into her first-person rhetoric of moral abstraction, she is able to define this alternative way of knowing:

> The names of qualities are interchangeable—vice, virtue; redemption, corruption; courage, weakness—and hence the confusion of abstraction, the proliferation of aphorism and paradox. In the human world, perhaps there are merely likenesses. Recognition, lack of recognition. Faces I know, faces I don't know. (52)

> Sometimes . . . I think that there are no qualities, that there are merely the things I do, the hands I know, the walls that I look upon. (53)

Faces I know, hands I know: this way of knowing returns from abstraction to material reality, from ideation to touch—in short, to a preverbal way of knowing what the other/mother means by the look on her face, the touch of her hand. It is only when Jane has moved to a perspective of contrasting verbal abstraction that she can *name* this concrete way of knowing. When she is embedded in sensuous activity, in the third-person narrative, no such generalizing view obtains. The reader is simply bombarded with words that convey physical sensations—hot, dry, wet, warm, cold, empty, full—as if Jane's body were dictating her text.

If images of proximity and touch convey physical closeness, water expresses an even closer connection, the unimaginable closeness "of infinitely neighboring entities . . . which makes the distinction between the one and the other problematical," in Irigaray's words ("Mechanics," 111). After Jane gives birth there, the bed becomes a preoedipal zone, the continuity of mother and child marked not just by the imagery of water, but by the literal fluids of birth: "Jane, sitting there in the bed with the small new child tucked in beside her, could feel the sweat of effort flowing unchecked into the sweat of a more natural warmth. . . . she could feel the blood flowing from her onto the white moist sheets" (9); " 'The bed's soaked,' said Jane. 'I'm sitting in a sea of sweat. The sheets are dripping' " (22). It is important that Jane accepts the fluids that envelop her and her child before she "drowns in a willing sea" (46) with James. Drabble does not privilege heterosexual sex as the initiation to female sexuality, but gives it the same stamp of fluidity as other female bodily processes. Before she lies "submerged" in love (37), "Jane let her whole body weep and flow, graciously, silently submitting herself to the cruel events [of giving birth]" (10). I emphasize this sequence in order to stress that the discourse of *The Waterfall* makes the female body itself, rather than the man's attentions, the source of female sexuality. Jane embraces her sexuality along with the other processes of her body.

The body of maternal experience becomes the semantic center of Jane's text, conferring meaning on sexual experience through metaphors of birth and nursing. Thus, for example, Jane first introduces lactation into discourse—"it seemed strange to her that so much natural instinctive force could flow through such a medium as herself" (16)—and later uses it as a metaphor for the power of sexual desire: "That a desire so primitive could flow through her, unobstructed like milk, astonished her" (46). In later passages, images of childbirth give sexual intercourse the mark of the preoedipal, erasing the lines of a traditional hierarchy that clearly distinguishes between the masterful lover and the supine female body he succeeds in activating:

> Her cry was the cry of a woman in labor. . . . The throes, the cries, the pains were his; and he could no more dissociate himself from them than from his own flesh. She was his, but by having her he had made himself hers. . . . He too had sweated for this deliverance. . . . A woman delivered. She was his offspring, as he, lying there between her legs, had been hers. (159)

As one would expect of a discourse based on the shifting relations of a preoedipal world, language ceases to draw a clear line between subject and object, liberating "words such as 'do,' 'have,' 'make' from a word order in which they describe . . . something one person does to another, and making them not only describe, but actually perform processes of reciprocity" (Greene, "New Morality," 61–62). Making labor the metaphor for sexual pleasure and lactation the metaphor for sexual desire gives maternity discursive priority over romance.

Thus one tactic that Jane uses to break out of the literary forms of romantic love that contain her in an alienated and idealized world is to create a discourse of female sensuality based on the flows of the maternal body. But this seemingly new language is actually permeated by George Eliot's imagery of desire. Brontë and Eliot—the mentors that Jane most frequently cites—repressed sex from the text of their heroines' responses to love. But both managed to represent sexuality while repressing it to meet the demands of the Victorian ideal of female chastity. They accomplished this difficult task by embodying sexuality in a character (Bertha) or a network of images (currents and tides) which they relegated to a territory outside the world of possibility. Jane Eyre and Maggie Tulliver inhabit a reality constructed by social and moral law, with sexual possibilities consigned to a world of dream (Maggie's trancelike state on the river) or nightmare (the mad world of Bertha's reality and Jane's dreams). Jane Gray brings these images back from the underworld of her predecessors' texts, restoring sexuality to the world of conscious narrative discourse.[4]

The extrasocial world constructed by the mergings and flows of sex and maternity in *The Waterfall* incorporates fragments from Maggie Tulliver's one excursion outside the social sphere, down the river with Stephen. Having left the world of clear social distinctions behind, Maggie allows herself to "drift" with the river, "borne along by the tide" (Eliot, *Mill*, 479); visions of fulfilled love "flow over her like a soft stream [that] made her entirely passive" (493). Tony Tanner sees Maggie's altered state of mind as an escape from the symbolic into a kind of preverbal flux, "a different kind of experience in which language is annulled and with it a grasp of the distinctions and intervals that are the separating and uniting rules of the society that Maggie inhabits" (68). Believing as she did in the value of a broad and vivid moral awareness, Eliot could create, but could not affirm, a state of mind where unconscious desire rules. She can imagine Maggie's abandonment of rational principle only as an abandonment of self, "the submergence of [her] personality by another" (*Mill*, 490). Thus she constructs the embrace of sexuality as entirely passive, a "yielding" to the man's desire (490). The possibility of Maggie's actively asserting her own sexual desire, the possibility that this newly discovered dimension of her personality might legitimately influence her conscious moral decisions, never enters the text.

By transforming Eliot's imagery Drabble creates a new language that can acknowledge and validate female sexuality; she turns Eliot's vocabulary into a metaphorical resource capable of expressing a female desire that is not merely passive. Drabble also preserves the connotations of submission and submergence attached to Eliot's floods and currents: "she began to live for his coming, submitting herself helplessly to the current, abandoning herself to it" (39). But this is no longer female submission to male desire: it is her own sexual desire that Jane gives in to. "She wanted [sex], she wanted it for hers. That a desire so primitive could flow through her, unobstructed like milk, astonished her. 'I want you,' she said" (46). By working Eliot's imagery of currents and tides into flows that originate within Jane's body, Drabble finds a way of imaging an active female desire. Jane's desire is no longer the pale and passive reflection of her lover's desire, but an expression of her own energy, an active force in determining her own decisions. Comparing her own choice with Maggie Tulliver's renunciation of *her* cousin Lucy's man—"She let him go. Nobly she regained her ruined honor, and ah, we admire her for it" (162)—Jane explains her decision to sleep with James thus: "I wanted James so badly . . . there was only one thing to do, and that was to have him" (161).[5] Articulating the voice of sexual desire that Eliot repressed, "I want you" shatters the position of woman as the passive object of male desire. The language of active.female desire thus subverts the gender positions of the romance plot, and indeed of Western narrative discourse, in which man is the active seeker, woman the recipient of love.

Becoming a Female Subject

The voice of female desire—the phrase "I wanted James" is the one constant in all the changing accounts of her love affair—is as much a product of Jane's active self-definition, written in response to those who have written of love before her, as it is a product of sexual desire. There is a connection between becoming the subjective center of one's own physical sensations and occupying the place of subject in language. These positions, "natural" as they may seem to a human being who speaks and who inhabits a body, are by no means given to women in male-dominant societies. Women must fight to overturn the position of object that a discourse constructed as a function of male desire assigns them—and then fight past internalized strictures on female self-assertion to attain the position of speaking subject.[6] Self-reflexive writing like Jane's, which draws attention to the writer's engagement in her writing by interjecting a running commentary on the relative truth or distortion of her own account, is a practice that makes visible the female subjectivity that spins out the text. When the writing also articulates, from inside, a woman's sensual impulses and responses, it makes visible too—and first of all to the writing woman herself—woman as subject of her own physical desire.

Jacques Lacan explains both the exclusion of woman from the position of speaking subject and the occlusion of female sexuality in a discourse created by male desire. The Name of the Father designates those who will inherit the father's social power as subjects of discourse; women, who do not get the father's name to keep, are by definition excluded from the place of speaking subject. "Lacking the phallus, the positive symbol of gender, self-possession and worldly authority around which language is organized, [women] occupy a negative position in language" (Jones, "Inscribing Femininity," 83)—a negative position whose incompleteness buttresses the subject's "manly reality" (Féral, 89).

The structure of sexual relations in patriarchy also excludes woman. A man relates not to his real partner, Lacan says, but to a projection of the signifier that stands for what he has lost—the joyous possession of the maternal body: "what he relates to is the *objet a* [the signifier of the lost object], and . . . the whole of his realisation in the sexual relation comes down to fantasy" ("A Love Letter," 157). In the Lacanian "imaginary," then, woman exists only as projection—and projection of a term that signifies a lack, at that. Thus Lacan can say, as he does with provocative frequency, "Woman does not exist" in any symbolic system, conscious or unconscious (Rose, "Introduction," 48; Lacan, "L'envers," 9–10).

The only way for women to enter the cultural system of representation is to accept the position of object constructed by male desire: "the problem of her condition is fundamentally that of accepting herself as an object of desire for the man" (Lacan, "Intervention," 68). "To imagine herself as men imagine her" (Lacan, *Encore*, 90) would then be the foundation of her self-representation—a prescription for inauthenticity. Jane initially suffers from just such an alienated self-concept, seeing herself as Woman in a number of male-determined scenarios: femme fatale (37–38, 102, 116, 169–70, 212), faithful woman waiting for her man's return (39, 139–41), sacred vessel of life (16), and "proper woman" who accepts her role as adjunct to her man, attendant on his will (80). Jane's antidote to the damage that living within a male-defined culture does to a woman is to construct, as we have seen, a discourse based on her own physical sensations; that puts her in touch with the concrete experiences of living in a female body, which the male-based version of femininity knows nothing about. As one would expect from Lacan's description of the forces arrayed against female subjectivity, the shift from male-defined object to self-defined subject is difficult. *The Waterfall* dramatizes writing not as a revolutionary moment, à la Cixous, when the woman grabs the pen and triumphantly assumes the active voice, but as a revolutionary practice from which emerges—gradually, laboriously—Jane's new position as subject in charge of her own narrative and her own sexual life.

Because *The Waterfall* is divided into third-person narratives and first-person versions of the same story, critics have tried to fasten different aspects of Jane to the different voices of her narration.[7] It is tempting to fit *The Waterfall* into the semiotic/symbolic split envisioned by Kristeva,

with the sensual discourse of the opening third-person sequence addressing the reader's body and the analytical "I" sections addressing the speaking subject enrolled in language and ideology. But no such easy dualisms
obtain in *The Waterfall*. Bodily response and ideological meaning are
intertwined. For example, Jane's body betrayed her in the selection of her
first husband:

> as he started to sing [the Campion love sonnet] I felt my hair rise, my
> scalp stiffen, my heart thud, my blood drain in one violent flow from
> me. . . . Love at first sight: I had heard of it, and like a doomed
> romantic I looked for it and found it, released into the air by the
> words of a long-dead poet. . . . it was for that moment that I married
> him. . . . I blame Campion, I blame the poets, I blame Shakespeare
> for that moment in *Romeo and Juliet* when he says, I'll have her,
> because she is the one that will kill me. And I . . . said to myself, I will
> have that note of suffering. (91–92)

If one cannot trust one's physical responses to reflect spontaneous feeling,
where is one to look for an index of authentic emotion? Yet Jane's body is
as compliant to literary allusion as her feelings, producing a checklist of
symptoms to fill out the cliché "love at first sight." Aligning her sensations
to Romeo's at the first sight of Juliet enables her to "recognize" them as
love.

This obedience of the body to literary indoctrination seems to invalidate the implicit contrast I have been drawing between the authenticity of
the flesh and the inauthenticity of internalized verbal patterns, as well as
the claim I have made that by making her sensations visible through
writing them down Jane recovers an immediate sensory channel to the
world, unmediated by ideological structures. How can the text that puts
Jane's sensuality into words be free of ideological contamination if the
very body it is based on is informed by literary designs? As Ann Rosalind
Jones puts it, Hélène Cixous's and Annie Leclerc's call on women to
"write the body" assumes that the female body escapes "the damaging
acculturation" that they describe so accurately, that it "exists somehow
outside social experience" (Jones, "Writing," 367). If women write from
the body, Cixous claims, they will articulate the values repressed from
culture, "nonassessed values that will change the rules of the old game"
("Medusa," 880).

In particular, the French feminists claim that female *jouissance* is a specifically female sexual pleasure that necessarily escapes male constructions

of sexuality. To write female *jouissance* into language is to explode the old order of discourse from within by forcing it to accommodate what it cannot express. But in practice, in Drabble's two-page description of Jane's first orgasm, the "new" language based on the female body and couched in metaphors of childbirth is infiltrated by old tropes that carry old values into Jane's text.

> It was like death, like birth: an event of the same order. . . . She had let herself be led here tenderly by the hand, garlanded with kisses, a sacrifice. . . . In her head it was black and purple, her heart was breaking, she could hardly breathe . . . then suddenly but slowly, for the first time ever, . . . she started to fall, . . . crying out to him, trembling, shuddering, quaking, drenched and drowned, down there at last in the water, not high in her lonely place . . . he had been as desperate to make her as she to be made. . . . he had made her, in his own image. The throes, the cries, the pains were his; and he could no more dissociate himself from them than from his own flesh. She was his, but by having her he had made himself hers. . . . He wanted her, he too had sweated for this deliverance, he had thought it worth the risk: for her, for himself, he had done it. Indistinguishable needs. Her own voice, in that strange sobbing cry of rebirth. A woman delivered. She was his offspring, as he, lying there between her legs, had been hers. (Drabble, 158–59)

Even if Jane (and Drabble too) has forgotten where some of these tropes come from, "the word [itself] does not forget where it has been and can never wholly free itself from the dominion of the contexts of which it has been a part," as Bakhtin reminds us (167). A glance at *Lady Chatterley's Lover* reveals that this discourse is not so new, after all. Lady Chatterley too was "born a woman" through the sexual ministrations of Mellors.

> She let herself go to him. She yielded with a quiver that was like death, . . . it seemed she was like the sea, nothing but dark waves rising and heaving, heaving with a great swell, . . . far down inside her the deeps parted and rolled asunder . . . till . . . the consummation was upon her, and she was gone. She was gone, she was not, and she was born: a woman. Ah, too lovely, too lovely! In the ebbing she realised all the loveliness. . . . 'It was so lovely!' she moaned. 'It was so lovely!' . . . And she moaned with a sort of bliss, as a sacrifice, and a newborn thing. (Lawrence, 162–63)

The source of the birth metaphor—as well as the language of sacrifice, death, and rebirth—is not Jane Gray's body at all, then, but a text. And that text was written by a man whose authority has imposed on women readers a definition of orgasm that their bodies find it difficult to live up to—another male-defined ideal of femininity that alienates women from their own spontaneous sensations. Drabble's waterfall borrows sublimity from Lawrence's watery floods and depths, and even her tone seems contaminated by Lawrentian hyperbole. She follows Lawrence's lead, too, in assimilating the multiple peaks of women's actual sexual experience to the single culminating climax of male orgasm: Jane's one orgasm is structurally as well as stylistically sublime, centrally positioned in the novel so that it serves in several ways as climax. (Even Jane's apparently spontaneous cry of sexual pleasure—"Lovely, lovely!"—was originally Lady Chatterley's.)

If Jane's task in writing out her experience is, on the one hand, to expose the conventions that determine her feelings and, on the other, to validate her body's sensations in order to open up a direct channel to experience, unmediated by ideology, we have to admit, confronting this passage, that the two are not so different. To write the body is to enter discourse, putting Jane immediately into an intertext. The way Lawrence's mystifications creep into a description of orgasm intended to proceed directly from Jane's body demonstrates how inadequate is the directive to "write the body." Cultural meanings are twisted into the roots of our feelings, even of our bodily sensations, so they necessarily pervade the "new" body-based text. Is there no escape from cultural formations, then—no physical or unconscious space that is free of them?

What is missing here is the debate with literary authority that marks Jane's account of her other experiences with love (like the argument with the moral example set by Maggie Tulliver). Jane (and Drabble behind her) does not recognize the influence of Lawrence's literary designs on her unconscious fantasy. (Margaret Drabble acknowledged in a conversation at the MLA Convention, 29 December 1988, that she knew *Lady Chatterley's Lover* well but was not aware that she had borrowed from Lawrence when she wrote this passage.) There is no way to struggle against male cultural hegemony if its hold remains unconscious. But if one becomes conscious of the imprint of literary design on unconscious fantasy, one can fight it. Jane Gray's dialogue with Jane Eyre is efficacious because she understands how the emotional configurations of *Jane Eyre* have patterned unconscious desire. She manages to dislodge Brontë's literary authority over her experience by "confronting a hegemony in the fibres of the self" (Williams, *Marxism*, 212)—and not merely by confronting it, but by conducting an extended dialogue with it.

Talking Back to Jane Eyre

Jane Gray twice breaks into the opening third-person account of her affair with James to blame Brontë for imposing the structure of her own fantasy onto Jane's reality: the narrative pattern of *Jane Eyre* (and other nineteenth century courtship novels) has seduced her, through the intensity of its focus on a single passion, into narrowing the story of her own life; in writing out her experience she has "omitted everything, almost everything, except that sequence of discovery and recognition that I would call love" (47).

"Reader, I loved him, as Charlotte Brontë said" (87).[8] Couching the protest of authentic feeling—"I loved him"—in literary allusion implies that Jane's emotions, as well as the love story she has just written, bear the imprint of Brontë's text. Jane calls up Brontë's vision of love as passionate intensity in self-deprecation to deride the way Brontë's world of fantasy has determined the shape of Jane's "real" experience. But Brontë's words do not simply fall into place as pieces of Jane's discourse: rather, the quotation imports the values of *Jane Eyre* into *The Waterfall*:

> Lies, lies, it's all lies. I've even told lies of fact, which I had not meant to do. . . . What have I tried to describe? A passion, a love, an unreal life, a life in limbo, without anxiety, guilt. . . . Reader, I loved him: as Charlotte Brontë said. Which was Charlotte Brontë's man, the one she created and wept for and longed for, or the poor curate that had her and killed her, her sexual measure, her sexual match? I had James, oh God, I had him, but . . . the world that I lived in with him—the dusty Victorian house, the fast cars, . . . the wide bed—it was some foreign country to me, some Brussels of the mind, where I trembled and sighed for my desires . . . with as much desperation as that lonely virgin in her parsonage. Reader, I loved him. And more than that, I had him. He was real, I swear it. (89)

Julia Kristeva maintains that the transposition of another text's system of meaning into a new text dispels the authority of the narrative voice in the recipient text and triggers a transformation of the narrative position. For the space of the quotation, the signifying system of the original text disappears, displaced by the quoted text's system of meanings and values. After the interstices, a new signifying system must be organized, with a new articulation for the narrative voice (*La révolution*, 340). So quotation involves the narrative voice in dialogue, thus change.

"The world that I lived in with him . . . was some Brussels of the mind." Jane's allusion is to an indisputably imaginary world—the world of Charlotte Brontë's mind, as she sat in the Yorkshire parsonage writing letters filled with adoration to a M. Héger in Brussels whom she reconstructed in the image of Byronic intensity.[9] Here the meaning seems unambiguous: if Jane has lived in a similar Brussels of the mind, she has occupied not even a fantasy world of her own, but the fantasy world created by another.

But Brontë's words will not lie still as objects of Jane's ridicule; rather, they challenge Jane to think again, send her discourse off in a contradictory direction—away from debunking toward validating the imagination as a transformative power that confers reality on its subject. "Which was Charlotte Brontë's man, the one she created and wept for and longed for, or the poor curate that had her?" The very process of questioning, as Jane Gallop has said, "is a specific dialectic shattering stable assumptions and producing contextual associations" that throw ready-made definitions into doubt (64). Shattering the binary opposition between real and imaginary that Jane's initial diatribe is based on—the certainty that lies and truth, fact and imagination are clearly distinct—Jane now questions what is "true": the ideal of passionate love for an imaginary figure, or the curate whose proximity was a dull accident produced by unimaginative circumstance, a reality in which Brontë could not invest her imagination.

Jane's "word," insisting on truth and reviling the falsifications of the imagination, alternates with Brontë's "word"—"Reader, I loved him"—which carries over from the world of *Jane Eyre* the absolute value of passionate love, regardless of the distortions it imposes on reality. The juxtaposition of the two discourses relativizes both. We cannot adhere to Brontë's words, "Reader, I loved him," with the single-minded intensity of a reader immersed in *Jane Eyre*; but by the time of the tag's second appearance we cannot scoff at its patent artificiality, either. The juxtaposition of discourses binds the two together "within a single ambivalent unity" (Kristeva, "Bounded," 51). If the energy of Jane's initial polemic—"Lies, lies, it's all lies"—sprang from a desire to draw clear distinctions between truth and fantasy, the dialogic method leads her to an embrace of contraries: "I must make some effort to comprehend. I am tired of exclusion" (90). The nonexclusive opposition between Jane Gray's text and Jane

Eyre's resolves not into a triumph of one position over the other, or into a synthesis that would restore a unitary truth, but into a "doubling" of meaning (Kristeva, "Bounded," 48). When the phrase "he [James] was real" appears at the end of the dialogue, the clearly opposed binary opposition between "real" and "unreal" has been replaced by a meaning that shimmers back and forth between "real" and "imaginary." Jane both loves James and makes it all up: she both "lies" and tells the kind of truth Brontë tells, investing the real with an imaginative intensity that makes it come alive. Jane's tendency to search for one absolute "truth" is thus softened and made more flexible by a dialogue that persuades her to make room in her notion of truth for the set of values that Mark Johnson articulates in another context: "without imagination, nothing in the world could be meaningful. Without imagination, we could never make sense of our experience" (ix).

This dance of alternation and alteration moves Jane from the fixed position of the woman in the romantic scenario who knows exactly what she thinks and feels—because she thinks and feels one thing only—to a more fertile ambiguity. The "in-between" that she now occupies—between Brontë's ideas on love and her own evolving position—is as fruitful as Winnicott's and Keller's transitional space between self and other (see chapter 6, above). Jane generates several different versions of her love out of the paradox implicit in "Reader, I loved him." Sometimes an account foregrounds the authenticity of passion ("I loved him"), sometimes the implications of "Reader"—an acknowledgment that her present account of authentic passion is a fiction addressed to a reader. Emerging from the dialogue with Brontë, "real" and "love" always have double meanings.

Thus, much later in the novel Jane takes first one side of the reality-illusion debate, then the other: one chapter debunks romantic love as an addictive and useless illusion, the next redeems it, fantasy and all. After Jane's harsh confrontation with material reality in the form of an automobile accident that almost kills James, she launches into a violent and unequivocal attack on romantic love:

> For what, after all, in God's name had they been playing at? . . . It had been some ridiculous imitation of a fictitious passion, some shoddy childish mock-up of what for others might have been reality—but for what others? For no others, as nonexistent an image they had pursued as God, as Santa Claus, as mermaids, as angels. . . . Romantic love. . . . How had they found so much to say about so great a delusion? The emperor's new clothes, discussed, endlessly,

stitch by stitch; and suddenly one looks in the light of undeceived day, and the man is naked. (213–14)

This chapter pulls to the surface the subtext of doubt that, in images of game, ritual, drama, fiction, and fairy tale, has shadowed all Jane's efforts to convey the authenticity of her love for James. Here love is but an imitation of a fictitious model, a pastiche of verbal formulas garnered from novels to fill the emptiness of lovers' lives. Robbed of the borrowed glamour of "being in love," "the things she had so admired in him, that had so moved her heart" crumble into "nothingnesses, shadows, mockeries" (214). But what Jane moves into the position of "real" here is equally a convention. She deconstructs love from the perspective of social law, which accepts as real only legal and financial contracts. What counts is who pays the bills and who has legal claims. "It was Malcolm that had . . . paid for her, . . . Malcolm, who . . . even in absence maintained financial fidelity, continuing to pay" (216–17): so Jane belongs to Malcolm. And "it was to Lucy and his children that [James] belonged" (216). "It was Malcolm that had endured her and paid for her, in cash and sorrow, [yet] . . . all her gratitude had been given to James, who had done nothing more for her than to change an electric plug and mend the brake of the pushchair" (216). Measured on a scale of social utility, passionate love is worthless.

But in the next chapter Jane restores love, illusion and all, to a reality guaranteed not by its roots, but by its fruits. If it was a mixture of need and weakness and irresponsibility and illusion that drove Jane and James together, their love was real enough, "serious enough, in its consequences" (221). One of its consequences was the life-giving richness that sprang from their mutual investment in each other:

We were starving, when we met, James and I, parched and starving, and we saw love as the miraged oasis, shivering on the dusty horizon in all the glamor of hallucination: blue water, green fronds and foliage breaking from the dry earth. Like deluded travelers we had carefully approached, hardly able to trust the image's persistence, afraid that it would fade into yet more dry acres as we drew nearer, believing ourselves blinded by our own desires; but when we got there . . . the image remained, it sustained my possession of it, and the water that I drank, the so much longed-for water, was not sour and brackish to the taste. Nor were the leaves green merely through the glamor of distance . . . they remained green to the touch, dense endless foresting boughs, an undiscovered country, no shallow, quickly exhausted, quickly drained sour well, but miles of verdure, rivers, fishes, colored birds, miles with no sign of an ending, and, perhaps, beyond them all, no ending but the illimitable, circular, inexhaustible sea. (221)

In a dialogic conclusion that embraces both positions of Jane's debate with Brontë, the metaphor of the mirage that is also a real oasis embraces the illusion together with the reality of love. The "reality" of love is produced by the lovers' commitment to it, their faith in what they create together, amalgam of their individual fantasies though it may be. This passage is an affirmation of the discourse Jane shares with her literary ancestors as well as an affirmation of love: poetic language can hold opposites together in a paradoxical mode that embraces more of the "truth" of love than the balance sheet of social utility that Jane used to figure debits and assets in the preceding chapter.

By constructing a dialogue between various cultural discourses that present her affair with James according to different paradigms, Jane—and the reader—is able to see what each discourse omits. Since ideology functions by smoothing out contradictions in order to present a coherent explanation of reality (Belsey, 57), the gaps and incoherence of any one discourse are usually hidden. Only the juxtaposition of contradictory discourses reveals what each omits, exposes the distortions of each. *The Waterfall* presents a complex answer to the question whether we can get outside ideology, escape the cultural framework of meaning that determines what we see. On the one hand, fantasy patterns stick. Jane is bound by desire to the elegant shape of the love story. In spite of her outrage at the simplifications it makes her impose on her own experience, she longs for the beauty of its concentrated passion: "I want to get back to that other story, that other woman, who lived a life too pure, too lovely to be mine" (70). And she slips back into the fairy-tale configuration of roles that grants agency to the man and reduces the self to a helplessly grateful female object: "when [James] touched me it was as though I had another body. . . . James changed me, he saved me, he changed me" (244). On the other hand, the continual shift between signifying systems throws Jane's identity into process. As she destroys each narrative frame, she destroys the self constructed by it: language, "deprived of its hallowed function as support of the law, . . . becomes the cause of a permanent trial of the speaking subject" (Kristeva, "Identity," 137). Unlike the figure of Mariana, who "only said, My life is dreary, He cometh not," Jane says various things at various times, each new discourse producing a new self: writing enables her to escape the stasis of obsession. She thus eludes the bounded contours of woman defined by the discourse of male desire as static object—as waiting woman—to become a self-in-process, continually exceeding definition to flow on toward unknown possibilities.

Outwriting Literary Forms

Though the somewhat stilted hyperbole of Jane's Lawrentian orgasm inscribes, unawares, the enclosure of female sexuality within male discursive designs, the metaphor of the life-giving oasis seems to express the exuberance of release from ideological containment. Here Jane finds her own metaphor for sexual love. As it spreads over the page, "dense endless foresting boughs, an undiscovered country, no shallow, quickly exhausted, quickly drained sour well, but miles of verdure, rivers, fishes, colored birds, miles with no sign of an ending, and, perhaps, beyond them all, no ending but the illimitable, circular, inexhaustible sea" (221), the oasis leaves behind first its metaphorical function as symbol of sexual love, then its origins in the desert; changing shape with the fluidity of water itself, the image proliferates into a multiplicity of life-giving forms—a celebration, finally, not so much of love as of sheer verbal fecundity. The vitality of this metaphor, together with its break from the rules of metaphorical reference, seems to confirm Michelle Montrelay's theory that a woman can experience a pleasure akin to orgasm from entering her sexuality into a discourse from which it has long been barred.[10] Finding her own metaphor for sexual love gives Jane's writing an exuberance that, like sexual *jouissance*, overflows the available limits for its articulation (Coward and Ellis, 115).[11]

The combined discipline of writing the body and writing a dialogue with the texts that have possessed her enables Jane to escape the prison of abstraction in which the romantic scenario initially encased her. At the end of *The Waterfall* her narrative embraces all the things that happen to her, including those outside the narrow "sequence of discovery and recognition that I would call love" (47). I believe that this is a result of writing sexuality into her love story. Sexual love displaces the absent—hence unchanging—idealized beloved with a body that is there and with sensual stimuli that shift from moment to moment. And writing that attempts to record sex must necessarily incorporate those changing physical sensations. Increasingly, as her writing validates physical sensation and response as a way of knowing the material world around her, Jane's sense of herself becomes grounded in her concrete daily actions. In the end she finds substance for her narrative in everything she does, rather than in a single static passion. Unlike Jane Eyre in the transcendent obsession that in the end closes out everything but Rochester—"I am my husband's life as fully as he is mine" (Brontë, 454)—Jane ends by attending to some trivial things that have nothing to do with passionate love. She cleans her house, hires an au pair girl to help with the children, and stoops to the mechanics of getting her poems published.

Like the oasis metaphor that destabilizes the fixed relation between vehicle and tenor by sprawling, expanding, changing shape on the page, *The Waterfall*'s ending reflects Jane's new fluidity and openness by transgressing discursive limits. Jane Gray emphatically refuses the romantic trajectory of a Jane Eyre, mounting in intensity toward a final ecstasy, by declining to make use of the potential for sublimity in her reunion with James by the side of a waterfall. Instead she keeps tacking on postscripts that dispel sublimity to reflect the way things happen in everyday life: just one thing after another.

This overrun of closure graphically demonstrates the changes that have taken place in Jane's art through combining sex and writing. In Ellen Cronan Rose's words, Jane has become "a woman writer" in the sense of evolving new fictional forms to catch the fluidity of female sexual experience (94–96). The mirror of Jane's prose style measures just how far she has moved emotionally, from the cold containment of the poems she wrote before giving birth to Bianca and loving James, poems "flawlessly metrical and . . . always rhymed . . . the end-stopped patterns of my solitude" (114), to the final overflow of closure. The ongoing fluidity of the conclusion both reflects her going beyond her former boundaries in sex and childbirth and affirms her faith in her open-ended potential for change.[12]

Jane's example demonstrates how vital a creative practice—not a creative act, but an ongoing creative discipline—can be to the process of reclaiming a woman's erotic energy for her own creative purposes. To find in sexual love a source of energy for creative work requires overthrowing habits of feeling, acquired through years of acculturation, that associate sexual excitement with finding one's whole meaning in a man. That is not the work of a moment, as the tenacity of Jane's debilitating identification with patterns of female dependency through the many drafts of her love story illustrates. Nor can sexual experience alone change a woman's orientation. Ann Rosalind Jones has convincingly argued that phallocentric habits of thought cling to even the most liberatory sexual practices ("Writing," 368). Only when sex is accompanied by a critical practice like Jane's writing, which seeks to expose the cultural scenarios that influence even her physical sensations, can sexuality help a woman escape the cultural fantasies that imprison her. Articulating her own sensations as the basis of her experience, over and over, helps Jane move her self—what she is actually experiencing—to the center of her story and the center of her consciousness, replacing the obsession with James. Perhaps even more important than the specific content of Jane's writing, though, is the very practice of writing which, with its constant demands on the self as the sole source of creative energy, shifts her attention away from James to the ongoing process of her own self-definition.

8 The Sexual Politics of the Unconscious

The Golden Notebook

WHY DOES *The Waterfall* stand virtually alone among contemporary female artist novels as an endorsement of the creative potential of heterosexual relations? Why do not more novels by women celebrate the erotic as (in Annis Pratt's expression) "a spring of creative energy that, activated in their sexuality, radiates to all of the facets of the fully realized personality" (88–89)? The psychoanalytic perspective presented above in chapter 6 frames an explanation that traces women's psychic patterns back to the warped power structures of the nuclear family. But women writers and readers are also quite simply skeptical of an ideal of merging that sounds suspiciously like the old romantic ideal of an ecstatic blending of two yearning spirits: given the imbalance of power between men and women in patriarchy, merging is likely to result in the absorption of a woman's self-interests and worldview into those of her man. A woman trained to the role of "angel of the house"—trained, that is, in the art of putting other people's needs and desires in place of her own—is more likely to lose track of her own interests than is a man trained to extend his abilities into the world, toward the achievement of his own projects. The traditional dominance relations are always there, pulling the ideal of a nurturing reciprocity back toward a one-way feeding of the male ego.

Doris Lessing's *The Golden Notebook* relentlessly exposes the destructive effects of a heterosexual model of relationship that gives man a dominant role, woman a supporting role. Lessing reveals the political where indeed it does the most harm—at the very base of the inner world, in the groundwork of the unconscious. *The Golden Notebook* is rich in psychological politics, offering a virtual encyclopedia of the emotional binds that women experience in patriarchy. But here I confine my discussion to the relationship between the two writers Anna and Saul contained in "The Blue Notebook" and "The Golden Notebook" sections of the novel.[1]

Anna, a writer who has written nothing for publication for a number of years, rents a room in her flat to Saul, an American writer. They sink into a love affair that is also a shared madness. Lessing herself, in a 1971 essay subsequently published as the preface to most editions of *The Golden Notebook*, identifies the Saul-Anna relationship as a merger: "Anna and Saul Green . . . 'break down' . . . into each other, into other people, break through the false patterns they have made of their past . . . dissolve. They hear each other's thoughts, recognize each other in themselves" (vii–viii). Destructive and creative aspects of this identification intertwine. What seems to be purely negative on the face of it—Anna's losing herself in the female parts that Saul requires her to play in his fantasies—turns out to be liberating: entry into Saul's unconscious fantasy world releases Anna from a solipsism that had immobilized her. Combined with Saul's direct pressure on her to write, this release from emotional fixation enables Anna to write a novel, *Free Women*. When at the end of "The Golden Notebook" section Anna gives Saul, and Saul gives Anna, the first line of a novel—a novel which each of them subsequently completes—they dramatize a new heterosexual exchange that replaces the hierarchy of sex roles with the mutuality of creative encouragement. But the poisonous basis of their love in what Lessing presents as the inevitably hostile power struggle between men and women in patriarchy makes their intimacy too destructive to maintain; having given each other this final creative push, they separate. The bottom line of Lessing's assessment is political: the dream of an ongoing sexual intimacy that daily nurtures the creative energies of both partners cannot be realized within a structure of sex roles that pits the members of one gender against the other in an unequal "sex war" (572).

The secluded world of Anna's flat becomes a demonic parody of the transitional space described in chapter 6 above, where it is safe for an artist to loosen her hold on ego boundaries and abandon everyday logic. Saul and Anna do regress into a world of shifting ego borders, where the violent changes and irrational links of primary-process thinking prevail; but rather than containing a boundless flux rich with new creative possibilities, the world of unconscious fantasy in which they "play" is heavily structured by cultural ideology, and the shapes that emerge from it are sharply differentiated male and female roles that prevent their becoming one or even understanding each other. Unlike the French feminists Kristeva and Cixous, who find in the unconscious a reservoir of revolutionary energy free from cultural inscriptions, Lessing peels away the organized conscious layer of personality to reveal an unconscious layer equally structured by ideology.

"[Saul] looked as if he were listening, as if the words he must say next would be fed to him from a play-back: 'I'm not going to be corralled by any dame in the world. I've never been yet and I never shall'" (631–32). These lines come from the paradigmatic scenario of male-female relations in our culture: a woman, unable to feel whole without a man, grasps at him as the absolutely indispensable prop to her being; understandably reluctant to take on the role of provider for all her sexual, emotional, and financial needs, the man runs the other way.[2] In spite of the schizophrenic rapidity with which Saul and Anna change personas, in many of their scenes each is locked into an emotional position dictated by the imbalance of power between them, so that a disturbingly repetitive emotional block to mutual understanding emerges. Saul cannot afford empathy, cannot afford to listen with understanding to Anna's feelings, because her emotional dependency threatens his freedom; in turn his defensive self-sufficiency exacerbates her need to make him hers in order to be a person at all. The logical extreme of a structure based on male dominance and female submission is, as Anna puts it, "the sado-masochistic cycle we were in": "He was directing a pure stream of hatred against me, for being a woman. . . . I felt in myself the weak soft sodden emotion, the woman betrayed. Oh boohoo, you don't love me, you don't love, men don't love women any more. Oh boohoo, and my dainty pink-tipped forefinger pointed at my white, pink-tipped betrayed bosom" (630). The balance of dominance can easily tip into cruelty, in which a man can indulge with impunity because of the woman's powerlessness to do without him; the woman, having relinquished control over her own happiness to the man, can only slide passively into despair, like Anna "luxuriating in her weakness" (630).

The sequence of subservient roles that Anna occupies is only the beginning of Lessing's analysis of the politics of merging. When Anna plunges into the play-world of unconscious fantasy, it is the world of Saul's unconscious fantasy that she enters. One reason she never gets good parts in their skits is that the scripts are dictated by Saul's unconscious—and that is dominated, as Anna realizes (581), by his obsession with an all-powerful, all-controlling mother figure. When he becomes the cunning and furtive child, determined to outwit his mother, she plays the imprisoning mother; when, guilty for having abused her, he becomes gentle and kind, she allows herself to be soothed and comforted; when he is sick and lonely, she becomes the giving, holding maternal comforter. And when he plays the role of unfaithful rake, she becomes the adult successor to the controlling mother: the jealous woman who spies on him, reads his diary, and tries (in vain, of course; that's part of the plot) to keep him from philandering.

"If I go out, you'll accuse me of sleeping with someone."
"Because that's what you want me to do." (583)

"If I've never been a jailer before, and if I've now become one, perhaps it's because you need one." (576)

Anna seems to have no fantasy life she can call her own: her fantasies are purely reactive. Like Lacan, Lessing extends the subjugation of women within patriarchy to the unconscious: "Lacan argues that woman can enter into the symbolic life of the unconscious only to the extent that she internalizes male desire (phallic libido)—that is, to the extent that she imagines herself as men imagine her" (Jones, "Inscribing Femininity," 83).[3] Anna's own fantasies betray her, constructing even the unconscious representatives of her self in accord with male patterns of desire—or hatred.

Anna suffers most from the confusions of living out Saul's versions of good mother and bad mother. Saul resorts to the most primitive of pre-oedipal fantasy mechanisms: splitting. Melanie Klein's study of infantile fantasy shows that splitting is an apparently universal reaction to the situation of exclusive mothering, where a mother is charged with the responsibility of meeting all an infant's needs. An infant sees the breast as the source of all goodness; but it is also constructed as destructive (when it is withheld). The infant then internalizes the image of a good breast and a bad breast. At a later stage, when the child is able to perceive persons as whole objects, it still cannot deal with the anxiety that would arise from imagining the mother as the source both of bliss (through the comfort of her presence) and of despair (through her absence or indifference). To protect the image of the good mother, the child projects both the negative traits it perceives in the mother and its own destructive rage onto a "bad" mother; it thus saves the image of the good mother from contamination, projecting its own loving feelings onto the "good" mother and continuing to imagine her as the source of all good things.[4] Splitting occurs in both male and female children, and both sexes internalize images of an all-powerful benevolent mother (such as Mrs. Ramsay in *To the Lighthouse*) and an all-powerful persecuting mother. But the boy's situation is further complicated by the addition, during the oedipal period, of an erotically tinged attraction that makes the mother both more desirable and, for that reason, more threatening to his precariously defended ego. The added intensity is likely to prolong his use of splitting as a defense mechanism. Lessing spreads out before us, via Saul's projections, the range of bad mother/good mother images that haunt the male unconscious in Western culture; and she lets us know, through Anna's self-imaging, the emotional effects of having to live up to the ideal of the all-perfect mother/woman and of having to bear the brunt of male rage at (inevitably) failing those expectations.

Forced to see herself in various embodiments first of the good, then the bad mother, Anna is filled first with self-hatred, then with confused desire:

> He's right to hate me. . . . I'm hateful. (587)

> I was aware of myself as he saw me, a woman inexplicably in command of events. . . . I disliked the solemnity, the pompousness of that upright little custodian of the truth. (584)

As in *Housekeeping*, we are in the realm of Lacan's imaginary, where the self seems to have its being in the other's mind and one's self-image is a composite of the other's projections. But the female imaginary in *Housekeeping*, marked by fantasies of mother-daughter mirroring, seems positively benign beside the self-denigration involved in looking at oneself disfigured by male projections.

Saul's desire for the perfect mother/woman puts Anna in an equally baffling double bind:

> I began to think of this other woman out there, kind and generous and strong enough to give him what he needed without asking for anything in return. . . . Then there was a moment of knowledge. I understood I'd gone right inside his craziness: he was looking for this wise, kind, all-mother figure, who is also sexual playmate and sister; and because I had become part of him, this is what I was looking for too, both for myself, because I needed her, and because I wanted to become her. I understood I could no longer separate myself from Saul, and that frightened me more than I have been frightened. . . . I knew this with my intelligence, and yet I sat there in my dark room . . . longing with my whole being for that mythical woman, longing to be her, but for Saul's sake. . . . I tried to get back to myself. . . . I could not. (588)

Since Anna is taken over by Saul's fantasy, she wants to have the object of his desire. But she also wants to *be* the object of Saul's desire, to make herself over to conform to the contours of his fantasy. Having and being are conflated, and desire becomes autoerotic, but in an alienated way. Stymied by the lack of an object outside the self to reach for, desire bumps up against a mirror: the woman wants herself, but she can only *be* herself, not *have* herself. Shulamith Firestone maintains that this kind of alienation is the general condition of female sexuality in a culture dominated by male viewers: having always before her the female body as an image of desire, a heterosexual woman can find satisfaction in intercourse only circuitously, by imagining how her body looks through the eyes of her lover or how it feels to penetrate her own desirable female body (158).

Yet so complex is Lessing's vision of the intertwined creative and destructive threads in the heterosexual weave that she finds possibilities for transcendence even in the decentering process of imagining oneself in the shape of the other's mental image:

> I was aware of myself as he saw me, . . . a woman inside time. . . .
> When he said: "It's like being a prisoner, living with someone who knows what you said last week, or can say: three days ago you did so and so," I could feel a prisoner with him, because I longed to be free of my own ordering, commenting memory. I felt my sense of identity fade. (585)

Indeed Anna has been too dedicated to order, an order that keeps the past and the Anna of the past intact. Her four notebooks separate the welter of actuality into watertight compartments: life in Africa, Communist party activities, love affairs, sketches for fiction. But merging with Saul, who can remember nothing, who lives in a present free of a determining past, teaches Anna to be spontaneous. Because Saul is unpredictable, Anna cannot prepare a response to meet him, but has to remain alert to whichever Saul emerges: "I heard Saul's feet coming up the stairs, and I was interested to know who would come in" (637). Practice in responding to the Saul of the moment carries Anna into a general willingness to accept what the moment brings and respond to it directly: "Saul wanted to see what would happen. And so did I" (631). Through this practice in spontaneity, Anna learns to accept whatever emerges from her own mind in direct response to her experience, "listening to hear what I would say, to find out what I thought" (626).

> He said: "Why do you have four notebooks?"
> I said: "Obviously, because it's been necessary to split myself up, but from now on I shall be using one only." I was interested to hear myself say this, because until then I hadn't known it. (598)

Because Saul's mind is *not* structured, but resembles the flux of primary-process thinking, it represents the mental chaos that Anna has tried to ward off in herself through the "acts of containment" represented by her four notebooks (DuPlessis, 101). But seeing mental chaos up close makes Anna realize its creative potential: Saul's mind is an "explosion of possibilities" (683). Immersing herself in it is equivalent to letting go of mental structures that defended her against new combinations of ideas.[5] In the "movie" sequence of her dreams, Anna accepts chaos, which yields in her, too, an "explosion of possibilities" (683).

What Anna calls a "film" is actually a projection of her own dreaming mind: asleep, she splits herself into a viewer of images from her past life and from the one novel she has published, and a sardonic projectionist of these images whom she understands to be Saul—a dream reflection of their having merged. The dream-Saul is, like his real-life counterpart, both a doer of damage and a bearer of new creative possibilities. (The label "projectionist" reminds the reader of Anna's debilitating imprisonment among the projections of Saul's hostile images of women; but his attacks on the structures of her fiction in the dream, like his attacks on her fixed emotional positions in waking life, break down old categories and enable her to see her own images with fresh eyes.)

If we take art to mean a vision communicated to an audience, Anna's "film" images are not yet art, as they belong to the closed, solipsistic world of dream. Because it *is* Anna's creativity at work, though, we can assume that the kaleidoscope of images both represents a stage of prewriting and adumbrates the qualities towards which Anna's prose style is moving. The dream images are thus in one sense art in potential; but in another sense they are already formulated, set down in a written sequence in the golden notebook—Anna's journal that doubles as the text we are reading. And this new form of writing reflects the changes brought about by the merger with Saul. Shifting from role to role to meet Saul's changing personas, Anna has learned a fluidity that shows up in the "film's" shifts from image to image; moving across ego boundaries has prepared her to imagine vividly the feelings of people she has known; and she is less inclined to impose patterns prematurely on her characters, for she has learned sponta-neity with Saul—learned, that is, to trust more to what happens, to let meanings emerge in their own time.

The initial movement of the film sequence, as of the waking experience with Saul, is destruction. Anna has to confront the distortions that her need for order has imposed on the shapes of her fiction:

> They [scenes from Anna's first novel] were all, so I saw now, conven-
> tionally well-made. . . . I knew that what I had invented was all
> false. . . . the projectionist . . . let the scenes vanish. . . . And now it
> was terrible, because I was faced with the burden of re-creating order
> out of the chaos that my life had become. . . . [The projectionist] was
> thinking that the material had been ordered by me to fit what I knew,
> and that was why it was all false. Suddenly he said aloud: "How
> would June Boothby see that time? I bet you can't do June Boothby."
> (619–20)

The projectionist's criticism is of course really Anna's own, an acknowledgment that her own anxious need for structure made her assimilate
the characters and situations emerging from her imagination to patterns
known in advance, rather than letting them develop fully in their own
time. It is perhaps a sign of the new creative ground upon which Anna has
entered that she can allow the figure of Saul to be creative as well as
destructive. Having played out, against Saul, all the male-female oppositions of her culture, Anna has at some level recognized the falsification of
dividing human qualities down the middle and portioning them out along
gender lines. Until the encounter with Saul she had denied her own destructiveness by projecting it, had "preferred to see the destructive principle outside her and in men only, in Tommy, Michael, the Pauls, Saul"
(Sprague, 83). This gender division has come increasingly under pressure
from her dreams of a figure she names "joy in malice, joy in a destructive
impulse" (Lessing, 477). This principle of destructive vitality appears as a
male figure—an old man (Draine, 82)—but the very fact that it emerges
in Anna's dreams means that it inhabits Anna.

When Anna incorporates Saul as the director of her dreams, the two
lovers "break down" into a single unconscious flow—an identification
even more complete than Anna's participation in Saul's fantasy life. The
collapse of the barrier between man and woman entails a collapse of the
strict gender division between nurturer and destroyer. Not only does
Anna now claim the destructive principle as her own by incorporating the
male sardonic voice of the destroyer into her dream life, but the line
between destructive and nurturing also disappears. In the dream quoted
above, it is only after the dream-Saul's withering criticism has annihilated
Anna's old fictional creations that there is room for his challenge to imagine something new:

> "How would June Boothby see that time? I bet you can't do June
> Boothby," at which my mind slipped into a gear foreign to me, and I

began writing a story about June Boothby. . . in the style of the most insipid coy woman's magazine. (620)

Anna can "do" June Boothby because of a general collapse of the walls between self and other. Having become "part of Saul" (587), having entered into "the chaos of Saul's imagination" (638) and survived, Anna can afford to give up her anxious defense of boundaries. She can become "part of" June Boothby, imagine more readily how June Boothby thinks, and slip into a style that expresses June Boothby's subjectivity. The merger with Saul, by relaxing boundaries of all kinds, has expanded Anna's capacity to empathize and thus to capture the inner life of people in her prose.[6]

The capacity for empathy—for "experiencing another's needs or feelings as one's own" (Chodorow, *Mothering*, 167)—is a capacity that people derive from having lived for a time indistinctly differentiated from another whose feelings they share, whose moods they absorb: for most people, that person is the mother. For whatever reasons, Anna, like Joanna Field, has felt the need to resist the partial dissolution of ego boundaries in empathy. If Field's experimentation with drawing was hampered by her emotional need to keep objects safely enclosed within clear outlines, Anna's writing has been hampered by her need to "name," to keep characters and events contained within well-defined verbal boundaries.[7] But through merging with Saul she has learned to enter without fear the transitional space between self and other where the artist can manage the "creative leap" of empathy (Keller, 99). Or, as Kohut has it, "the creative individual . . . is less psychologically separated from his surroundings than the non-creative one; the 'I-you' barrier is not as clearly defined. The intensity of the creative person's awareness of the relevant aspects of his surroundings is akin to the detailed self perceptions of the schizoid and the childlike, . . . near to some schizophrenics' experience of their body" (259). Indeed, Anna seems now for the first time to perceive others' motions with the immediacy usually reserved for perceptions of one's own bodily movements:

I watched, for an immense time, noting every movement, how Mrs. Boothby stood in the kitchen of the hotel at Mashopi, her stout buttocks projecting like a shelf under the pressure of her corsets, patches of sweat dark under her armpits, her face flushed with distress, while she cut cold meat off various joints of animal and fowl, and listened to the young cruel voices and crueller laughter through a thin wall. . . . I saw Mr. Lattimer, drinking in the bar, carefully not-looking at Mr. Boothby, while he listened to his beautiful red-haired wife's laughter. I saw him, again and again, bend down, shaky with drunkenness, to stroke the feathery red dog, stroking it, stroking it, stroking it. (634–35)

Field's argument that relinquishing the clear demarcation between self and object is the prerequisite for an art that is "alive" (83) seems to be confirmed by the vivid quality of Anna's new images. Replacing the dry, repetitive abstractions of Anna's earlier debates with herself, physical gestures and facial expressions communicate people's feelings with the immediacy of concrete detail. The flow of sensual images conveys the sense of Anna's expansion past solipsistic boundaries—"past the limits of what had been possible" (619)—into an empathic identification with the people around her.

Anna's vivid representation of people's innermost feelings seems to confirm Keller's contention that empathy is a valid way of knowing. Overcoming ego boundaries, as Anna does with Saul, does not lock one forever into fusion but rather provides an entry into all the stations along a continuum between fusion and differentiation, the continuum traveled by mothers and infants. Children do not stay fused with the mother, but approach and then slide away from a recognition of the mother as a person in her own right, a person with aspects that do not necessarily fit in with the child's needs and desires. Saul's way of merging may lock him into an early stage of infantile fusion that limits his vision, freezing the figure of the other into a projection of his own desires, a figment of his own fantasy world. But the clarity with which Anna sees persons from her past or from her fiction testifies to her having moved through the stages of differentiation to a point where she can see the other as a person in his or her own right. Judith Kegan Gardiner clarifies the difference: "Empathy [is] an adult process in which a mature person takes on the position of the other person. . . . empathy is not the same as but opposite to the position in which a person sees the other as an extension of oneself" (*Rhys*, 165). The mark of Anna's arrival at a position of "vicarious introspection" (Gardiner, *Rhys*, 165) is her ability to see even her former lovers, Willi and Paul Tanner (a stand-in for Michael), as subjects with lives of their own.

I heard Willi's humming, . . . the tuneless, desperately lonely humming; or watched him in slow motion . . . look long and hurt at me when I flirted with Paul. Or I saw Mr. Boothby . . . look at his daughter with her young man. I saw his envious, but un-bitter gaze at this youth. . . . I saw Paul Tanner coming home in the early morning, brisk and efficient with guilt, saw him meet his wife's eyes, as she stood in front of him in a flowered apron, rather embarrassed and pleading, while the children ate their breakfast before going off to school. Then he turned, frowning, and went upstairs to lift a clean shirt down from a shelf. (635)

Seeing her lovers as they exist apart from her, in aspects of their lives beyond the range of her desire, signals Anna's move through empathy as fusion to empathy as vision. Anna has been able to transform the regressive infantile merger with Saul into a different kind of unity: a sympathy that allows the other his or her integrity while maintaining a connection based on shared human emotions.

The kind of attention Anna practices here is close to the flexible objectivity Keller proposes to replace the "static" objectivity that is the norm of the scientific community: "dynamic objectivity is not unlike empathy, a form of knowledge of other persons that draws explicitly on the commonality of feelings and experiences in order to enrich one's understanding of another in his or her own right" (117). Although Keller directs her redefinition of objectivity to the scientific world, it sums up the conditions for producing art that catches the life of its objects. The vitality of physical gesture that conveys Willi's or Paul's complex emotional state convinces us that if Anna were to write a novel now, it would no longer be her psychological need for a bounded order that forced alien patterns onto her text; rather, its shape and meaning would emerge from the experiences of her characters, vividly felt.

"Changed by the experience of being other people" (602), Anna is able to extend the range of empathy still further, past cultural as well as gender limits:

I was not Anna, but a soldier. . . . I saw dark glistening hair on my bronze forearm which held a rifle on which moonlight glinted. I understood I was on a hillside in Algeria, I was an Algerian soldier and I was fighting the French. Yet Anna's brain was working in this man's head. . . . Then Anna's brain went out like a candle flame. I was the Algerian, believing, full of the courage of belief. Terror came into the dream because again Anna was threatened with total disintegration. (601)

Breaking through rigid ego defenses also suggests a resolution to Anna's writer's block. As a good Marxist, she had previously censured herself for writing "subjectively" about personal emotions rather than "objectively" about social reality.

At that moment I sit down to write, someone comes into the room . . . and stops me. . . . It could be a Chinese peasant. . . . Or an Algerian fighting in the F.L.N. . . . Why aren't you doing something about us, instead of wasting your time scribbling? (639)

The ability to express the personal feelings of an Algerian soldier should resolve this ideological conflict by enabling her to write politically, to encompass social issues within the experience of the individual. Readers would have to live out, on the plane of vicarious personal experience, the moral dilemmas that confront a fighter who kills in a just cause.[8]

It is significant that Anna does not actually write the novel about the Algerian revolutionary but instead makes Saul a gift of her inspiration:

"You want me to give you the first sentence of your novel?"
"Let's hear it."
"On a dry hillside in Algeria, the soldier watched the moonlight glinting on his rifle." . . .
"Write the first sentence for me in the book." . . .
"Why?"
"You're part of the team. . . . There are a few of us around in the world, we rely on each other even though we don't know each other's names. . . . We're a team, we're the ones who haven't given in, who'll go on fighting. I tell you, Anna, sometimes I pick up a book and I say: Well, so you've written it first, have you? Good for you. O.K., then I won't have to write it."
"All right, I'll write your first sentence for you." (639–42)

Anna writes this first sentence in the golden notebook itself, whose contents form "The Golden Notebook" section of the novel we are reading. The notion of Anna and Saul as a "team" may surprise the reader, who has been propelled through the labyrinth of Anna's and Saul's mutual destructiveness as they enact the damaging sex roles of their culture. But the golden notebook as artifact, as object in the world of Anna and Saul, embodies their teamwork. It begins with an epigraph written by Saul, continues through Anna's description of her dream-films, and ends with a summary of the novel Saul wrote from the first line that Anna set him in the scene quoted above. The golden notebook is thus transitional space made concrete, a space where the two merge. Lessing comments: "In the inner Golden Notebook, which is written by both of them, you can no longer distinguish between what is Saul and what is Anna" (viii).

More specifically, the golden notebook embodies the creative mutuality that is the other side of their male-female enmity: as writers, they nurture and encourage each other's creativity. The text of "The Golden Notebook" chapter is composed of the two art works born of their union: the journal description of the dream-films that heralds Anna's shift toward a more lively, concrete, sensuous writing, and the summary of Saul's novel about the Algerian soldier. After the outline of Saul's novel that ends "The Golden Notebook" section comes a section of *Free Women*, a novel written by Anna from the first line given her by Saul, in the complementary half of the dialogue quoted above:

> "Anna, I'm going to force you into writing. Take up a piece of paper and a pencil. . . . It doesn't matter if you fail."
>
> My mind went blank in a sort of panic. I laid down the pencil. . . .
>
> "I'm going to give you the first sentence then. . . . 'The two women were alone in the London flat.' . . . You're going to write that book, you're going to write, you're going to finish it."
>
> "Why is it so important to you that I should?" . . .
>
> "Well, because if you can do it, then I can." (639)

As if to emphasize the mutuality of this creative cooperation, Lessing builds it in perfect symmetry: Anna's first line/Saul's finished novel balances Saul's first line/Anna's finished novel. If Saul's assaults jolt Anna out of the fixed position of "writer's block," Anna also gives Saul a push past his insistent solipsism—the "I, I, I" (628–30) of an egotism heavily defended against connection with others—by challenging him to identify with the Algerian soldier. Thus their creative union has all the reciprocity and equality that was lacking in their sexual union.

I do not mean to imply that Lessing resolves the paradoxes of heterosexual relationship through a happy ending of creative togetherness: Anna and Saul can imagine no liberating ending but separation. Limited by the structure of male dominance in which it is grounded, the alliance of Saul and Anna inevitably produces a contradictory blend of generative nurturing and hostile destructiveness. On the one hand, merging with a man means that a woman pours her creative energies into fleshing out his fantasies, gives up her own vision to become the object of his, and circumscribes her potential self within the rigid confines of his reductive and negative image of woman. Yet despite her distrust of heterosexual dynamics, Lessing's presentation of the creative process is fully embedded in relationship. Anna could not have risked the necessary breakdown into formlessness without the touchstone of another person's reality, however unstable; alone, she could not have experienced the dissolution of bound-aries between self and other that enables her to enter empathically into a vividly imagined reconstruction of others' feelings. Although the thorni-ness of Anna's relationship with Saul makes the world they inhabit to-gether seem far indeed from the comforting transitional space described in chapter 6 above, where loving care makes it safe to create imaginary worlds, their merging in sex and play does produce both creative break-throughs and concrete works of art.

Reflections on Ideology and Change in *The Waterfall* and *The Golden Notebook*

The Waterfall and *The Golden Notebook* both abjure the either/or choice offered women writers by narrative tradition: either an "ambition" script with a pattern of relentlessly austere autonomy that enables a woman to paint or write while depriving her of sexual and emotional relationship; or a romantic love script that confirms the central doctrine of patriarchy—the inferiority of women, the superiority of men—by making the man rather than the self the center of a woman's existence and subordinating her creative powers to the single task of ensnaring him into a permanent alliance. Lessing and Drabble answer Phyllis Rose's call for "more and more complex plots. . . . We need literature, which, by allowing us to experience more fully, to imagine more fully, enables us to live more freely" (*Parallel*, 9). Their stories resist easy solutions to encompass the whole range and complexity of women's experience within patriarchy.

It is sometimes difficult to discern whether Lessing and Drabble are aware of the cultural origins of their characters' emotional binds or whether they themselves are caught up in the patriarchal myths that blind their characters. Feminists have taken Lessing to task for Anna's general-izations about women, which, because "Lessing has so conceived the book that nowhere within it are Anna's and Ella's judgments of their experiences implied to be anything but unavoidable" (Morgan, 480), stand as unquestioned truths.[9] Anna accepts culturally defined ideals—"a real woman," "a real man," "a real orgasm"—which tend to discredit a woman's own spontaneous feelings by measuring them always against cultural definitions (see especially Lessing, 215–16). Similarly, Drabble's presentation of Jane's emotional bondage to James has disturbed many feminists.[10] In one published interview Drabble seems to endorse Jane's belief in James as her savior when she speaks of "grace" coming to Jane "through James" (Hardin, 283–84).

Whether or not they measure up to feminist standards of awareness, Lessing and Drabble do record and so expose to reflection and analysis the various forms of women's alienation under patriarchy. *The Waterfall* and *The Golden Notebook* offer compelling evidence that fantasies subordinating women to men are integral to women's experience of heterosexual relationships. They warn us against embracing uncritically the idea of a return to preoedipal merging as a prelude to change: given the unconscious structures of male dominance that inhabit us, some awareness of the power of ideology to infiltrate our most personal fantasies is necessary to prevent the ideal of a fruitful exchange of selves from becoming a one-way incorporation of the woman into the man's fantasy life.

Indeed there is some danger of Jane's remaining in her room, enslaved to James's fantasy of having a mother/woman always in bed, always at his disposal; there is some danger of Anna's remaining enclosed within Saul's fantasy world. But Drabble and Lessing instead affirm the potential in experience itself—and especially in the experience of intimate relationship—for working through the fantasies that imprison us. By playing out against their lovers' roles the male-female scenarios of their culture, Anna and Jane open up for scrutiny the fantasies that enforce unconscious compliance with social norms. If they cannot delete these fantasies from their unconscious life, they can understand and so resist their pull. Jane works toward a recognition of her own myths by living them out and writing them out, learning to recognize the "lies," or ideological warps, that distort her vision of her own experience. Anna and Saul, by giving themselves over for a time to the emotions of the cultural personas that inhabit them, gradually become aware of the social determination of their responses. After playing out the lone stranger and the controlling woman for the last time, they look at each other with recognition: "Well, we'll never have to say that again" (632). Lessing evidently shares Freud's optimism that making the unconscious conscious gives people control over their behavior. *The Waterfall* and *The Golden Notebook* thus dramatize the possibility of change through "a struggle at the roots of the mind—not casting off an ideology, or learning phrases about it, but confronting hegemony in the fibres of the self and in the hard practical substance of effective and continuing relationships" (Williams, *Marxism*, 212).

9

Eros as Creativity:
The Extended Family
in *The Color Purple*

THE COLOR PURPLE extends the meaning of the term "erotic" to creative work and to the libidinal bonds formed by creative work—both between those who work together and between the creator and the user of a product. The novel centers on a couple, Shug and Celie, whose sexual intimacy awakens and energizes their creativity—that possibility so elusive among female artist novels. But their relationship is only part of the larger erotic movement of their extended family to integrate more and more diverse individuals into an "expanding network of connection" (Gilligan, 39).

Although I will be describing them separately, the lines of individual and family expansion run parallel. The novel begins at the nadir of both personal and family erotics. Celie, alone and deprived of communication and love by the abusive father who silences her, lives out the desperate extreme of isolation possible within the patriarchal nuclear family. As Celie expands her creative and libidinal ties with various people, the family broadens, too, drawing in more and more colorful personalities. The energy generated by this multiplicity of human connecting goes into making things together—quilts, pants, shirts, songs, a house—that in turn enrich the life of the family.

A Maternal Erotics

The Color Purple begins at the destructive extreme of a masculine erotics of dominance and moves toward a maternal erotics in which sexual love fosters personal growth. It opens with the rape of the fourteen-year-old Celie by her father (later discovered to be only her stepfather). To make a tale of incestuous rape into an exemplum of male sexuality may seem an exaggeration unfair to men; but as an expression of the power of man over woman, as "an act of domination" (Hartsock, 165), rape represents the logical extreme of a sexual power imbalance that dictates conquest for the man, submission for the woman. Jessica Benjamin contends that the male desire for control over his sex object prevalent in our culture stems from the assertion of absolute autonomy characteristic of male development. Although boys need to deny fusion with their mothers in order to assert the independence from mother that is the basis of male gender identity, they do not by a single stroke of will liberate themselves from the need for fusion.

> Since the child continues to need the mother, since the man continues to need women, the absolute assertion of independence requires possessing and controlling the needed object. The intention is not to do without her, but to make sure that her alien otherness is either assimilated or controlled, that her own subjectivity nowhere asserts itself in a way that could make his dependency upon her a conscious insult to his sense of freedom. (Benjamin, 80)

Celie's stepfather asserts just this kind of absolute control over Celie. As he denies her autonomy physically by assimilating her body to his own uses, he also tries to erase the evidence of her subjectivity by silencing her story of the rape: "You better not never tell nobody but God" is the opening line of the novel. It is more difficult to deny a woman's subjectivity if one has to listen to her view of things; denying women speech, as Hartsock notes, enables men to avoid "the reality of women as fellow human beings" (171).

When Celie is passed from father to husband, there is little change: her sexuality and her subjectivity are still denied expression. That the husband's orientation toward Celie as sexual receptacle and domestic worker is not different in kind from Celie's stepfather's indicates that Walker is concerned with incestuous rape not as an isolated problem, but as part of a continuum of male sexual attitudes that dehumanize and objectify women.

Celie, oppressed, plays out the female side of sexual objectification. In an early conversation with Shug, she describes conjugal sex thus:

> He git up on you, heist your nightgown round your waist, plunge in. Most times I pretend I ain't there. He never know the difference. Never ast me how I feel, nothing. Just do his business, get off, go to sleep. (79)

As if acceding to the ban on female subjectivity, Celie withdraws her consciousness from the act altogether—"I ain't there." Internalizing the masculine instrumental view of women, she makes of herself a passive vessel for male uses. Shug draws attention to the outrageous distortion that comes of defining the vagina exclusively in relation to what the penis is doing: "Do his business. . . . Do his business. Why, Miss Celie. You make it sound like he going to the toilet on you" (79). As so often in *The Color Purple*, Walker lampoons phallocentric logic by drawing it out to a parodic extreme. In a phallocentric symbology the female genitalia are construed as mere accessories to the penis, as a receptacle for male emissions—hence, in this passage, a toilet.[1]

The brutality of Celie's sexual exploitation in her original family can thus be seen as the point of departure for the construction of a masculine erotics characterized by the suppression of female self-expression. Against this male sexual dynamic Walker plays off an alternative maternal orientation that fosters the other's self-expression, both sexual and creative. I insist on the connection between the sexual and the creative because Walker does. Celie's father's violation of her body is simultaneously a violation of her creative spirit:

> I did love to cut hair, I say to Shug, since I was a little bitty thing. I'd run go git the scissors if I saw hair coming, and I'd cut and cut, long as I could. (109)

> one time when mama not at home, he . . . told me he want me to trim his hair. . . . While I trim his hair he look at me funny . . . he grab hold of me and cram me up tween his legs. . . . How it hurt and how much I was surprise. How it stung while I finish trimming his hair. (108–9)

Thereafter Celie recoils from the instruments of her craft, become the instruments of sexual violence: "every time I saw him coming with the scissors . . . I start to cry" (109). In the relation with Shug the sexual and the creative continue as aspects of the same libidinal force, but turned now in the direction of growth: Shug both guides Celie to a discovery of her sexual identity and channels her creative energy into making pants.

The maternal erotics I wish to construct here, based on Sara Ruddick's analysis of "maternal thinking," can be seen as a response to the same problems of mother-child fusion as the masculine Eros outlined above—an answer to the dilemma of needing the other, yet needing the other to be separate. But a maternal erotics is grounded in a mother's attitudes toward her child rather than in infantile attitudes toward the mother. A mother knows from the start what the infant has to learn, painfully and slowly: that the other to whom she is intensely connected has an existence independent of her. In fact, maternal devotion to the other ideally includes a dedication to the other's eventual autonomy: in Nancy Hartsock's words, "The power of the mother over the child, and the sensual and erotic relation with the child, issue (in healthy relations) in the creation of an independent and autonomous being. The point of having power over another is to liberate the other rather than dominate . . . her" (257). In place of the need for control of the other that Benjamin claims goes hand in hand with the male assertion of absolute independence, the maternal attitude, bred in the course of trying to preserve and develop another being whose essence is unpredictable, changing, and always growing away, is governed by an awareness of the limits of one's power over another being.

Where a masculine erotic orientation seeks to annul the subjectivity of the other in order to control her, working effectively with a child over time depends on an understanding of what is going on in his or her mind: "A mother, in order to understand her child, must assume the existence of a conscious continuing person whose acts make sense in terms of perceptions and responses to a meaning-filled world" (Ruddick, 344). A maternal erotics, then, would oppose a recognition and appreciation of the other as a person with his or her own subjective reality to the masculine assertion of control and denial of the other's subjectivity. (Following Ruddick's example, I am describing attitudes that arise from the practice of mothering, from the demands that a child's existence makes on its mother. If one began theorizing instead from a psychoanalytic standpoint, one could argue that because of the difficulty in determining boundaries that Chodorow and others attribute to women, a mother can easily fail to recognize that her child possesses a separate consciousness. As Alice Miller has compellingly argued, this confusion of ego boundaries, combined with the vulnerability of a child's position, can produce a mother who uses her child to satisfy her own emotional needs and ignores the child's own spontaneous feelings.)

A mother's task is not just to recognize her child's subjective world but to contribute to its development, to foster her child's physical, emotional, and intellectual growth. An erotics derived from maternal attitudes would then imply each lover's stake in the creative development of the other. Power viewed as the power to enable the other's growth as a person, an erotic and sensual relation viewed as the ground of autonomy—if such attitudes underlay the feelings of sexual partners toward each other, loving would involve liberating each other's powers of self-expression rather than trying to suppress them.

Celie and Shug establish a sexual relationship on the basis of a reciprocal nurturing. From the first, when Celie's husband brings his deathly ill and evil-tempered mistress into the house, Celie's erotic attraction to Shug is inseparable from a maternal impulse to preserve her life:

> Come on in. I want to cry. To shout. Come on in. With God help, Celie going to make you well. (50)

Not "I alone," but "with the help of God." Celie's desire to heal and protect is tempered by what Ruddick calls maternal humility: a recognition of the imponderable forces arrayed against the preservation of a fragile life. While the masculinist desire for control over the loved one expresses a confidence in one's power to subjugate external reality to one's will, maternal practice, because it is embedded in the daily struggle with events and persons that elude control, produces humility—"a profound sense of the limits of one's actions. . . . 'We cannot dominate the world'" (Ruddick, 343, quoting Murdoch, 99). Throughout their relationship, Celie maintains her sense of limits in the face of forces beyond her control, starting with Shug's autonomy: "Shug got a right to live too. She got a right to look over the world in whatever company she choose. Just cause I love her don't take away none of her rights. . . . Shug bound to live her life and be herself no matter what" (236).

But a respect for each other's autonomy does not preclude Celie and Shug from creating a maternal space for each other where ego boundaries temporarily overlap.

> I wash and comb out [Shug's] hair. . . . I work on her like she . . . Olivia [Celie's daughter] or like she mama. I comb and pat, comb and pat. First she say, hurry up and get finish. Then she melt down a little and lean back against my knees. That feel just right, she say. That feel like mama used to do. Or maybe not mama. Maybe grandma. . . . Start hum a little tune.
> What that song? I ast. . . . Something come to me, she say. Something I made up. Something you help scratch out my head. (57)

Both partners draw on memories of their mothers to reenter this space of nurturing sensuality. Shug gives up her insistence on boundaries to "melt down . . . against [Celie's] knees," relaxing into the diffuse space between self and (m)other where, the need to meet the demands of reality lifted for a moment by the loving other's protective presence, the creative self is free to play. This release from ego control to wandering impulses results in the creation of something new: a song that Shug subsequently names "Celie's song" (75) in acknowledgment of the creative collaboration between she who nurtures and she who creates.

Reciprocally, Shug becomes an enabling presence for Celie. In response to Celie's male-identified description of the vagina as a receptacle for male excretions (quoted above), Shug begins a redefinition of sex in the context of female experience, which Celie picks up and completes. "You never enjoy [sex] at all? [Shug] ast, puzzle. . . . Why, Miss Celie, she say, you still a virgin" (79). As Molly Hite points out, Shug's redefinition of "virgin" makes the woman's own sexual enjoyment rather than male penetration the index of sexuality, eroding an important category in men's classification of women. Shug goes on to explain that "Right down there in your pussy is a little button that gits real hot. . . . It git hotter and hotter and then it melt" (79). Hite comments that this is "a mixed metaphor from the point of view of mainstream discursive practice, which of course has only recently begun to acknowledge the existence of buttons that behave in this way" ("Writing," 128). Shug's discourse in fact overturns the accepted view of female genitalia as "a hole that requires plugging" by substituting "a button that gets hot and finally melts" ("Writing," 128).[2]

What Shug begins, Celie completes, defining a sexual identity that does not depend on what a man does to her but on the whole span of her sensual experience, from early erotic ties to her mother's body to the orgasmic sensations of nursing her babies.

> [Shug] say, Here, take this mirror and go look at yourself down there. I bet you never seen it, have you? . . .
> And us run off to my room like two little prankish girls.
> You guard the door, I say. . . .
> I lie back and haul up my dress. Stick the looking glass tween my legs. Ugh. All that hair. Then my pussy lips be black. Then inside look like a wet rose.
> It a lot prettier than you thought, ain't it? she say from the door.
> It mine, I say. Where the button?
> Right up near the top, she say. . . .
> I look at her and touch it with my finger. A little shiver go through me. . . . She say, While you looking, look at your titties too. I haul up my dress and look at my titties. Think bout my babies sucking them. Remember the little shiver I felt then too. Sometimes a big shiver. Best part about having the babies was feeding them. (79–80)

By claiming the sensations that spring from nursing and autoeroticism as her own Celie turns away from the phallocentric restriction of female sexuality to those activities that involve a man.

Feminist theorists have described the cultural model of asexual motherhood that impoverishes women's sensuality. According to Niles Newton, coition, nursing, and giving birth produce similar muscular and neurohormonal responses; but women tend to "deny the evidence of their senses by repressing the component of sexuality in the maternal role" (Rossi, 169). When Celie embraces the orgasmic sensations derived from her babies' suckling—"best part about having the babies was feeding them" (80)—she retrieves an element of her sexuality from this culturally imposed fragmentation. Later, when Celie feels Shug's mouth on her nipple, she is able to locate her sensations on a continuum of her own experience: "Then I feels something real soft and wet on my breast, feel like one of my little lost babies mouth" (109).[3]

Celie also manages to integrate the memory of her mother's body into adult sensuality:

> Me and Shug sound asleep. Her back to me, my arms round her waist. What it like: little like sleeping with mama, . . . little like sleeping with Nettie. . . . It warm and cushiony, and I feel Shug's big tits sorta flop over my arms like suds. (110)

Although "the mother is, after all, the first love object for the girl as well as the boy," as Jane Flax says, so that "all of us carry the memory of the experience of our mother's body—her softness, smell, comfort"—homophobia pushes women to suppress their sensual memories of their mothers' bodies. "A powerful source of women's sexuality—the memories of early infantile gratification—is denied" (Flax, "Conflict," 183). Women who internalize the approved feminine sexual identity are thus cut off from the roots and branches of their sexuality—from the memory of their mother's body on the one hand and from fully realized sensual connection to their children on the other. As a result their sensual responsiveness as a whole is reduced. Celie's example shows how, on the contrary, integrating memories of erotic experience from the whole span of a woman's life can enrich the sexual experience of the present.

One component of a maternal erotics is thus a redefinition of female sexuality to encompass all of a woman's sensual experience. While it could be argued that sexual intimacy with another woman more readily evokes memories associated with the mother's body than heterosexual sex, or that a relationship between women facilitates their thinking in terms that elude male-imposed parameters, I wish to argue instead that a maternal erotics is possible in heterosexual as well as lesbian love. The crucial factor in Shug's and Celie's re-vision of female sexuality is not that they are both women but that they refuse the sensual impoverishment that comes of limiting sexual excitement to those activities that require a male intermediary between a woman and her body. The expanded female sexuality that Walker constructs could be accessible to a heterosexual woman, too, if she could break free of the cultural hegemony that classifies as "sexual" only those sensations released by intercourse (or the prelude thereto). Were a woman able to admit the range of her own sensations freely, as Celie does, erotic memories of being in touch with her mother's body could enrich the pleasures of lying next to her lover, whether that lover's body were male or female; and accepting the sensual aspect of nursing her babies could later enhance heterosexual caresses as well as homosexual caresses. (For example, in *The Waterfall* Jane's and James's sensual life together— see chapter 7 above—seems rich in part because sex evokes associations with giving birth, nursing, and being close to a mother's body.)

Shug's power as a facilitator in this scene suggests a maternal dynamic that focuses on enabling the other's development. Unlike the romantic lover who awakens the woman's sexuality with a kiss, Shug creates a safe space where Celie can discover her sexuality for herself—a space guaranteed by Shug's watchful presence but not violated by her. Shug stays in the background, only reflecting from the doorway the discoveries that Celie makes for herself: "It prettier than you think, ain't it?" (80). Shug enables Celie to recover her body from the world of male instrumentality and to reclaim its pleasures for her own delight: "It mine." The incident recalls Winnicott's paradigm of a maternal figure who "does not violate one's space but permits the experience of one's own desire, who recognizes it when it emerges of itself" (Benjamin, 96).

This enabling role extends to Celie's creativity: it is Shug who suggests that Celie make pants, and when Celie's aptitude for sewing emerges Shug provides her with literal space in her Memphis home:

> I sit in the dining-room making pants after pants. I got pants now in every color and size under the sun. Since us started making pants down home, I ain't been able to stop. I change the cloth, I change the print, I change the waist, I change the pocket. (190)

Characteristically, Walker does not explain in so many words the relation between this creative exuberance and Shug's sheltering presence but offers a spatial representation of their interconnection in the close of this letter to Nettie:

> Your Sister, Celie
> Folkspants, Unlimited.
> Sugar Avery Drive
> Memphis, Tennessee
>   (192)

Evidently Shug has, with characteristic self-determination, wrested from the city fathers the power to name her own street; Celie nestles the basis of her autonomy—her own creative enterprise—within this woman-defined space.

Walker thus constructs an alternative fantasy both to romantic love and to the fantasy of austere autonomy that characterizes most female artist novels. To the romantic model of excitement radiating from a male figure *The Color Purple* opposes an excitement that proceeds from within, from what a woman spins out of her own creative potential. To female artist novels like *Violet Clay* and *To the Lighthouse*, which assume that sensual pleasure precludes the autonomy necessary for art, she opposes the notion of a maternal sensuality that nurtures the other's creative autonomy. Celie develops the ability to stand alone, both financially and emotionally, on the basis of her creative work, but her productivity is always grounded in relationship.

Walker's commitment to interdependency as the basis of personal autonomy can be read in the name of Celie's "private enterprise": "Folkspants" recognizes the intersubjective character of Celie's work by naming the "folk" who both inspire her designs and, by wearing her pants, complete her work. In *The Color Purple* art is embedded in a network of others.

"Every Stitch I Sew Will Be a Kiss"

Every creation in *The Color Purple* represents a nexus of interconnection between the one who makes it and the one who receives it. That includes God's works and the letters that constitute the text we are reading, as well as the artifacts that the characters make. According to Shug's doctrine, God makes something to get our attention, to arouse our love and admiration, and "just [to] share a good thing" (178). Thus every flower in a field becomes the center of a personal transaction between God and me:

> More than anything else, God love admiration. . . . I think it pisses God off if you walk by the color purple in a field somewhere and don't notice it.
> What it do when it pissed off?
> Oh, it make something else. (178)

Like a lover, God is "always making little surprises and springing them on us when us least expect" (178). The Creation is not a finished product, then, but an ongoing process, powered by love.

The epistolary framework of the very art work we are reading continually reminds us that each narrative is motivated by love and destined to a loved other: "Dear Nettie, . . . Your loving sister, Celie" (217); "Dear Celie, . . . Your devoted sister Nettie" (163). (*The Color Purple* is itself "a letter of love" to Zora Neale Hurston, as Henry Louis Gates sees it (244); images from *Their Eyes Were Watching God* are incorporated into Walker's text, so that the novel itself expresses a recognition of personal connection.)[4]

The artifacts within the novel likewise acknowledge connection. Each is a gift—a tribute—to a loved one, created out of loving attention to who that other is. Thus the purple frog that Celie's husband carves for her (at the end of a long and arduous development away from his initial male chauvinism) incorporates in *his* self-expression something central to Celie. That he chose to carve a frog signifies his acceptance of the view of men she articulated earlier: "Take off they pants, I say, and men look like frogs to me. No matter how you kiss 'em, as far as I'm concern, frogs is what they stay" (224). Injurious as such a sentiment might once have been to Albert's defensive pride in his masculinity, his carving attests to his having moved beyond egocentrism to turn his full attention on Celie and to grasp her view of the world. Before, Albert needed to control Celie to make her play her part in the drama that shored up his masculine self-esteem. Now he bases his art work on who she is in the context of her own subjective reality.

Celie designs pants for Shug in the same spirit: they fit the actuality of Shug's life, outside the sphere of Celie's wishes and needs. Rather than imposing control like the (male-designed) designer jeans that are "form-fitting" only in the sense that they demand that the female body conform to their pattern of slimness, Celie adapts her pants to the idiosyncrasies of Shug's life.

> Then finally one day I made the perfect pair of pants. For my sugar, naturally. They soft dark blue jersey with teeny patches of red. But what make them so good is, they totally comfortable. Cause Shug eat a lot of junk on the road, and drink, her stomach bloat. So the pants can be let out without messing up the shape. Because she have to pack her stuff and fight wrinkles, these pants are soft, hardly wrinkle at all. . . . And they full round the ankle so if she want to sing in 'em and wear 'em sort of like a long dress, she can. (191)

This design is based on an acceptance of the world Shug inhabits when she is outside Celie's ken, implying both a recognition of the loved one as a person with her own reality and a flexible empathy with a dynamic human being who changes in response to the varying demands of her concrete life conditions.

Art works in *The Color Purple* are thus creations of a particular kind of love, one that retains connection with the other through empathy but that relinquishes the desire for control. As Winnicott says about a stage of differentiation that enables the child to see the mother, and the mother to see the child, as a person in her own right: when the individual can locate its object "outside the area of omnipotent control," outside the borders of projective fantasy, then the reality of the other "can feed back other-than-me substance into the subject" ("Use of an Object," 89, 94).[5]

In *The Color Purple* it is this capacity to take in and respond to "other-than-me" material that produces the work of art. Celie's receptivity to the truly "other" reality of a loved one enables her to make pants that "fit" him or her in all senses of the word.

> I start to make pants for Jack. They have to be camel. And soft and strong. And they have to have big pockets so he can keep a lot of children's things. Marbles and string and pennies and rocks. And they have to be washable and they have to fit closer round the leg than Shug's so he can run if he need to snatch a child out of the way of something. And they have to be something he can lay back in when he hold Odessa in front of the fire. (191–92)

Recognition of the other is the source of Celie's design. The pair of pants she makes expresses her individuality as maker, but the wearer's personality as well.

Marx envisioned art taking place in just such an intersubjective dimension. In an economy based on use rather than exchange, it would be not only the maker who would "objectify in [his] production [his] individuality and its peculiarity," but also the user who would find in the object an expression of *him*self (or herself): "In my expression of my life I would have fashioned your expression of life, and thus in my own activity have realized my own essence, my human, my communal essence" (Marx, quoted in McLellan, 31–32; McLellan in Hartsock, 5). Celie makes pants that no one else could make; but this formal expression of her own creative self expresses Jack's essential self as well. The pants are modeled on the capaciousness of his acceptance of children's play and children's needs. This is no vision of Jack's essential self divorced from time and place, "clear and complete, the essence sucked out of life and held rounded here" (Woolf, *Lighthouse*, 181); rather, Celie perceives Jack dynamically, as he relates to others in the family network. And she envisions her finished work entering the round of intertwined lives. Art is not set apart, in the abstract space of a museum, but "has its source in human ties and its end in human change" (DuPlessis, 103). Viewing life as a web of connection (Gilligan, 32) enables Celie to think of both her creations and the people to whom she destines them as dynamic, evolving through ongoing personal interchanges.

The aesthetic of *The Color Purple* makes artistic creativity an extension of care. What Celie makes—first diapers for her baby, then cotton shifts for Shug, then quilts and pants—ties her creativity to a tradition of mothers who have always made things to wrap around and warm their loved ones. "Every stitch I sew will be a kiss" (192), she promises Nettie, as she imagines the pants she will make "to beat the heat in Africa. Soft, white, thin. Drawstring waist. You won't ever have to feel too hot and overdress again" (192). As in maternal thinking, knowing the other is a matter of meeting the other's physical need where that other lives, in the material conditions of his or her daily life. Walker does not so much reverse the terms of the reigning cultural dichotomy that distinguishes art that counts —art conceived in some "pure autonomy of mind" (Adorno, 26; quoted in DuPlessis, 104)—from its humble domestic counterpart, which is designed for use and destined for consumption, as challenge dichotomous thinking altogether. *The Color Purple*'s aesthetic brings together maternal work and artistic work, suggesting a way of healing the divisions that make the artist daughters in the novels described in chapter 6, above, put as much distance as they can between themselves and their mothers. As

Rachel Blau DuPlessis says in elaborating the "poetics of domestic value" that she finds in some other female artist novels, the "labor of love" involved in creating art works destined for loved ones heals the split between work and love.[6]

The Extended Family

The Color Purple is not so much a *Bildungsroman* about Celie's creative and sexual growth as it is about the *Bildung* of the family, its expansion into an extended family network that is resilient, flexible, and supportive. To turn a vocabulary meant for persons to the description of a literary text: the energy that gives *The Color Purple* its momentum is not so much the narrow form of Eros that aims at gratification within the unit of the sexual couple, as the broader instinct that Freud called Eros—"the instinct to preserve living substance and to join it into ever larger units" (*Civilization*, 118). When Celie toward the end of the novel expresses the creative impulse of Eros—"So much in the habit of sewing something I stitch up a bunch of scraps, try to see what I can make" (249)—she is articulating not just the erotic impulse of the individual artist, but the drive that moves her family to "make one out of more than one" (*Civilization*, 108), to bring ever more diverse personalities into the web of family relations. Although the exact cause for the lift of spirit that *The Color Purple* gives its reader is difficult to pinpoint, my speculation is that it comes from the reader's participation in this erotic movement "to establish ever greater unities" (Freud, *Outline*, 148): the novel moves from an opening confinement in the nuclear family unit toward an ever-widening circle of affiliation.

Walker's text also puts into practice the meanings of the erotic articulated by Herbert Marcuse and more recently by Audre Lorde: the erotic gives life to work, and shared work creates libidinal ties.[7] In the world of *The Color Purple*, creative work is a natural expression of erotic bonding. When a new friendship sparks between Sofia and Celie, they immediately begin a quilt; Shug and Celie design a house together to inaugurate their life together in Shug's Memphis home; and Celie and her husband renew their relationship on a new structural basis—one of equality—when he sews shirts to match the pants she makes. Quilting both creates family solidarity and serves as its symbol. As metaphor, quilting represents the activity of connection, the piecing together of disparate scrappy personalities into a flexible whole. On the literal level, quilting bonds the quilters: because they share a single objective for the length of the project, or because they sit side by side for hours, sewing together opens up lines of communication. Celie begins to understand Sofia, her opposite in many ways, while she quilts with her (62); and as Albert sits sewing with Celie he learns to listen to her and to understand the way she sees the world.

The novel's drive toward expansion begins in the loneliness of the patriarchal nuclear family, where Celie is cut off from all communication and support by her father's silencing: "You better not tell nobody but God." When she is passed from father to husband, she becomes "mother" to her husband's children, but she is still treated as sexual receptacle and domestic beast of burden. Acting the part of mother in this parodic extreme of patriarchal family organization, she passes her oppression on to the next generation. When Harpo, her stepson, asks her how he can make his wife Sofia obey him, Celie answers, "Beat her" (42).

The act of quilting with Sofia forms Celie's first bridge out of the isolation of her position in the nuclear family. Angry at her mother-in-law's betrayal, Sofia returns the curtain materials Celie had given her: "Just wanted you to know I looked to you for help. . . . Here your curtains. . . . Here your thread" (45). But rejection is followed by a breakthrough into communication.

> What you say ["Beat her"] for? she ast. . . .
> I say it cause I'm a fool, I say. I say it cause I'm jealous of you. I say it cause you do what I can't.
> What that? she say.
> Fight. I say. . . .
> What you do when you git mad? she ast.
> . . . I can't even remember the last time I felt mad, I say. . . . Couldn't be mad at my daddy cause he my daddy. Bible say, Honor father and mother no matter what. . . . Well, sometime Mr. ——— get on me pretty hard. . . . But he my husband. . . . This life soon be over, I say. Heaven last all ways.
> You ought to bash Mr. ——— head open, she say. Think bout heaven later.
> Not much funny to me. That funny. I laught. She laugh. Then us both laugh so hard us flop down on the step.
> Let's make quilt pieces out of these messed up curtains, she say. And I run git my pattern book. (46–47)

Laughter is a sign of rupture—a release of energy that signals a breach, first, with an inner psychic order that keeps certain disruptive possibilities under repression;[8] and second, with the social code that that inner order mirrors—here, the Law of the Father (Honor thy father and thy husband) that keeps Celie oppressed. The forbidden idea of the wife beating the husband turns on its head the principle of male dominance that both psychic and social orders are founded on, and so overthrows the hierarchical vision of the world that has kept Celie imprisoned in habits of obedience and self-suppression. As always in *The Color Purple*, emotional movement is immediately transformed into physical movement. At this toppling of the old oppressive order Celie and Sofia fall down laughing, rolling on the porch like children; a moment later they put the energy released from repression into quilting together, their positions side by side representing the female reciprocity and mutuality that replaces the old male-female hierarchy. Sofia and Celie make a quilt based on a pattern called "Sister's Choice" to mark their new commitment to support each other against male oppression. But already the quilt itself prefigures a larger circle of women: they piece into it a flashy dress donated by Shug, as well as fragments of Celie's old dress and Sofia's curtain material. Finally Shug joins in the quilting.[9]

Shug's inclusion in the family begins the eclipse of its patriarchal lineaments. The wife (Celie) does not rule out, or even object to, her husband's mistress (Shug) moving in; nor does the husband become the focus of the two women's jealous rivalry. Rather, the wife loves and protects the mistress, and their relationship becomes central. The shift in family relations is pictured in material terms—as are all the emotional shifts in *The Color Purple*: Celie and Shug quilt together with Albert next to them, arrayed against the patriarchal figures (Albert's father and brother) who try to restore the forms of conventional family life. "I see myself sitting there quilting tween Shug Avery and Mr. ———. Us three set together gainst Tobias. . . . For the first time in my life, I feel just right" (61). As Sofia and Celie consolidated their overthrow of the Law of the Father by making a quilt, the line of mistress-wife-husband quilting together ranges itself against a return to patriarchal arrangements.

If it is making things together that binds people into new social configurations, it is the relationships between them that inspire their creative production. The very differences that make the quilt an appropriate metaphor for the patchwork of variegated personalities in this evolving family also create a field of creative energy between them, "a fund of necessary polarities between which [their] creativity can spark like a dialectic" (Lorde, "The Master's," 99). Celie starts from the position of submissive female, while Shug is at first "mean and nasty" (237), "evil" (51), "hateful" (53); she pushes away both food and love in her determination to remain wholly self-sufficient. Celie grows toward Shug, in the direction of self-assertion: she learns both to confront her tyrannical husband with an assertion of her right to live her own life and to grapple actively with her materials, shaping them to her designs. Shug grows by becoming more like Celie, learning to accept maternal care and the inspiration that springs from it and to reciprocate; it is from within a maternal embrace ("me and Shug sleep like sisters") that Shug launches Celie on her career: "Let's make you some pants" (136).

When, after Sofia's departure, the family circle expands again to include Harpo's mistress, Squeak—"a nice girl, friendly, . . . [who] do anything Harpo say" (83)—she is drawn to her opposite, the defiantly self-deter-mining Shug. Inspired by Shug's example, Squeak turns her unlikely voice ("it little, it high, it sort of meowing," 96) into a seductive instrument with which she wins over the audience at Harpo's juke joint. Squeak thus changes through identification with Shug. But this identification is not the regressive coalescence with the image of the other that Lacanian psy-choanalysis presents as a static interplay of mirrors; rather, it is a step toward change, along a path of development that would be closed to a more rigidly self-enclosed individual. "First she sing Shug's songs, then she begin to make up songs her own self" (96). If growing toward Shug enables Squeak to discover her voice, practice in expressing her own idio-syncratic talent through singing enables her to become self-defining. She refuses the diminution of Harpo's nickname to insist on her real name, Mary Agnes (95, 183), thereby claiming a position of autonomy:

> Squeak, Mary Agnes, what difference do it make? [says Harpo.]
> It make a lot, say Squeak. When I was Mary Agnes I could sing in public. (183)

Unlike the white middle-class artist novels that construe autonomy as the antithesis of close relationship, in Walker's novel affiliation inspires cre-ative self-expression and sustains its development; creative expression, in turn, becomes the basis of self-definition. Relationship, creativity, and the autonomy that emerges from them are mutually enhancing rather than mutually exclusive.

Walker's vision of the extended family provides for the practical support as well as the emotional sustenance of creativity. If Shug's encouragement has given Squeak the courage to sing in public, Sofia's offer to take care of her child makes it possible for Squeak to pursue her career in Memphis.

Go on sing, say Sofia, I'll look after [Suzie Q] till you come back.
You will? say Squeak.
Yeah, say Sofia. (185)

Because child care is a responsibility shared by all the mothers of this family circle, the group can survive the departure of any one mother. This arrangement encourages autonomy even in mothers. It continues to promise them nurturance, too. Though all the women in *The Color Purple* at one point or another leave to pursue their own individual fortunes, they all return for emotional sustenance to the family circle.

The Color Purple reflects not just the extended network of mutual aid that is characteristic of African American families but also the genesis of that structure in necessity. It has been suggested that spreading responsibility for domestic functions over a number of individual households related through the children is a response to the economic pressures of poverty and racism (Stack, 113–15; N. Tanner, 153–54). In a racist society black men cannot always find work, and when they do it is likely to be impermanent; so black women have to work outside the home. Sharing domestic responsibilities among a large number of adults makes an extended family network relatively impervious to individual comings and goings—a necessary adaptation to the stresses of living in a racist society, as the episode of Sofia's arrest and near-death in jail demonstrates. Where the institutions of law and order threaten to destroy the individual rather than protecting him or her, the family would disintegrate if it depended for its life on the presence of any one family member. In *The Color Purple* the "circle" of family and friends is first drawn together around the kitchen table by survival needs, namely the threat of Sofia's imminent death at the hands of her jailers. "Us all sit round the table after supper. Me, Shug, Mr. ———, Squeak, the prizefighter [Sofia's lover], Odessa and two more of Sofia sisters" (90).

Squeak has lost a few teeth to Sofia's old-fashioned jealous rage—they both claim Harpo as lover—but she subordinates her personal erotic investment first to Sofia's survival (she plays a major role in getting Sofia out of jail and into service in the mayor's home) and second to the communal responsibility of caring for Sofia's children.

Wonder if she still mad Sofia knock her teef out? I ast.
Yeah, she mad. But what good being mad gon do? She not evil, she know Sofia life hard to bear right now.
How she get long with the children? ast Mr. ———.

They love her, say Harpo. She let 'em do anything they want.

Oh-oh, I say.

Besides, he say, Odessa and Sofia other sisters always on hand to take up the slack. They bring up children like military. (96)

In a flexible network of child-rearing, what one parent lacks in the way of disciplinary backbone is compensated by others' strictness: the lack of censure in Harpo's tone reflects the relatively relaxed atmosphere of a world where the responsibility for the way children turn out is shared. Whereas the individualistic bias of middle-class ideology places wholly on the mother the onus of her child's care as well as the responsibility for her child's whole personality structure and success in life, in *The Color Purple* the parental generation assumes collective responsibility for bringing up the younger generation. Nettie brings up Celie's children, Celie brings up Annie Julia's children, Sofia cares for Squeak's child, and, Squeak, Jack, and Odessa raise Sofia's children.

Even Albert, Celie's tyrannical husband, is finally absorbed into the pattern of domestic cooperation. That Albert can change is an index of Walker's optimistic faith in the power of interpersonal relations and shared creative work to change a person's fixed attitudes. For, as Celie's title for him, "Mr. ———," implies, Albert's self-definition is rigidly affixed to the role of dominant male; his identity depends on the traditional family hierarchy that gives him absolute power over his wife. "Wives is like children," he explains. "You have to let 'em know who got the upper hand. Nothing can do that better than a good sound beating" (42).

The manner of Albert's transformation illuminates the mechanisms of change that operate throughout the novel, beneath the apparently disconnected interactions between individuals, to transform this brutal version of patriarchal hierarchy into a circle of nurturing "mothers." Walker's vision of change is erotic rather than revolutionary, depending on the power of shared domestic and creative work to open libidinal channels between people so that each begins to identify his or her interests with the other's and to understand how the other sees the world. It is true that Albert's construction of the family has to be destroyed by revolution, so to speak—by Celie's angry defiance of his power to control her life, followed by her move to Memphis—before he can open up to change. But after his patriarchal identity collapses along with the institutional dominance that supported it, two erotic events change his fundamental attitudes.

Albert is rescued from sliding into madness, amid the stench and mess of an unkempt house, by an extension of the emerging family organization of male and female mothers. His son Harpo abandons his own former insistence on a hierarchy of sex roles to act out a domestic role of nurturance; he cleans his father's house, bathes him, cooks his meals, and holds him in his arms to calm his mad fears. A further extension of the family constellation clicks into place when Sofia discovers Harpo in this maternal role. Alienated by Harpo's attempts to impose the dominance relations of the patriarchal family on her, she had left him. But when she discovers "the two of them . . . just laying there in the bed fast asleep. Harpo holding his daddy in his arms," Sofia "start to feel again for Harpo." And, as we have learned to expect, this erotic charge sparks a new creative project: "Pretty soon us start work on our new house" (201). Being encircled by his son's care and watching his son learn to exercise his considerable domestic talents apparently break down Albert's determination to stick to the dominant role: now "he clean that house just like a woman. Even cook . . . and wash the dishes when he finish" (199).

But it takes sharing creative work with Celie to convert him definitively to a view of human cooperation that transcends sex roles.

> . . . he come to visit me while I was sewing and ast me what was so special about my pants.
>
> Anybody can wear them, I said.
>
> Men and women not suppose to wear the same thing, he said. Men spose to wear the pants.
>
> So I said, You ought to tell that to the mens in Africa. . . . People in Africa try to wear what feel comfortable in the heat . . . men and women both preshate a nice dress. . . . And men sew in Africa, too, I say.
>
> They do? he ast. . . . When I was growing up, he said, I use to try to sew along with mama cause that's what she was always doing. But everybody laughed at me. But you know, I liked it.
>
> Well, nobody gon laugh at you now, I said. Here, help me stitch in these pockets.
>
> But I don't know how, he say.
>
> I'll show you, I said. And I did.
>
> Now us sit sewing and talking and smoking our pipes. (238)

The sewing connection enables Celie to liberate Albert's creativity from the vise of role differentiation that once suppressed it. Sex roles disappear along with the scaffolding of patriarchy that once made them functional. Like earlier social realignments in the novel, this new structure of gender-free egalitarianism is no abstract concept philosophically elaborated; it takes shape immediately in a concrete pattern of creative activity: "Now us sit sewing and talking and smoking our pipes" (238).

In the context of this book-long family expansion, the return of Celie's sister Nettie together with Celie's two children at the end of the novel seems less an arbitrary and contrived happy ending than part of a continuing movement toward inclusion. Just as a collapse on the spatial plane expressed the overturn of family hierarchy when Sofia's suggestion that Celie beat her husband dropped them both, laughing, to the floor, so the shock of reunion after nearly fifty years of separation plunges Nettie and Celie down to the level of "babies" lying on the porch.

> When Nettie's foot come down on the porch I almost die. I stand swaying. . . . Then us both start to moan and cry. Us totter toward one nother like us use to do when us was babies. Then us feel so weak when us touch, us knock each other down. . . . Us sit and lay there on the porch inside each other's arms.
> After while, she say *Celie*.
> I say *Nettie*. (250)

The restructuring of the family, from a system of male dominance based on the repression of women's voices[10] and the exploitation of their bodies to an institution modeled on sisters' solidarity, is capped by Celie's and Nettie's moving into a house of their own. They take over ownership of the house they grew up in, once a bastion of the most abusive form of patriarchy. To inaugurate their entry into this transformed family home Celie and Nettie go backwards, "tottering" toward each other "like us use to do when us was babies," finally regressing to a preverbal unity, lying "inside each other's arms"; only then do they stammer toward speech. After nearly half a century of using each other's names to address an absence ("Dear Celie," "Dear Nettie"), they have to learn all over again to affix the signifier to the bodily presence of the other ("she say *Celie*. I say *Nettie*"). Thus everything is finally rendered concrete in *The Color Purple*: even the signifiers that frame the novel's epistolary discourse—"Dear Celie", "Dear Nettie"—are resolved back into concrete presence.

The structural change in the family, from patriarchal hierarchy to an inclusive circle where all are of equal importance, has a parallel on the cosmic plane. Shug replaces the great white father in the sky with a continuum where everything is divine and everything is connected: God is in "everything" (178), "inside you and inside everybody else" (144). Shug's "feeling of being part of everything—not separate at all," so that "if I cut a tree, my arm would bleed" (178), parallels the interconnectedness that is the unspoken basis of the family network. The opening of Celie's final letter—"Dear God. Dear stars, dear trees, dear sky, dear peoples. Dear Everything. Dear God" (249)—expresses the widest compass of love. Celie writes to the spirit of divine vitality in everything rather than in a single reified patriarchal symbol, and she writes to everyone, not just to Nettie. The wide embrace of this salutation introduces a view of the family similarly expanded to its broadest circumference. All its far-flung members having returned—Shug, Squeak, Nettie, Samuel, Olivia, Adam, and Adam's new wife, Tashi—the family celebrates its reunion in a feast that Walker identifies explicitly as an alternative family ritual:

> Why us always have family reunion on July 4, say Henrietta. . . .
> White people busy celebrating they independence from England July 4th, say Harpo, so most black folks don't have to work. Us can spend the day celebrating each other. (250)

While white America celebrates the national virtue of independence, Celie's family celebrates interdependence.[11]

A Feminist Materialist Epistemology

Nancy Hartsock maintains that "a community structured by forms of eros that express women's experience might take quite different form" from male-defined social relations (210). *The Color Purple* creates community by means of the erotic potential in women's work in the home: the material work of providing for the family's physical well-being and the spiritual work of love. The task of fostering children's mental and physical development gives rise to specific forms of caring such as creating things to enhance the other's comfort and investing in the other's creative development.

At the center of their families, responsible for keeping the lines of communication and cooperation between family members open, women tend to see the larger world too as "a network of connection," "a web of relationship," as Carol Gilligan has persuasively argued in *A Different Voice*: "An awareness of the connection between people gives rise to a recognition of responsibility for one another, a perception of the need for response" (30). Were a community to be structured along the lines of a female Eros, then, we might expect it to look something like the extended family in *The Color Purple*: an expanding network of persons bound by affective ties and responsive to each other's needs, physical and emotional.

Women are not just subjects of practice, but subjects of culture too— subject, that is, to cultural influences that direct erotic energy exclusively toward the unit of the romantic couple. But if women's thinking *could* circumvent cultural hegemony, if women *were* free to base their vision of the world on their concrete practices in the home—on the experience of linking people together and expressing care in material terms—they would likely understand human connection in the way *The Color Purple* does: not as a concentration of erotic intensity within isolated, self-contained couples, but as an extended network of erotic bonds.

3 Changing the Family

10 Family Circles

Beloved, The Middle Ground,
A Weave of Women, Housekeeping,
Little Women, and The Color Purple

THE FAMILY IS difficult to think about clearly, Jane Flax points out, because "in no other area of our existence are ideology, feeling, fantasy, wishes, and reality so complexly intermingled" ("Family," 223). This chapter and the next separate out one strand from this complicated web, following the thread of fantasy in more speculative directions than previous chapters: backward, from fictions of family life in women's novels to the structural peculiarities of the authors' own family lives; and forward, from the alternative family configurations in contemporary women's novels to the influence these fantasies may have on readers' desires for their own lives.

Preceding chapters on *Jane Eyre* and various female artist novels have referred to the imprint of oedipal fantasies on authors' minds and, by implication, on the minds of the readers who love the novels they write. Thus *Jane Eyre*, in spite of its complexities, reveals an underlying assumption that a woman's happiness depends on being affirmed and accepted by a man rather than on the processes and products of her own creative autonomy. That schema reflects the value structure of the patriarchal nuclear family, where the father—powerful, authoritative, mysterious—is the center of attention and excitement and a girl is called upon to accept the role of object of his attention, rather than become a subject in her own right. What I have described as an alternative oedipal resolution is equally a product of this skewed power relation: the young girl assumes the role of active subject, but at the cost of repudiating her mother's subordinate role and so risking the withdrawal of her mother's love. The unconscious fantasy pattern that results—the choice between love and autonomy that structures many female artist novels—is also damaging to women, requiring as it does that a woman lop off some of her capacities and needs so that another set of abilities may flourish. The principle underlying these analyses is that unconscious fantasies reflect basic patterns of family interaction.

Women writers searching for a less damaging principle of family organization than the phallocentric norm may reach back further, past oedipal patterns, to images imprinted by early mother-daughter relations. Assuming the principle of development that informs this study—that earlier developmental stages remain available to us as platforms for evolving alternative approaches to life—I argue that these women reach back in order to move forward into a better future: primitive fantasies can be transformed toward more mature and viable patterns of living. Obviously nostalgia is not enough: to aim at a recovery of preoedipal fusion would be to aim at a state of arrested development. Some of the examples cited here—*Housekeeping, Beloved*—demonstrate the dangers of stagnation inherent in a desire to restore the original mother-child continuity. But the desire still attached to these early patterns can also be mobilized to create experimental social forms based on the old configurations, as in *Little Women, The Color Purple, A Weave of Women*, and *The Middle Ground*. The advantage of the preoedipal configuration is that it is *there*, in the unconscious of writers and readers who have been brought up in a situation where mothers have primary responsibility for child care.

Reimagining the Family

In the novels surveyed in this chapter, facial or gestural modes of communication reinforce an ethic of reciprocity and remind family members of their similarities, in contrast to the Word of the Father that lays down the law of differences. Faces mirror the expressions of other faces, enhancing a unity of feeling (*Little Women, Beloved*). Music—most often a mother's lullaby, but sometimes a shared chorus of song—reverberates within both singers and listeners, joining them (*Little Women, Housekeeping*). Learning takes place in a dimension often overlooked by logocentric discourse: a physical identification with the other through imitating her walk and gestures (*Housekeeping, Beloved, The Color Purple*). The nonverbal character of these interactions suggests an origin in preoedipal times.

The family pattern that emerges most often as a challenge to patriarchal family structure is the circle. Mothers and daughters are often grouped in a circle that represents in spatial terms the lateral and reciprocal character of their relations, as opposed to the hierarchies of the patriarchal family. I hazard the guess that the circle images the preoedipal illusion of completion, the sense of seamless continuity with the mother. Although the figure of the circle may derive immediately from being enclosed within the mother's arms, the emotional content of being encircled is broader, signifying a unity without beginning or end that seemed to be the truth of things before the self began to emerge from primary identification. In the novels under examination here, the circle is enlarged to include more daughters, but it often retains the quality of an undifferentiated female bond.

"She had always known a thousand ways to circle them all around with what must have seemed like grace" (Robinson, 11). *Housekeeping's* picture of the three sisters (Ruth's mother and aunts) peaceful within their mother's enveloping presence can serve as a paradigm of the preoedipal circle, presenting both its beauty and the danger of its pull toward stasis.

> When their mother sat down with her mending, they would settle themselves around her on the floor, . . . with their heads propped against her knees . . . their mother felt them leaning toward her, looking at her face and her hands. Never since they were small children had they clustered about her so, and never since then had she been so aware of the smell of their hair, their softness, breathiness, abruptness. It filled her with a strange elation, the same pleasure she had felt when any one of them, as a sucking child, had fastened her eyes on her face and reached for her other breast, her hair, her lips, hungry to touch, eager to be filled for a while and sleep. (11)

In this preverbal space the unity of bodies rather than their separation is the ground of communication. The mother knows her daughters through smell ("the smell of their hair"), through touch ("their softness"), and, yet more intimately, through a bodily awareness of the elemental rhythms of their bodies ("breathiness, abruptness") (11). The mother does not differentiate between her daughters, and the text likewise presents them undifferentiated, in a "cluster."

Measured in terms of its own preoedipal values, this picture is all harmony. But a distonic note in the description of this world's maternal time sounds a warning:

> They had no reason to look forward, nothing to regret. Their lives spun off the tilting world like thread off a spindle, breakfast time, suppertime, lilac time, apple time. . . . if immortality was to be this life held in poise and arrest, and if this world purged and this life unconsuming could be thought of as world and life restored to their proper natures, it is no wonder that five serene, eventless years lulled

my grandmother into forgetting what she should never have forgotten. (13)

Time shares the quality of maternal space: the encircling presence of the mother is also an encircling present; the moment being full, there is no reason to look forward or back. And time cycles rather than progresses. Seasonal and diurnal cycles ("breakfast time, suppertime, lilac time, apple time") are reinforced spatially by the spherical shapes of the turning world and its simile, the spinning wheel; the world spins off a time that is all continuity, with no divisions, no markers by which to measure temporal progression. But this latter property of time—that it marches on—is "what [my grandmother] should never have forgotten": for suddenly "the children had disappeared, every one" (25). Within the temporal frame of *Housekeeping* there is no allowance for a forward movement, so the girls' growing up and leaving home is described as a sudden vanishing. From a preoedipal perspective in which presence fills the whole time-space continuum, the advent of linear time, in which events succeed each other, can only usher in loss.

But if one steps outside *Housekeeping*'s frame of reference, one can see what is missing in this view of time as "a monumental temporality, without cleavage or escape, which has so little to do with linear time (which passes) that the very word 'temporality' hardly fits," as Julia Kristeva characterizes one mode of "Women's Time" (34). The girls who continue to take in their mother orally, "hungering" for "her breast, her hair, her lips," are no longer babies, but adolescents; in the developmental account of time, they ought to be pushing towards individuation, establishing separate lives. They have avoided the painful crimp and repression dictated by oedipal charts of female development, but by falling out of linear time altogether they have failed to grow. The image of "perfect serenity" (13) that crystallizes the beauty and harmony of a mother-daughter erotics is also an image of perfect stasis.

On the other hand, Margaret Drabble in *The Middle Ground* develops the mother-child circle into a family configuration whose flexibility and responsiveness to change make it adaptive rather than retrogressive— adaptive, that is, to the loss of permanence in contemporary family life. Kate at the end finds herself unexpectedly "the center of a family circle" characterized by spontaneity and mutability.

The Middle Ground starts by depriving its protagonist, Kate, of a whole range of sustaining structures. More unsettling than the dissolution of her marriage or her loss of faith in the significance of her work is her sense of having lost the thread of meaning that tied together the stages of life. Kate has gone through "marriage, children, love, divorce, illness, ageing parents, lost love, rejection"—all "the expected phases of life," but they "no longer seemed to make sense" (10). Thrown out of a shared cultural understanding of the human life cycle into the contemporary chaos of values, Kate has lost what Erik Erikson claims to be the basis of confidence in the meaning of one's actions, "an all-enveloping world-image tying past, present and future into a convincing pattern" (116). "A link has been broken, and the past no longer seems to make sense, for if it did, how would it have left her here, in this peculiar draughty open space?" (Drabble, 10). The novel works towards an affirmation of this "draughty open space": Kate learns to embrace the infinite possibilities of chaos, to welcome whatever chance sweeps her way, including the motley array of old friends, children, and borrowed children that suddenly—and only for a moment—coalesces into a family circle:

> even as she was thinking this, looking around her family circle, feeling as she sat there a sense of immense calm, strength, centrality, as though she were indeed the centre of a circle, in the most old-fashioned of ways, a moving circle—oh, there is no language left to describe such things, we have called it all so much in question, but imagine a circle even so, a circle and a moving sphere, for this is her house and there she sits, she has everything and nothing. (255)

The piling up of dependent phrases, the sudden shift from social surface to a peak of spiritual exultation, even the phrase "feeling as she sat there" to introduce a sudden access of feeling, recall Virginia Woolf's style. The "old-fashioned" idea that the present age has "called into question" is the idea of family. And Drabble here rewrites that apotheosis of patriarchal family life, the dinner scene in *To the Lighthouse*.[1]

In that scene Mrs. Ramsay has just engineered the engagement of Paul and Minta, so that the dinner becomes a celebration of her power to impose marriage and the permanence it enshrines on her entourage. Floating in the element of family unity that emanates "from husband and children and friends," Mrs. Ramsay feels a moment of joyous security—the analogue to Kate's—when she is convinced that her creation, this human order, will triumph over the forces of time and change: "It partook of eternity . . . there is a coherence in things, a stability; something, she meant, is immune from change" (Woolf, 158). The visual image that contains the immutable order of marriage and family is the "infinitely long dinner-table" (Woolf, 125) with mother and father posted at each end, marshaling the ranks of children and friends who line the two sides.

To the stability of this rectangle *The Middle Ground* opposes "a moving circle," "a moving sphere," meant to integrate suggestions of fluidity and change with the notion of unity—a temporary unity, that is, governed by the same openness to change that brought it into existence. Kate's family circle is constituted by the principle of inclusion, her solution to the contemporary dissolution of old structures. Having no containing structure means being open to all possibilities, as the last lines of the novel emphasize: "Anything is possible, it is all undecided. . . . It is unplanned, unpredicted. Nothing binds her, nothing holds her" (Drabble, 257). Kate's practice of keeping the door open to whatever chance brings her way bestows on her this gathering of possibilities, this heterogeneous family that mixes up old friends and new acquaintances, her own children with children borrowed from other mothers, other countries (an Iraqi boy, a French girl). The scene ends, like that in *To the Lighthouse*, with a disintegration of the family gathering: "the circle broke up into its various spheres of activity" (Drabble, 255), as in *To the Lighthouse* "a sort of disintegration set in; they wavered about, went different ways" (Woolf, 168). But in *The Middle Ground* this dissolution is accepted in advance, integrated into the notion of a "moving sphere," a space wherein the family not only flourishes but embraces change and moves with it into the future.

Whereas *The Middle Ground* disperses unity almost as soon as it is formed, the rites and ceremonies of the community in *A Weave of Women* are meant to give continuity and a sense of permanence to the alternative community of women: rather than a "moving circle," the women inhabit "a stone house." "It is a story of women who are ceremonious and correct with each other, who celebrate sermons and hermans, birth rites, death rites, sacrificial rites, exodus rites, and exorcism rites" (9). More explicitly than the other family circles surveyed here, the "ring of women" in Broner's novel (48) is conceived as an alternative. Its rituals are proposed as substitutes for the rites and values of orthodox Judaism that exclude and devalue women.

"Holy Body Day" is a rite that affirms the female body, in direct opposition to the surrounding male culture that constructs women's bodies as instruments of blasphemy and sacrilege. The novel makes clear, through several scenes in which one or another of the women stumbles in on exclusively male religious rites, that the presence of a female desecrates the men's holy day (64–65, 253)—including the exclusively male rite of the gynecological convention. When women protesters intrude on a conference of gynecologists and produce banners proclaiming WE ARE OUR BODIES, a rush to cover them over with tablecloths expresses the urgency of the men's desire to undo the sacrilege of seeing and being seen by women: "They are the Evil Eye, these women. They are the shouting mouth. Veil the eye, muffle the mouth" (154–55).

Holy Body Day is a "counterholiday" that the women create out of opposition to this veiling, "to the shyness of the world, where everything is lidded—eyes, cooking pots, windows and shades. . . . There in the bathhouse nakedness prevails. Bellies undulate, breasts point and flop, ankles are sunk into flesh or bracket the legs. Thighs shake or saunter, knees dimple or are bony. Everything stares: eyes, navels, nipples, opened mouths" (256–57). This display amounts to a corporeal declaration of women's right to possess their own bodies, to show them and to see them. The language of multiplicity suggests an undifferentiated sea of bodies—a "forest of hair, scales of nails, desert sands of smooth bodies" (257)—a vision of female bodily continuity that has its spiritual correlative in the community of purpose that unites these women. When they arm themselves to avenge the stoning of Deedee, they form "one body" (152–53). Broner thus evokes images of preoedipal merging to give energy to her description of a female solidarity that protects and heals its members from the environing patriarchal order, which she portrays as hostile to female sexuality, female values, and even female lives.

Unlike the mature versions of female solidarity and fluid family life evolved from images of preoedipal continuity in *The Middle Ground* and *A Weave of Women*, Toni Morrison's *Beloved* presents the dangers of a mother-daughter erotics that is unexamined and unreconstructed. The destructive effects of the preoedipal hungers in *Beloved* serve as a corrective to this study's emphasis on the creative potential of the preoedipal.

Beloved: A Corrective to Idealizations of the Preoedipal

I am reluctant to diminish the scope and significance of Toni Morrison's *Beloved* by reducing it to just a preoedipal parable. Denver, Beloved's sister, seems to be passing on a warning from her author when she responds to the question, "You think [the ghost] sure 'nough your sister?"

with the admission, "At times. At times I think she was—more" (266). Beloved *is*, I believe, Denver's sister—the baby her mother killed to save from a return to slavery; she has come back in the body of a young woman to share the house with Sethe (her mother), Denver (her sister), and Paul D, the ex-slave who shares Sethe's bed. But she is also "more," as Denver says: a victim of slavery, Beloved embodies the pain and anguish of all those killed or maimed through racial violence. Stamp Paid, whose communal consciousness functions as a depository where the count of blacks killed by whites accumulates—"whole towns wiped clean of Negroes; eighty-seven lynchings in one year alone in Kentucky; four colored schools burned to the ground" (180)—hears in Beloved's voice a whole chorus, the "roaring" of "the black and angry dead—the people of the broken necks, of fire-cooked blood and black girls who had lost their ribbons" (180–81). Her presence draws out the memories that Paul D and Sethe have repressed, memories of a past marked by sufferings under slavery. As Gayle Greene says, "*Beloved* is about bringing what's dead to life" ("Feminist Fiction"). Although reliving the mutilations of slavery is painful, "nothing heals without pain," as Amy Denver tells Sethe (78): the remembering that Beloved's presence triggers is necessary and beneficent.

So Beloved is much more than a preoedipal devouring child; but she *is* that, too. Killed when she was about one year old,[2] she returns to haunt her mother clothed in the body of a twenty-year-old. A preoedipal child cannot tell its fantasies, for the preoedipal is, by definition, the preverbal. Klein and Winnicott reconstruct infantile fantasies from traces left in the fantasy life of their patients. But through the stratagem of the ghost story, which bestows on this infant revenant a body equipped for speech, Morrison gives voice to preoedipal desire.

Beloved functions almost entirely in terms of oral drives: she wants to possess her mother totally. The urge to incorporate into the self what the baby perceives as good is one of the two original drives, according to Freud. Expressed "in the language of the oldest—the oral—instinctual impulses, the judgment is: 'I should like to eat this' . . . and, put more generally, 'I should like to take this into myself.' . . . the original pleasure-ego wants to introject everything that is good and to eject from itself everything that is bad" ("Negation," 237). Beloved manages to structure the family along the lines of her desire. Her drive to eject the bad—Paul D, whose presence blocks her unqualified possession of her mother—is fueled by the supernatural power she derives from her ghostly status: "She moved him" (114, 121)—out of her mother's bed, out of her mother's house, out of the family. And her mother's burden of guilt and love gives

Beloved the leverage to make her mother comply with the infantile demand for absolute attention: Sethe gives up all distractions, both man and job, to "play with Beloved. . . . Anything she wanted she got" (240). Beloved lives by incorporation, a preoedipal version of growth: feeling herself tenuous, insubstantial—she is subject to "two dreams," the dream that her body is fragmenting and the dream of being swallowed (133)[3]— she tries to increase her substance by taking in supplements. She constantly eats sweets, and she virtually succeeds in incorporating her mother, becoming literally "bigger, plumper by the day" while Sethe diminishes, the flesh on her hands becoming "thin as china silk" (239).

Beloved reminds us that a family structured by preoedipal impulses in their original form, unreconstructed by a mature imagination, must collapse under the weight of its own contradictions. Because a preoedipal child's desire for its mother is not under the sway of the reality principle (Chodorow, *Mothering*, 79), it is insatiable. Demanding the totality of the mother, it can never get enough: "Beloved . . . never got enough of anything: lullabies, new stitches, the bottom of the cake bowl, the top of the milk. . . . When Sethe ran out of things to give her, Beloved invented desire" (240). It must be admitted that these are special circumstances: Sethe killed her child and so carries around more than the common burden of maternal guilt and love. But the dynamic of mother-child relations is only exaggerated thereby: the child demands, the mother gives, the child demands more. "Beloved lapped up devotion like cream" (243) and asked for more. But even a nursing mother—and the relation between Sethe and Beloved is a nurseling's fantasy writ large—does not have magically self-generating powers of sustenance, although the infant may think she does. A mother too must get fed, emotionally as well as physically. The symmetrical shrinking of Sethe and fattening of Beloved rewrite in a concrete body language appropriate to Beloved's mental age the feminist complaint that mothers are always called upon to nurture without getting nurtured in return.[4] Her stores depleted, Sethe, like Mrs. Ramsay before her, seems about to die of inanition: "the bigger Beloved got, the smaller Sethe became . . . Beloved ate up her life, took it, swelled up with it, grew taller on it. And the older woman yielded it up without a murmur" (250).

So powerful is the oral drive embodied in Beloved that she converts even words into her own currency, into things to eat. Denver feels "like a lover whose pleasure is to overfeed the lover" (78) when she tells her sister stories of their mother's past, "word-shapes" that Beloved consumes as if they were parts of the mother.

When Beloved herself speaks, language becomes a tool of assimilation.

The substance of family life within the charmed female circle is rendered in a succession of three monologues in which each woman speaks her desire, followed by a dialogue between the three that becomes in effect a monologue, too, as their voices and identities merge.

> Will we smile at me? . . .
> I love your face . . .
> I needed her face to smile . . .
> I want her face . . .
> she is the laugh; I am the laughter. . . .
> You are my face; you are me. . . .
> You are my face; I am you. (215–16)

To assure herself that she exists Beloved depends on the mother's mirroring face. Her liveliness is constructed by the liveliness of her mother's expression. Her mother's smile is her well-being; if the mother laughs, she is the laughter.

While a spoken dialogue (ideally) leads to movement, the differences voiced by one speaker moving each other speaker out of his or her original position, a dialogue of faces only confirms presence and identity. You are me, therefore I exist. Or, alternatively, you are not there and I am nothing. "You are my face; I am you. Why did you leave me who am you?" (216). With this statement Beloved completes the limited and stubborn logic of the preoedipal, which excludes absence: if I am you, there is no leeway for separation.

Beloved's insistence on assimilating the (m)other prevails as the three voices merge in a single claim to the totality of the other:

> You are mine
> You are mine
> You are mine (217)

The statement of identity—"you are mine"—expresses the bare minimum of distinction between subject and object necessary to speech. The most slender of copulas, "are," links them; then differentiation is wiped out altogether as the separate positions of "you" and "me" slide into the possessive, "mine." Language functions as appropriation, and once the appropriation is complete, it ceases.

An epistemology that merges self and other undermines the singular positions that anchor language and also the structures of bipolar opposition that govern logic: insofar as the language of *Beloved* reflects the influx of preoedipal instincts, it is revolutionary in the Kristevan sense (see Introduction and chapter 4, above). But the other face of the preoedipal is stasis: "And the One Doesn't Stir without the Other," as the title of Irigaray's essay on mother-daughter fusion has it. If one is fused with the other, one cannot move in the direction of growth, which entails differentiation. Nor can one move out into the world to confront its larger challenges.

The preoedipal circle that in other novels in this survey offers the promise of transformation and renewal becomes in *Beloved* a circle of repetition that blocks forward movement. The figure for this debilitating interdependency is the "falling-down circle" of mother and daughters on the ice. Sethe, Beloved, and Denver have only three skates between them—a dramatization of the economy of scarcity that prevails when family members feed on each other rather than taking in "other-than-me" substance from the outside world. One daughter skates on two skates, one daughter on one, while the mother—predictably self-deprived—has to make do with none. A brittle circle, the wavy, breaking line of the three women gives spatial form to the edginess and final collapse of a circle of dependency where everyone leans on everyone else but no one can stand on her own two feet: "Making a circle or a line, the three of them could not stay upright for one whole minute, but nobody saw them falling. Each seemed to be helping the other two stay upright, yet every tumble doubled their delight" (174). They all delight in falling. But what delights does not necessarily sustain: "Walking back through the woods, Sethe put an arm around each girl at her side. Both of them had an arm around her waist. Making their way over hard snow, they stumbled . . . but nobody saw them fall" (175). Unlike the solidarity of female bodies moving as one in *A Weave of Women*, this monolithic block of bodies impedes progress, reduces movement to repetition: falling and getting up and falling down again.

Hunger triggers the dissolution of this family circle—hunger of a healthier kind. Denver leaves the closed circle to get food for her mother—real, substantial food from the outside world in place of the fantasy consumption of one another. Denver's search for food is associated with her old "hunger" for learning: after a year spent learning to read, she had retired from language, becoming a deaf-mute to avoid hearing that her mother was a murderer. But she remembers that "original hunger" (118, 121) that could be satisfied only by "the wonderful little *i*, sentences rolling out like pie dough, and the company of other children" (121).

When she leaves the closed world of mother and daughters—"it was she who had to step off the edge of the world and die because if she didn't, they all would" (239)—she goes straight to the place of verbal nurturance, the house of Lady Jones, who had taught her to read. Denver's developmental path leads out into the world, then, by way of the symbolic. Like Lucille, the "other sister" in *Housekeeping*, Denver takes the normal route to separation, substituting signifiers for a physical connection with the mother's body. But this is no routine progress from preoedipal to oedipal: no father figure saves her; nor does she have to break into a world of harsh separation and abstract representation. Rather, Lady Jones's caring ushers her into a larger world of maternal nurturing. "'Oh, baby,' said Mrs. Jones," in compassion for Denver's tale of her mother's starving, "'Oh, baby.' . . . it was the word 'baby,' said softly and with such kindness, that inaugurated her life in the world as a woman" (248). Denver replaces the closed and self-consuming maternal circle with an enlarged maternal embrace: individuals in the community provide food for the family, bringing them into a communal give-and-take that replaces the self-consuming fantasy of feeding on the mother.

The preoedipal fantasy of total union with the mother, unreconstructed, does not work as a principle of family life. Beloved's story "is not a story to pass on," the epilogue says (274–75), whereas Paul D gets to "put his story next to Sethe's" (273). Paul D's story has a social function, to reveal the self to the other and to trigger a reciprocal telling that will reveal the other to him. When Beloved put *her* story next to Sethe's, Sethe's story got swallowed up. Outside social law, the desire to merge is subject to no limits and so engulfs the lives it loves. Beloved is finally cast out of the social realm altogether, to wander in a limbo of fantasy. "This is not a story to pass on" is of course ambiguous, meaning both that it is too terrible to find resolution in any narrative and that it will not die, either ("pass on"). But this story also cannot be told because preoedipal desire lies outside the social realm of communication through language.

Fantasies of Strong Mothers and Shared Parenting

Most preoedipal fantasies feature a strong mother figure who has a central position in the family. Before an understanding of the overarching patriarchal power structure awakens a child to the "real" lack of power in the mother's position, the mother seems, as the source of physical comfort, pleasure, food, and emotional sustenance, to be all-powerful. Although such a perception is out of touch with social reality in a patriarchal culture, the image of a powerful mother can produce fantasies that redress the imbalance of power accorded maternal love and paternal authority in traditional families. In *Little Women* and *The Color Purple* especially, the respect granted the mother has a secondary effect on family politics: once nurturing is liberated from its debased status as an attribute of a servile female role, other family members come forward to share the work of fostering others' development. The result, in both novels, is an extension of the responsibility for nurturing to a whole circle of "mothering" people. Instead of one woman's being charged with encouraging everyone's growth while neglecting her own, as in patriarchal arrangements, *Little Women* and *The Color Purple* picture mothering as a reciprocal activity, everyone nurturing and getting nurtured in her (or his) turn.

In *Little Women* Marmee is pictured as the center of a circle of adoring daughters, the "sun" whose light and warmth is reflected in their "brightening faces" (163). Because the mother is so highly valued, the girls take over the maternal role in relation to each other. Meg and Jo consciously "mother" the two younger girls (68), and all encourage each other through a facial mirroring associated with maternal encouragement. The three sisters "beam" their delight at Beth when she overcomes her shyness to set a crippled boy at ease (187). And the three sisters' faces reflect Jo's glory in her published story, reassuring her of its worth; their enthusiastic responsiveness redoubles the narcissistic energies that she can then channel into more writing. So when the mother is not there, the circle remains, its diffuse bonds extended to a circle of equals who take turns nurturing each other.

Similarly, a respect for mothering extends the maternal role to everybody in *The Color Purple*: Jack and Harpo, especially, are respected for their domestic abilities. The distinction between generations starts to blur too, in the sense that everybody gets the emotional nurturing that everybody, parent and child alike, needs to grow towards autonomy and a full expression of his or her creative potential. More generally, love itself appears to be a sufficient organizing principle of family life. Paternal authority in the novel is reduced to the stature of Albert's father—even physically a little man—who tries to push his son's family back into patriarchal shape by throwing Shug, his son's mistress, out of the household. But his effort to get the wife and the mistress back into the separate categories where they belong is ineffectual in face of the love for Shug that is the one thing that connects husband and wife, providing the basis for a newly viable family life.

Little Women and *The Color Purple*, then, offer usable fantasies: a powerful position for the mother and a family structure that spreads the work of mothering among several figures.

Creative Ways of Thinking

By means of some admittedly speculative discussion of the relation of Alcott's and Walker's families to the fantasy patterns dramatized in their novels, I would like to suggest that growing up in such alternative child-raising structures can produce in the child alternative ways of thinking. Evelyn Fox Keller has argued that developmental processes structure mental processes. Nancy Hartsock believes that in the case of a boy, the "construction of identity as differentiation from his mother sets a hostile and combative dualism at the heart of . . . the masculinist world view by means of which [a man] understands [his] life" (240). The same principle applies to those girls who define themselves through hostile opposition to their mothers (see chapter 6, above). If a daughter's dawning awareness of the demeaned and demeaning female role requires a sharp break with the mother who embodies that role, the necessity of distinguishing herself sharply from her mother must lead her, too, to construct reality in terms of bipolar oppositions, in the image of that original me/not-me distinction. The dichotomy between love and art that structures most female artist novels is just one example of this kind of dualistic thinking.

If no break with the mother is required because the mother's role is respected, development is constituted less by a sharp division between self and mother and more by a slide back and forth between identification and differentiation, as in the pattern of development envisioned by Winnicott, Keller, and Benjamin (see chapter 6, above). That developmental flexibility can generate a mental flexibility, a habit of seeing the continuities between things as well as their differences. Such a mindset may well be more useful for creative purposes than habits of dualistic thinking. According to Albert Rothenberg, Joy Guilford, and Arthur Koestler, the key to creative thinking is the capacity to hold two or more contradictory ideas in a single mental embrace. Although they have different names for this process, they agree that creative breakthroughs depend upon "the capacity to conceive and utilize two or more contradictory ideas, concepts, or images *simultaneously*" (Rothenberg, 313). The habit of marking off the world into antithetical structures that mime the absolute quality of the original self/mother division must exclude or at least diminish such a fruitful play of opposites.

The structure of the patriarchal family as a whole reinforces the tendency of its mother-rejecting daughters to think in terms of bipolar oppositions. The clear bifurcation between paternal authority and maternal nurturance, between the autonomy and power associated with the father and the dependency and subordination associated with the mother, is the source of another developmental polarization: either I can be my mother and remain enfolded within nurturing symbiotic relations and within the life of the house; or I can imitate my father, move outside the world of relationships, and (maybe, if no one notices that I'm not my father—that is, not male) establish autonomy and a position of respect. But in a family where child-rearing and breadwinning tasks are shared around a circle of family members, patterns of continuous thinking are reinforced. Seeing a continuum of parenting faces, children are more likely to construct reality as a continuum, taking note of the similarities that unite even things that the culture keeps strictly separate.

In spite of the vastly different historical and ethnic contexts that separate Alcott's childhood in white middle-class nineteenth-century New England from Walker's childhood in a black family of sharecroppers in the rural South, both women grew up in families that were not organized by a strict hierarchy of sex roles. The mother and father shared the burden of making a living (in Alcott's case, it was the daughters and the mother who became breadwinners); the mothers in both families occupied a position of power and respect; and Alcott's and Walker's autobiographical writings attest to strong feelings of unbroken continuity with their mothers. The multiplicity of factors that influence an individual's way of thinking makes it impossible to posit a simple cause-effect relation between family structure and thought structure, but it is striking that the fictions produced by both these authors are organized not by bipolar oppositions, but by continuities. In fact both works demonstrate a facility in conflating categories whose separation the culture holds sacred: the erotic and the maternal, the sexual and the religious, male and female in *The Color Purple*; "high" abstract art and domestic arts, love and work in *Little Women*.

The conditions of Alcott's growing up were idiosyncratic largely because of the peculiarities of her father, Bronson Alcott, an educational reformer and utopian idealist who was never able (or, apparently, willing)[5] to provide for his family. He often withdrew from family life, either to his own intellectual space—in 1834 he "took a room of his own across the street from the Philadelphia library in order to read and continue his writing" (Elbert, 27)—or to journeys of intellectual stimulation, across the United States and in England. Even when he was in residence, he seems to have been nearly as abstracted from the concrete life of the family as the absent father in *Little Women*.[6] The responsibility for making a living devolved onto Louisa's mother and the four sisters, who worked and contributed what they could. As the family lacked both a working father and a mother who could devote full time to child care, paternal and maternal duties were distributed around the family circle. Louisa especially became increasingly the breadwinner, as her stories sold, and increasingly the confidante to her mother, taking over roles that a different father would have filled.[7] Thus the hierarchies and dualities between genders and between generations were blurred.

Spared the oedipal devaluation of the mother and the oedipal displacement of preoedipal adoration and respect onto the father, Louisa could afford to keep her ties with her mother intact. Unlike girls entangled in matrophobia, she did not need to define herself against the maternal role in order to secure a modicum of power and self-esteem. She could step into the vacant masculine role of protecting and providing for her mother, as a poem dated from her tenth birthday attests:

I hope that soon, dear mother,
  You and I may be
In the quiet room my fancy
  Has so often made for thee, . . .

The desk beside the window
  Where the sun shines warm and bright:
And there in ease and quiet
  The promised book you write;

While I sit close beside you,
  Content at last to see
That you can rest, dear mother,
  And I can cherish thee.
                                    (Cheney, 24)

Reversing the pattern of matrophobia that keeps mother and self, love and art, poles apart in artist novels based on an oppositional developmental pattern, "writing the promised book" and "sitting close beside you" are fused in a single picture, so there is no distance at all between mother and self, writing and maternal nurturance. Indeed mother and daughter are fused in a single wish: it is of course Louisa who wants a room of her own and wants to write a book,[8] but the dream is projected onto the mother and satisfied by way of extending Louisa's loving presence around the mother who sits writing. Feelings of continuity with her mother, expressed together with the desire to provide for her comfort, were constant. At seventeen, Louisa wrote in her journal: "I think she is a very brave, good woman; and my dream is to have a lovely, quiet home for her, with no debts or troubles to burden her" (Cheney, 62). After her mother's death she wrote in an addendum to the poem quoted above: "The dream came true, and for the last ten years of her life Marmee sat in peace, with every wish granted, even to the 'grouping together'; for she died in my arms" (Cheney, 24).

It was in part the pressures of poverty that erased the hierarchical distinction between women's work and men's work in Alice Walker's family: "[my mother] labored beside—not behind—my father in the fields" ("Search," 98). The dominant note in Walker's "In Search of Our Mothers' Gardens" is the note of respect entwined with love that one hears in other African American women writers' testimonials to their mothers' strength and creativity. "She made all the clothes we wore, . . . she made all the towels and sheets we used. . . . She spent her winter evenings making quilts enough to cover all our beds" (98): domestic work, the labor of love, is not distinct from creative work in Walker's tribute.

> After years of listening to my mother's stories of her life, I have absorbed not only the stories themselves, but something of the manner in which she spoke. . . . But the telling of these stories . . . was not the only way my mother showed herself as an artist. . . . my mother adorned with flowers whatever shabby house we were forced to live in. . . . Whatever she planted grew as if by magic. . . . A garden so brilliant with colors, so original in its design, so magnificent with life and creativity, that . . . people drive by our house in Georgia . . . to stand or walk among my mother's art. (100)

Rachel Blau DuPlessis has said that twentieth-century women novelists heal the old breach between art and love by embedding art in a tradition of maternal creativity. I differ from her in distinguishing two different trends in modern female artist novels: middle-class white authors tend to perpetuate the split between art and love that reflects the original polarized choice between autonomy and mother; but black women authors recognize their mothers with pride as models for their own creativity. Thus Paule Marshall and Dorothy West, like Walker, praise their mothers' creativity and credit them with passing on to their daughters a sense of entitlement to the powers of language (Washington, 150–60). As Mary Helen Washington says, "the long chain of presences that inhabit the literature of black women does not convey inferiority, or submissive femininity, or intellectual powerlessness: what these mothers passed on would take you anywhere in the world you wanted to go" (161). The need to move outside the ring of maternal love in order to establish the autonomy necessary for creative work disappears when the mother is already defined as a creative person, doing work that is valued by others.

Remarkable as these African American mothers were as individuals who retained their self-esteem in the face of persistent social discrimina~~tion~~ their position of strength and the corresponding lack of ambivalence in their daughters' respect for them is part of a family system that rests on "a strong, resourceful mother with a structurally central position" (N. Tanner, 151).[9] Without in any way condoning the systematic racial and economic discrimination (chiefly, the scarcity of employment for black men) to which black American family systems are the response (see chapter 9, above), we can look to African American culture for alternative family structures—structures that do not produce daughters divided against themselves.

Nancy Chodorow's survey of mother-daughter relations in the family structures of Java, Atjeh, and East London confirms the idea suggested by Walker's and Alcott's lives. In cultures where mothers have a female support system and where they have decision-making powers in important spheres of life, maternal self-esteem is high and daughters can identify with the female role without losing self-respect: "Acceptance of her gender identity involves positive valuation of herself, and not an admission of inferiority. In psychoanalytic terms, we might say it involves identification with a preoedipal, active, caring mother" ("Family Structure," 63). Chodorow's phrase applies equally to Walker and Alcott: where mothers and the work of mothers are esteemed, a daughter need not see her "preoedipal, active, caring mother" differently when she rounds the oedipal turn and so need not deny her bond with her. The mother's oedipal fall from power is socially constructed, then, the result of the patriarchal system's need to deny or delegitimate the real power of mothers.[10]

Ignoring for the time being the claim that originality is the province of individual genius and adhering instead to the notion that runs throughout the present work, that fantasy structures bear the imprint of family structures, I argue that the continuities that structure *The Color Purple* and *Little Women* stem at least in part from their authors' lack of radical division from their mothers and from the relative fluidity of the generational and gender roles in their families. Both novels tend to present things on a continuum. They thus perform a revolutionary function, undermining the logic of bipolar opposition that buttresses patriarchal epistemology.

In *Little Women* and *The Color Purple* the bipolar opposition between art and family that tends to keep women in their places in the domestic world is ignored in favor of a creative cycle. Just as Jo's plays and stories find their first audience among her sisters, so she imagines an artist's career in the wide world as a return to her family on the investment they have made in her creativity: "'In time I may be able to support myself and so help the girls.' For to be independent and earn the praise of those she loved, were the dearest wishes of her heart" (212). Jo is able to encompass her desire for loving connection and her desire to be a self-supporting author in a single sentence, avoiding the split between love and autonomy that characterizes most female artist novels. A similar creative cycle prevails in *The Color Purple*. A network of family relations boosts the artist's self-confidence, supports her work, and in turn is nurtured by the art works themselves: Celie's pants, Shug's song, the quilts they make together return to enrich the life of the family.

In both novels love and creative work are joined through an ethic of use: a created work can be an object of household utility, yet still be respected. Both texts thus undermine another fundamental dichotomy of Western patriarchal culture: that between "high" (abstract) art and "low" (domestic) crafts. In one of *Little Women's* tableaux of group creativity, the arts are no more hierarchically arranged than the circle of sisters: "Meg sat . . . sewing daintily with her white hands. . . . Beth was sorting the cones that lay thick under the hemlock near by, for she made pretty things of them. Amy was sketching a group of ferns, and Jo was knitting as she read aloud" (190). Not even a separate sentence privileges the high art of drawing over the domestic art of knitting; Beth's and Amy's "artistic" arrangements occupy a continuum with Jo's knitting and Meg's sewing. Similarly, *The Color Purple's* creative processes are embedded in a domestic context, their products designed for incorporation in the household round.

The distinction between high art, created in some "pure autonomy of mind" (Adorno, 20; cited in DuPlessis, 104), and the low arts of the household supports gender hierarchy by marking off a world of abstract mental work done by men from a world of concrete material labor populated by women.[11] Dissolving the distinction between high and low art thus threatens to erode the hierarchical division of the world into separate spheres. If no line is drawn between the value of domestic work that women do and the value of mental work that men do, the rationale for the most fundamental division of labor crumbles—the rationale for "the subjection of wives to their husbands' labors," as Mrs. Ramsay articulates the code she lives by in *To the Lighthouse* (20). Mrs. Ramsay's willingness to carry the whole burden of shoring up the domestic foundation of life so that her husband, freed from household worries, can devote himself to writing books, rests on her conviction that "of the two he was infinitely the more important, and what she gave the world, in comparison with what he gave, negligible" (Woolf, 62).

But once one starts valuing women's creative activities equally with men's, it begins to seem that everyone, male and female, has talents that deserve support (that is the basis for equality in *The Color Purple*). And once one begins to value work in the house as creative, the reason for exempting one gender from housework becomes obscure. So embedded in bipolar oppositions are the presuppositions that support patriarchal institutions that an epistemology that emphasizes continuity threatens to bring them down.

Thinking of male and female persons on a continuum—everybody creative, everybody needing love and capable of giving care—leads to the kind of family circle created in *The Color Purple*, a sort of continuum of gender on which being male is not so very different from being female (no one is more maternal than Jack, no one more gifted in the arts of domesticity than Harpo) and being female is not so very different from being male (Shug is self-determining and independent, Sofia is aggressively self-assertive). Celie undoes the distinction between genders when she disputes Albert's assertion that Sofia and Shug are "manly": they aren't "womanly," either, she says—only "different from you and me" (236) (Hite, "Writing," 129).

Rather than claim any special knowledge of the way Walker's and Alcott's families worked, I intend only to suggest that in families where a mother's work receives as much credit as a father's (perhaps more), where the labors of love seem as important as work in the outside world, there is no need for a daughter to establish and defend an absolute delineation between self and mother. She can afford the luxury of ranging along all the degrees of being together and being separate on the developmental continuum. And, assuming with Keller that developmental processes structure mental processes, her thinking will be less inclined to absolute distinctions and oppositional structures, more capable of bringing contradictory ideas together in a single mental embrace. If this flexibility of mind is the key to creativity, as Rothenberg, Guilford, and Koestler claim, it can be argued that changing the family in the direction of the family circles described in this chapter—toward sharing tasks across gender lines and giving mothers positions of power and respect—could produce not only healthier, but more creative daughters.

Conclusion

Reflections on Families
and Fantasies

FANTASIES ARE IMPORTANT because they set before us objects of desire. If women are to change the way they live, they need to change what they want, so that the energy of desire can be mobilized in the fight for a better life.

Unconscious fantasy structures pose the most formidable opposition to change, for they seem immutable, channeling desire forever into recreating old patterns of relationship. The fantasy of romantic love, especially, holds unconscious desire hostage in patterns that lead a woman to recreate in her adult life the imbalance of power between male and female figures that she first experienced in her father's house. This final review of the possibilities for changing unconscious fantasy structures moves in the direction of hope: from a review of the retrogressive fantasies generated by the patriarchal family, through some guesswork about the different kinds of unconscious fantasies different kinds of family structures might produce, toward an open-ended question: can families be altered by fantasies? That is, can readers make the alternative family patterns in novels their own, thus changing the direction of desire so that they will want to create new family structures in their own lives?

The structural peculiarity of women's traditional fantasies of love is that a man, rather than the woman herself, is central. It seems inevitable that the myths generated by a male-defined culture should feature men as heroes. But it is a curious and damaging effect of male cultural hegemony that even women's fantasies about their own lives center on a male figure rather than on the self. The woman waits at the margins of her own life, keeping the central space open for the man's appearance. Thus the Bennett women in *Pride and Prejudice* wait eternally for the smoking-room door to open after dinner and the men to enter: "the story, the glow, will begin with the opening of the door" (Auerbach, 38). When Rochester rides into the picture, Jane Eyre's fantasy of autonomy is effaced—along with all her other desires and concerns—to clear center stage for the potential lover.

What can have led women to imagine themselves as marginal in their

own lives? What process so deforms women's desire that they are persuaded to put aside the natural strivings of the self and put a man there,
where the action is? I want to answer this question by way of literary
fantasy, turning again to a children's novel popular over many generations
to find a reflection of a family pattern shared by many readers. In *Little
House in the Big Woods* and *Little House on the Prairie*, Laura Ingalls
Wilder's father fills her world.[1] *Little House in the Big Woods* records in
minute detail the way both her pioneer parents make things, but it is what
the father does that is stimulating, exciting, magical. The mother makes
good things to eat, it is true, and her daughters are charmed by the little
pats of orange-colored butter and the flapjack-men she makes. And "Ma
sometimes cut paper dolls for them. . . . But the best time of all was at
night, when Pa came home" (33). All her father's actions are illumined by
Laura's admiration. What he makes is not merely functional but beautiful,
like the carved bracket he makes for Ma. And even his daily chores are
privileged by their connection with his exploits in the harsh outside
world: Laura and Mary are rapt in contemplation of his making bullets
and loading his gun. The games he plays with the girls are tumultuous,
frightening, stimulating (*Woods*, 35–36, 39). He sings and plays the fid-
dle, entrancing Laura and Mary. And while Ma reads from the Bible—
only passing on the Word, in stories that Wilder's narrative does not
bother to record—Pa tells stories of his own or his father's adventures in
the wilderness. These stories are incorporated into the text, recounted in
Pa's voice. The strict division of labor by gender in Laura's family is thus
reproduced in the grown-up Laura's narrative, where her own account of
the domestic world she shared with mother and sister is divided off from
the interpolated male narratives of her father's adventures in the exciting
world outside.

The Little House on the Prairie continues the drama of Pa making and
Laura watching: here building the house is the central event. Laura's
admiration for her father's skills is translated into a painstaking account,
through three chapters, of his labors. Sometimes she is allowed to help
him and is rewarded with his praise: "I had a fine little helper!" (*Prairie*,
105). Pa extends his house over Laura, literally making her world; and his
flute-playing, from the threshold of the house, mediates her connection
with the outside world. She imagines that he plays to the stars outside
and the family inside (*Prairie*, 131); and his singing seems to carry "the
night and the moonlight and the stillness of the prairie" into the house
(*Prairie*, 79).

Without the father's inspiriting presence, the world is empty and desolate: "he was gone and everything was empty and lonely" (*Prairie*, 208). His return is the return of life and plenitude: "He hugged her. Everything was all right. The house was cozy with firelight . . . and Pa was there. . . . Everything was all right when Pa was there" (*Prairie*, 221–25).

Later volumes in Wilder's series focus more on Laura's activities, and Pa tends to praise her for what she does for herself. I limit my discussion here to the two *Little House* novels because narrative structure so neatly reflects family structure, indicating the relative positions of father and daughter in a traditional patriarchal family. Laura occupies a peripheral position in her own story, looking on with wonder at her father's feats. As author, Laura Ingalls Wilder reproduces the position of admiring daughter: unlike her father, who told tales about his own adventures, Wilder makes her father's actions the center of her story (*Prairie*) and his tales the center of her narrative (*Woods*).

Attributing agency to the father and deriving self-esteem from his affection and praise prepare a girl to depend for self-esteem on a man's approval rather than drawing satisfaction directly from a sense of work well done. We can see this father-daughter pattern repeated in the romantic fantasy of *Jane Eyre*. Jane's vivid imagination takes shape in paintings and drawings; but we readers are not privileged to see her in the act of creation. Instead her paintings appear only as objects of Rochester's approbation. He orders her to show him her portfolio, judges which paintings are worthy of his attention, and interprets them. The reader's interest centers not on the content of Jane's paintings and what they reveal of her inner life, but on Rochester's interpretations—especially the promise contained therein of a potential intimacy between Jane and Rochester. His comment, "Where did you see Latmos? for that is Latmos," draws the reader's attention away from the paintings themselves to the mystical bond between these two strangers that enables her to paint what only he has seen (130). The value of her paintings is reduced to their power to intrigue and attract Rochester. Subsequently Jane's talent is always instrumental to the love interest: by drawing portraits of Blanche Ingram and herself, she objectifies herself and Blanche as rivals for Rochester's love; and she draws a picture of Rochester not for the satisfaction of making something but to supply the gap created by his absence.

The family pattern reflected in *The Little House on the Prairie* leads directly to the kind of subordination of female creativity to the purposes of attaching a man that we encounter in *Jane Eyre*. Seeing the father as the main agent of effective action and subordinating her creativity to his direction and approval trains a girl to accept the man-centered ideology of romantic love.

Even within family life as it is now structured, there is the potential for a healthier focus on the self in relation to the other, in what Jessica Benjamin calls a "holding fantasy." This pattern springs not from the relation with the exciting father, but from the steady, soothing presence of the mother. In Winnicott's terms, the presence of the (m)other enables one to accept one's impulses, claim them as one's own, and integrate them into an ongoing sense of selfhood; protected by the (m)other's presence from the demands of reality, one is free to play with the figments of one's imagination. This first relationship embeds "the wish for a holding other whose presence does not violate one's space but permits the experience of one's own desire, who recognizes it when it emerges of itself" (Benjamin, 96). In romantic fantasy, new life is visited upon the woman from outside, as she is "swept away" by the passion and power of the other; in the "holding" fantasy the other's nonintrusive presence unlocks what lies deeply hidden, enabling a woman to bring out the potential for new life from within.

In my own search for such an enabling heterosexual fantasy, I found the fictional field so bare of examples that I had to turn to life for a better plot—to Eliot's "How I Came to Write Fiction." In the creative space provided by George Lewes's presence, George Eliot's drive to create fiction could emerge. She could play with the idea of writing a novel ("I imagined myself writing a story of which the title was—'The Sad Fortunes of the Reverend Amos Barton,'" 407), and she could make her desire real to herself by articulating it. Lewes's enthusiastic response—"What a capital title!"—mirrored back her ambition in a form she could assimilate and eventually convert into reality.

Why are there not more literary expressions of this fantasy?[2] It is available, presumably, to all who have been infants playing in the space sheltered by the mother. We can only guess that in a male-dominant culture the fantasy associated with the mother is denigrated and dismissed along with the mother herself to make way for a structure in which the exciting man is central. It is striking that in the fiction produced by the women in this study who were brought up in mother-affirming families, the fantasy of a transitional creative space is preserved. In *The Color Purple* Celie recreates maternal space for Shug by brushing her hair—"That feel like Mama used to do" (57)—and so releases Shug from self-enclosure into a creative flux from which a song emerges, "something you help scratch out my head" (57). Shug reciprocates by extending a literal shelter over Celie, giving her space in her Memphis home to make pants.

Although the individual circumstances of Toni Morrison's upbringing were different from Walker's, her fiction is marked by the same African American family tradition of respect for strong mothers (see especially Eva in Morrison's *Sula*). In such a family structure there is no reason either to rub out the holding fantasy or to turn away from the mother who first offered it. In *Beloved* heterosexual resolution is a matter of establishing a protected space for creating stories. Paul D, who is "blessed" with the gift of enabling women to express their feelings, offers Sethe a version of creative space. Early in the book he literally holds her and so enables her to tell her sadness (17). At the end he offers her a shared space for self-expression: "He wants to put his story next to hers" (273). Thus sexual completion takes the form of creative collaboration in which her story will complement and complete his.

The underlying fantasy patterns of *Beloved* are quite different from those of *The Color Purple*, discouraging easy generalizations about the fantasies that arise from life in African American families. On the other hand, it can be argued that both these novels ignore oedipal developments and retain intact earlier holding fantasies; they thus reflect, in different ways, a family tradition in which mothers are perceived as strong and central. It seems that their authors never had to experience the oedipal devaluation of the mother or shift their allegiance to a father with a monopoly on autonomy and self-esteem. In these novels growth comes not through turning from a denigrated mother to an enabling father but through emerging into a larger maternal circle. Denver in *Beloved* is not rescued from maternal symbiosis by a male savior; rather, she moves from a self-consuming maternal circle that can no longer sustain her into the larger embrace of a nurturing community, which literally gives her more substantial food. Even her graduation into language is not a matter of separating her self from her objects so much as a matter of finding more wholesome food—"the wonderful little *i*, sentences rolling out like pie dough" (121); and language lessons are presented as a different kind of nurturing, provided by a woman who calls Denver, in compassion, "Baby."

Although it is dangerous to generalize from so few novels, I hazard the guess that in families where maternal love and maternal work are respected equally with paternal authority and paternal work, there is in effect no oedipal turn and hence no residual oedipal fantasy. Louisa May Alcott, because of the idiosyncratic family structure described above in chapter 10, never had to shift preoedipal adoration from mother to father. Consequently *Little Women*, like *The Color Purple* and *Beloved*, lacks the oedipal themes that I have traced in this study—the abandonment of nurturing love for self-respecting autonomy, or the dependence on male attention for a sense of self-worth.

Where the family for one reason or another escapes the imperatives of male dominance, there is no need for an oedipal stage. The oedipal stage is not necessary to development, then, but only to the maintenance of patriarchy. If the value system that sustains male dominance did not require that girls learn to love submission and that boys learn to derogate women and women's work, there would be no oedipal stage. Where men and women are perceived as equally competent and receive equal respect for work in the world and in the home, there is no set-up for the oedipal turn from a devalued mother to a paternal "knight in shining armor" who "represents freedom, the outside world, will, agency, and desire" (Benjamin, 86).

By ignoring the oedipal stage, Winnicott and Kohut (and the later Chodorow) similarly imply that it is not necessary. They represent development not as a sudden break for separation and autonomy but as a continuity in which differentiation occurs always within a relational context: an affirmative parental presence continues to reflect back a child's feelings and accomplishments in a form it can integrate into an evolving identity. The continuities of *Little Women*, *The Color Purple*, and *Beloved* reflect such an experience of development by presenting change as growth *toward* others and *with* others rather than as a sudden overthrow of old patterns of dependency.

Perhaps the current mass movement of women into the job market will eventually break down the traditional division of labor by gender. Certainly the strain on the old parenting structure is great, as women try to balance home and career. One needs, in fact, a bit of the optimism of fantasy to foresee a breakdown in the traditional family's distribution of work, given the results of Heidi Hartmann's study of housework and Arlie Hochschild's more recent *Second Shift*. Their research shows that women's entrance into the world of paid employment has not significantly altered the division of responsibilities at home: it seems that only the working woman is forced to change, usually by adding an eight-hour workday onto her household duties. Nevertheless the pressures to change are there; perhaps one day the old gender division of labor will break down, so that men and women will work and parent equally. It is, after all, the social function of fantasy to introduce possibilities not immediately visible to a survey of the gray probabilities: we can work toward actualizing only that which we have first imagined.

Let us imagine growing up in a nuclear family in which mother and father are perceived equally as workers in the world and as care-givers. In a family where gender definitions were thus loose, a daughter could identify with either mother or father as a subject of effective agency who integrated a range of human capacities for effective work and nurturing care. Jessica Benjamin maintains that a child around the second half of the second year (in my terms, a child emerging from the preoedipal confusion between self and mother into a clearer sense of its own separateness) feels helpless because it has lost omnipotence along with the illusion that its mother was an extension of its will. What it needs to defend against a crushing sense of inadequacy is to identify with a powerful other who says, in effect, "You are like me." It will be immediately apparent that as the patriarchal family is traditionally constituted, this path toward individuation is open only to a boy. As Benjamin says, both mother and father encourage a boy's identification with his father, who as provider and actor in the outside world presents an image of effective agency. A girl may try the same gambit: Chodorow says that a girl originally turns to the father to get a measure of his autonomy, mobility, and power (*Mothering*, 121, 124). But that doesn't work: rather than accept his daughter's identification with him as an effective actor in the world, a father tends to mediate society's gender expectations by rewarding his daughter with love for demonstrating her "feminine" coyness and submissiveness (*Mothering*, 118–19), thus turning her into the object of his affections. The mother cannot offer a girl a model of agency and desire because on the one hand she is the object of the father's desire, and on the other hand, as a properly self-effacing mother she has no right to desires of her own. As things stand now, "Being the I who desires is routed through identification with [the father]," and that route is closed to the girl (Benjamin, 88).

But in a family where gender lines were not so tightly drawn, where mothers and fathers were perceived equally as subjects bent on projects of their own and as nurturing parents, a girl could identify either with a strong and effective woman or with a strong and effective man. What fantasies would arise from identifying *with* a subject of desire and agency, rather than as the object of his attention? Contratto's survey of daughters' feelings about their fathers, cited in chapter 1, shows that Laura Ingalls Wilder is not alone in idealizing her father as a figure of excitement. In a traditional patriarchal nuclear family fathers carry with them the glamour of the outside world and of relative inaccessibility; and they tend to play more roughly and vigorously with their small children than do mothers. So "father[s come to] stand for outsideness, novelty, stimulation, and excitement" (Benjamin, 86). As things stand now for girls, excitement remains attached to the male figure. The experience of awaiting the father's homecoming each day and perceiving experience shared with him as special, haloed by his superior power and prestige, leads a girl to attach excitement to a man's presence. This is the relational structure behind romantic love: excitement is what you wait for when you wait for a man to enter the scene; excitement is what you get when he turns the light of his attention on you.

For a boy, it is different. Benjamin says that as a boy develops his identification with his father, the source of excitement shifts from the object ("she is so attractive") to the desiring self ("I want her"). If a girl could also identify with the figure of excitement, with a subject of desire, she too could learn to locate the source of excitement within herself. Identifying oneself as the source of energy and desire would give rise to unconscious fantasies that feature the self, rather than the man, at the center of things. A self-definition as the subject who acts is the basis for what I have called fantasies of creative autonomy, in which excitement is generated by what one does for oneself—more specifically, in artist fantasies, by spinning out one's inner life into concrete external forms. Whereas the fantasy of romantic love makes the man the agent of a woman's happiness, so that only his actions count, the fantasy of making things and sending them out into the world affirms a woman's sense of agency and competence, her ability to affect the world around her.

These speculations on the fantasies arising from alternative family structures are meant to be suggestive rather than inclusive. This study is limited in part by the parameters of my own experience, growing up as I did in a heterosexual, white, middle-class, traditionally organized patriarchal American family. I have only begun to speculate here—and from the tentative position of an outsider—on the traces in African American women writers' texts of a family tradition in which the mother is honored and parenting is shared. It remains for those who are more conversant with other cultures than I to analyze the fantasy structures shaped by other family arrangements. What would be the unconscious formations of a child growing up in the kind of family *The Color Purple* ultimately envisions, where women as well as men pursue their own career objectives and men as well as women enjoy child-rearing? What kinds of literary fantasies do the children of kibbutzim write? What is needed is a cross-cultural study, a kind of literary parallel to Nancy Chodorow's survey of alternative mothering structures in East London, Java, and Indonesia ("Family Structure," 60–66).

Any discussion of alternative family and fantasy structures brings us back to the question of whether unconscious fantasies can be changed. If unconscious desire is forever locked into patterns that reflect one's original family, good ideas for alternative family structures will fall away, impotent and irrelevant: desire will still and always move persons to recreate in their adult lives the circumstances of their growing up. And since most people in a patriarchal society are raised in male-dominant structures, these will always be reproduced—in fact as well as fiction.

To reverse the direction of inquiry now: can fantasy change the shape of the family? Can readers take in the images of alternative family patterns in literature, make them their own, and thus mobilize desire to construct new family arrangements in their own lives?

In chapter 2, above, I described a model of unconscious reading that allows girl readers to assimilate fantasies of autonomy. Is this process valid, as well, for adult readers? To recapitulate briefly: Pinchas Noy asserts that the primary processes are always in play, assimilating new experience into the self-structure. These unconscious mechanisms work by means of "thing-presentation," rather than "word-presentation," says Freud. Therefore, material that comes clothed in vivid "thing-shapes"—concrete objects or physical actions—is already adapted to primary-process thinking and can be readily assimilated.

If literature can change our minds, then surely *The Color Purple* shows how. As the novel moves from the abuse of patriarchal power in Celie's original family toward the expansive family circle of the ending, each new bonding or shift in communal organization is given body through immediate, concrete action. When Sofia and Celie give up envy and rancor for friendship, they translate their new-found solidarity into making a quilt together. Celie and Albert sit "sewing and talking and smoking [their] pipes" (238), representing in concrete action the downfall of gender boundaries that has just occurred in their conversation (238). Before Celie and Nettie reenter their childhood home to build an egalitarian family in a house where the cruelest form of authoritarian patriarchy once oppressed them, they start over again physically: they fall down on the porch, lose the power of speech, and crawl around like babies. New social configurations thus always take the concrete form of "thing-presentation." A reader can take in each step in the process of creating a more flexible, less gender-bound family network.

Most memorable, because most oft-repeated, is the image of *The Color Purple*'s extended family as a circle around the dinner table, united by the effort to survive and to tend its children. That image of an expanded circle that accepts idiosyncrasy and integrates difference evolves, as I argued in chapter 10, from an infantile image of the mother-child circle of completion. If desire for a lost maternal unity is evoked in the reader by the image of bodies joined in a circle, can that desire be attached to the new verbal structure in the novel and so transformed toward a new pattern of living? Marshall Alcorn says it can: "A self-system may undergo radical change as deep strata of affect and repression become evoked and then networked and anchored to new verbal systems. In this case the self-structure may itself change. This change, indeed, may be experienced as a kind of 'freedom.'" ("Rhetoric," 149). The images of alternative family life in the novels reviewed in chapters 9 and 10 evolve the mother-child circle toward a more adaptive formation, a family circle that in each case encompasses change and difference. They thus offer readers a fantasy pattern that both evokes repressed desire and transforms it.

But finally, making a new fantasy one's own probably rests on the strength of one's desire to do so. Children, with their undiminished faith in the possibilities of life, their eagerness to try on new experience, and their proximity to the age of permeable ego boundaries, may read novels with a passionate identification closed off to adult readers. On the other hand, the model of the split reader elaborated in part 1 of this study locates the hope for change in the unconscious, in buried preoedipal drive energies. If the unconscious is home to desires left over from preoedipal times, it contains the oral drive to introject what is good in the outside world—the drive identified by Freud as one of our two most primitive impulses ("Negation," 237). Many adults are still "voracious" readers, "devouring" books. This common idiom points to the Beloved in all of us, to the part of each reader that wants to take in something of the external world and make it his or her own.[3]

The unconscious desire to assimilate the other-than-me is aided and abetted by the conscious and wholly realistic desire of women saddled with today's overburden of work, family, and guilt to find new ways of organizing child care. Given this harmony of conscious and unconscious wishes, it seems likely that the concrete images of a different family presented in contemporary novels *can* transform desire, giving women patterns of family life that they can assimilate and use.

Notes

Introduction

1. In the psychoanalytic lexicon *preoedipal* refers to the earliest stages of development, when the mother-infant dyad is central and the distinction between self and other has not yet become firmly established. The derivative character of the term, which seems to deny the preoedipal a legitimate existence of its own and makes it point instead to the primacy of the oedipal, reflects the circumstances of its emergence as an afterthought to Freud's work on the Oedipus complex—as his work on female psychology in general was an afterthought to his male-centered vision of psychosexual development. Feeling obliged late in his career to say something specific about female sexuality, he looked back on a girl's early relations with her mother and acknowledged their central significance in female development. But because the Oedipus complex continued to be of central importance to him as "the nuclear complex of the neuroses" (Laplanche and Pontalis, *Language*, 329), Freud always seemed to be gazing at the preoedipal from a base in the oedipal: "Our insight into this early pre-Oedipus phase in girls comes to us as a surprise, like the discovery, in another field, of the Minoan-Mycenaean civilization behind the civilization of Greece" ("Female Sexuality," 226). The oedipal period is like Greek civilization—known, reliable, fundamental, the reference point in terms of which the preoedipal appears shadowy and irrational. The preoedipal is relevant mainly as it "underlies and explains the form and content of the feminine oedipus complex" (Chodorow, *Mothering*, 95).

Setting age limits on the preoedipal is tricky and possibly misleading, because girls tend to remain within preoedipal modes of relationship longer than boys—Freud says that some girls retain their preoedipal attachment to their mothers beyond the fourth year of life ("Female Sexuality," 226)—and because there is no cutoff point for preoedipal modes of relationship and cognition. The preoedipal literally means everything before the Oedipus complex, and the Oedipus complex is thought to dominate the period between three and five years. The most common usage limits the preoedipal to the first two years of life.

In this study I have followed the practice begun by Freud in the "oceanic" passage, quoted above, of conceptualizing the preoedipal as an ongoing mode of perception and self-definition, forever shadowing the dominant vision of self and world as separate and self-contained. Lacan and Kristeva extend this notion of interplaying registers of being, Lacan assuming that the imaginary is an ongoing dimension of adult personality and Kristeva constructing a person as a dialectic between semiotic and symbolic registers.

2. Norman Holland claims, without regard to gender, that "the single most common fantasy-structure in literature is phallic assertiveness balanced against oral engulfment" (*Dynamics*, 43). The terms of his description—a valiant phallus tak-

ing arms against a sea of encroaching engulfment—represent a widespread male resistance to the fantasy of merging. From Nancy Chodorow's account of male development as a movement away from the mother and all she represents, a movement to define the self as safely separate from the original symbiosis with her, one would expect that the notion of moving back toward some version of that maternal merger would threaten male identity. Indeed the specific merging fantasies that Holland lists are tinged with the fear of losing the self: "In literature, this earliest phase appears as fantasies of losing the self, of being engulfed, overwhelmed, drowned, or devoured, as in Poe's stories of being buried alive" (*Dynamics*, 35). In contradistinction to these tales of terror, novels by women tend to present fusion as desirable, indeed natural. In keeping with Chodorow's idea that girls tend to remain longer in a state of diffuse connection with their mothers and therefore perceive returns to preoedipal states as less threatening to their identities, characters in women's novels like *Mrs. Dalloway*, *Surfacing*, *The Awakening*, and *Housekeeping* experience an expansion past ego boundaries into the environing world as a "bath of blisse" rather than a drowning (Chaucer, 230; cited in Holland, *Dynamics*, 35); they seem to feel more secure, more fully themselves, when they feel part of the surrounding world.

3. Andrea Nye theorizes this problem and Kristeva's solution to it in "Woman Clothed with the Sun." Paula Treichler's essay "Escaping the Sentence" deals with the oppressions of patriarchal language and women's options for disrupting it. The exchange between Carol Neely, Karen Ford, and Treichler recorded in the "Notes and Queries" section of *Tulsa Studies in Women's Literature* 4 (Fall 1985) was very useful to me in thinking about women and language. (See in particular Karen Ford's response, " 'The Yellow Wallpaper' and Women's Discourse.") Teresa de Lauretis, recognizing woman's exclusion from language, from the position of "producer of signs," suggests that she become a troublemaker in language: "The woman cannot transform the codes; she can only transgress them, make trouble, provoke, pervert, turn the representation into a trap" (35). "The only way to position oneself outside of the [dominant] discourse is to displace oneself within it—to refuse the question as formulated, or to answer deviously (though in its words), even to quote (but against the grain)" (7). Patricia Yaeger, more optimistic about the possibilities for women as language users, sets out to show in *Honey-Mad Women* how women have appropriated male language to their own uses, how they have played with language, how they have "spoken of their pleasure and found pleasure in speech," how they have used a second language to articulate what they cannot voice in the dominant discourse (40).

4. Although, as Laplanche and Pontalis say in "Fantasy and the Origins of Sexuality," "we shall find a marked ambiguity [in Freud's notions of unconscious fantasy] as new avenues open out to him with each new stage in his ideas" (6), one can see reflected in their account Freud's persistent need to find structure in the unconscious. For example, an early letter conveys his excitement at finding what he thinks is the single fantasy structure that explains a patient's whole psychic life: "Buried deep beneath all his fantasies we found a scene from his primal period (before twenty-two months) which meets all requirements and into which all the surviving puzzles flow" (Letter 126, quoted in Laplanche and Pontalis, "Fantasy," 15). Freud took up one after another various theories that enabled him to think of

the unconscious as organized in a reliable and stable way. Before he arrived at the idea of the Oedipus complex as the organizing center of unconscious fantasy life, he entertained the idea of *Urphantasien*, original fantasies such as primal scene, castration, seduction, that everyone shares: whether they are inherited through racial memory or arise through some other means, the unconscious fantasies come first; they structure the desire of the subject (Laplanche and Pontalis, "Fantasy," 17). Beneath all Freud's fantasies of the unconscious can be glimpsed the need for finding in the unconscious "a structural field which can be reconstructed, since it handles, decomposes and recomposes its elements according to certain laws" (Laplanche and Pontalis, "Fantasy," 16).

5. These are my examples, meant to illustrate Lacan's pronouncements. (1) On the desire to be the other's desire: "To put it in a nutshell, nowhere does it appear more clearly that man's desire finds its meaning in the desire of the other, not so much because the other holds the key to the object desired, as because the first object of desire is to be recognized by the other" (*Language*, 31). (2) On the relation of need, demand, and desire: "It must be granted that it is the concrete incidence of the signifier in the submission of need to demand which, by repressing desire into the position of being faultily recognized, confers on the unconscious its order" ("Théorie du symbolisme," 1959, unpublished seminar; quoted by Wilden in Lacan, *Language*, 143 n. 143).

6. Lacan's famous statement, "The unconscious is structured like a language," does not in my opinion mean that the unconscious functions by means of language and secondary-process thinking; rather, the "language" of the unconscious operates by rules of substitution and combination peculiar to it. But in some instances linguistic and unconscious processes are analogous: first, Lacan claims that metonymy and metaphor in language reproduce the unconscious operations of displacement and condensation; secondly, he insists with some vehemence that the unconscious is not a cauldron of seething drive energies but operates by means of signifiers.

First, metaphor and metonymy: metaphor effectively superimposes one signifier on another, as the primary process of condensation pulls two disparate things or ideas into a single image. Metonymy implies moving across the signifying chain (from "boats," say, to "sails") in imitation of the movement of displacement from object to object. (See "Letter," 160, and "Subversion," 298.) But as contemporary French theorists Jean Laplanche and Serge Leclaire caution: "To proclaim hastily that Freudian displacement *is* metonymy and condensation metaphor is to choose to ignore much information . . . and to skip . . . numerous mediations" (177).

Secondly, Lacan insists that the unconscious functions by means of signifiers that represent specific drive energies. This is not different in kind from Freud's observation that "the ideational representative of the instinct [is] denied entry into consciousness . . . the representative in question persists [in the unconscious] unaltered from then onwards and the instinct remains attached to it" ("Repression," 147). In other words, in both Freud's and Lacan's model, a drive, or instinct, can enter mental life only through becoming attached to a representative (image or word); the energy of the particular drive continues to be attached to that signifier in the unconscious.

Words operate in the unconscious quite differently, then, from words in linguistic systems: as representatives of particular desires. In a dream analyzed by La-planche and Leclaire to illustrate the workings of the unconscious, for example, words function just like images: thus the word "Lili," the phoneme "Li," the image of sand, the image of horn, and the image of beach compose a medley that represents the interplay of the dreamer's various desires and fears. Words no less than images are counters in this game of desire. In another formulation, La-planche and Leclaire declare that the language of primary process "treats words not as words but as things" (151).

To take a similar example cited by Lacan: a patient of Freud's, "to achieve sexual satisfaction, needed a certain shine on the nose (*Glanz auf der Nase*); analysis showed that his early, English-speaking years had seen the displacement of the burning curiosity that he felt for the phallus of his mother . . . into a 'glance at the nose,' in the forgotten language of his childhood" ("Letter," 170; from Freud, "Fetishism," 149). The word "glance" in his original tongue, English, persisted in the unconscious as a representative of desire for his mother; in the permutations of learning German it had become *Glanz*—a shine on the nose.

When words become representatives of desire in the unconscious, as in the examples above, they do not behave like words in a linguistic system; "glance" (or *Glanz*) and "Lili" have become detached from language networks and operate exactly as images in the unconscious do, as "things" or tokens signifying particular drives. Thus, as Laplanche and Leclaire conclude, the "language" of the uncon-scious "can by no means be assimilated to our 'verbal' language. The 'words' that compose it are elements drawn from the realm of the imaginary" (162). Similarly, Robert Silhol in "Language and the Unconscious" shows the differences between Lacanian psychoanalytic and linguistic models, concluding: " 'The unconscious is structured like a language' cannot in any way be replaced by 'the unconscious is a language' " (28). See also Mark Bracher ("Four Discourses") for a lucid explana-tion of the relation between "master signifiers and the entire signifying apparatus" and "what has been left out of discourse," "the *a*, unconscious fantasy, cause of desire" (47, 48). As Ragland-Sullivan sums it up: "Lacan viewed language and the unconscious as distinct, closed systems that work by different kinds of logic" (15).

7. This summary oversimplifies the text of *Jane Eyre*, which is powerfully attrac-tive just because it is so rich in ambivalence. One can make an equally convincing argument that the text offers a reader a position of conscious identification with the invariably moral and upright thinking of that good girl Jane, while giving the reader's repressed rage against the stultifying enclosures of patriarchy the satisfac-tion of burning down the house with Bertha.

8. Annis Pratt describes women's choosing a merger with nature over life with a man in Sarah Orne Jewett's "A White Heron," Ellen Glasgow's *Barren Ground*, and May Sinclair's *Mary Olivier* (16–21). In Margaret Atwood's *Surfacing* the narrator rejects conventional love and marriage to enter the natural world with a commitment so absolute that, as Roberta Rubenstein says, she "tests the very boundaries between human and nonhuman" (*Boundaries*, 83), giving up language to eat, sleep, and bear offspring like an animal. In an essay on "avoiding self-definition," I argue that Woolf's Mrs. Dalloway similarly feels most content, most herself, not when she is "in love" but when she expands into the world around

her—"being part, she was positive of the trees, . . . of the house . . . part of people she had never met; . . . laid out like a mist between the people she knew best . . . it spread ever so far, her life, herself" (12).

Chapter 1

1. Dianne Sadoff points out the father-daughter configurations in *Villette* and *Shirley* as well as *Jane Eyre*, arguing persuasively that Brontë's dependence on her own father as well as her angry need to free herself from that dependency inspired several variations on the father-daughter theme. Sadoff focuses on a different set of parallels with father-daughter arrangements than I do, highlighting patterns of fathers abandoning and punishing their daughters and daughters in turn punishing their fathers in "narrative castrations [that] appear to be an exaggerated attempt to free [Brontë's] heroines from dependence on fathers" (*Monsters of Affection*, 151). Sadoff argues convincingly that Brontë's relationship with her father was the cornerstone of her emotional life: "She remained emotionally tied to him—dependent upon him even when he was dependent upon her—for life" (152). And his "paradoxical absence and hovering presence somewhere in the godlike upper reaches of the parsonage" (139) endowed him with power, mystery, and distance.

In "Incest Patterns" David Smith maintains that a battle between incestuous desire and the incest taboo occupies Jane's unconscious and structures the novel. His analysis of the Red Room incident in terms of the incest theme is especially interesting.

2. In Lacan's paradigm desire is also produced by lack. As Juliet Mitchell succinctly explains in her introduction to *Feminine Sexuality*: "The object that is longed for only comes into existence *as an object* when it is lost to the baby or infant. Thus any satisfaction that might subsequently be attained will always contain the loss within it. Lacan refers to this dimension as 'desire.' . . . Desire persists as an effect of a primordial absence and it therefore indicates that, in this area, there is something fundamentally impossible about satisfaction itself" (6). Tony Tanner brings together de Rougemont, Freud, and Lacan to theorize desire in *Adultery in the Novel* (87–95).

3. Chodorow says that "the father . . . is a fantasy figure whose contours, because they are less tied to real object-relational experiences for the child, must be imagined and are often therefore idealized" (*Mothering*, 80). Susan Contratto similarly finds that in her female patients' experience fathers' "more limited presence allowed for heightened idealization" ("Father Presence," 141). Jessica Benjamin thinks the idealization of the father is at the base of what she calls "ideal love": "This early love of the father is an ideal love; . . . this idealization becomes the basis for future relationships of ideal love, the submission to a powerful other who seems to embody the agency and desire one lacks in oneself, someone who can be a mirror of one's ideal image of the self" (85–86).

4. Contratto's essay "Father Presence," although it deals with only a small sample of white women from middle-class and working-class families (her female

patients), captures the tonality of a daughter's feelings toward mother and father as a result of the skewed power structure of a traditional home. All her patients' fathers worked outside the home while their mothers took care of the children. In spite of differences in wealth and class and the different ways in which the father's superior power was made clear to the children, all these daughters felt that the father "represented excitement, competence, fun, and power. . . . In contrast, mother was always around. She did not do special things. . . . mothers/women were boring, fathers/men exciting" (153). Many of Contratto's patients' accounts concern the excitement of the father's homecoming (143). Contratto's account ties the excitement attached to fathers to their relative scarcity and to the privileges accorded one who has a position in the outside world.

5. Rachel Brownstein, like Rich, insists that "by widening the period of time in which a girl is interesting, beginning Jane Eyre's story with the crucial events of her childhood, Brontë effectively argued . . . the case for a heroine as a developing individual, not a creature made at puberty for a man" (156).

6. The intensity of female waiting in *Pride and Prejudice*, as described by Nina Auerbach, is paradigmatic for the nineteenth-century courtship novel: "Waiting for the entrance of the gentlemen, [the women's] shared world is a limbo of suspension and suspense, which cannot take shape until it is given one by the opening of the door" (38).

7. Holland elaborates this model throughout *The Dynamics of Literary Response* (esp. 189, 311–14). Jameson restates Holland's theory in "Reification and Utopia," 136.

8. I am indebted to Gilbert and Gubar's *Madwoman in the Attic* for a sense of the psychological and emotional resonance of architectural metaphors in nineteenth-century novels by women. They point out that because women writers felt both literally contained (within their fathers' houses) and psychically constricted by "woman's place," the "spatial imagery of enclosure and escape" occupies a central place in their novels (83–87). They also demonstrate brilliantly how Bertha, "Jane's truest and darkest double," acts out Jane's anger against Rochester on several fiery occasions. Her final incendiary feat actualizes "Jane's profound desire to destroy Thornfield, the symbol of Rochester's mastery and her servitude" (360).

9. In *Loving with a Vengeance* (83) Tania Modleski describes a similar combination of unconscious fantasy with rational social analysis in Mary Wollstonecraft's *Maria*. Modleski's analysis of the male-dominant family patterns that underlie the fantasy structures of Harlequin Romances and modern Gothics was inspiring and helpful to me in writing this essay.

10. Essays by Gayatri Spivak and Laura Donaldson have focused on Bertha. Spivak claims that white middle-class feminist critics "colonize" Bertha, the "native woman," the woman of color, by turning her into Jane's dark double. She is given the position of the other whose presence serves only to define, by contrast, the one—Jane as central female identity. Bertha's own identity is excluded from the evolving female norm (245). Donaldson argues that although Gilbert and Gubar's construct of Bertha as Jane's dark double may deprive Bertha of "independent textual significance" (66), Spivak goes astray when she casts Jane in the (proto-

male) position of individualist subject. Donaldson argues that it is important to notice all oppressions, sexist as well as racist: Jane is not in the position of subject, but in the subject(ed) position of oppressed woman in a sexist society.

I see Jane and Bertha as doubles who, suffering from the same set of patriarchal oppressions, lodge a common protest against patriarchy. Though Brontë overtly acknowledges the connection between Jane and Bertha only once—"'It is not because [Bertha] is mad that I hate her. If you were mad, do you think I should hate *you?*' 'I do indeed, sir'" (303)—the reader is encouraged to make unconscious pathways between the two women. As I explain in detail in the next chapter, unconscious scanning picks up affinities between Bertha and Jane that a conscious reader intent on plot coherence might overlook: the scattered images of fire and room that dot both Bertha's and Jane's stories with reminders of what they share—oppression and rage.

11. In *Reader, I Married Him*, Patricia Beers also says this is "a marriage of equality as well as ecstasy" (107). Adams presents a comprehensive analysis of the complex class, status, and economic issues interlocking with the romantic dream, to conclude, as I do, that questions of economic status and autonomy are finally secondary to "the fantasy that love is a fusion of souls" (157).

12. Terry Eagleton analyzes the complex blend of submissiveness and control in Jane's power relations with Rochester in *Myths of Power*. Sadoff says that Rochester's "symbolic castration represents the daughter's surreptitious punishment of the domineering master-father . . . and gains the daughter a qualified mastery over him" (145).

13. Despite this underlying pattern of oedipal surrender, no one could seriously accuse Jane of becoming an object of desire merely; the active passion of her narrative voice makes her emphatically a subject of desire. As Patricia Spacks says, she "chooses passion over action" (81), Rochester over St. John, because "she believes in the primacy of feeling . . . Jane, passionate in every sense of the word, like Rochester, finds in Rochester for this reason above all her natural mate, and St. John's lack of passion, his ability to imagine a wife as nothing more than a comrade in a good cause . . . makes him repellent" (72). Rachel Brownstein similarly emphasizes that "Jane marries in the active voice" (157), choosing for herself: Jane's marriage "defiantly affirms not the heroine's transformation but her remaining herself" (156–57).

14. As Judith Newton and Helene Moglen have argued, Brontë's early submission to her father's and her brother's domination prepared her for a lifetime of depending on men to confirm her self-esteem (Moglen, 41, 225); the desire to submerge herself in a man's life was always in tension with her desire for self-definition and autonomy (Judith Newton, 98).

Chapter 2

1. In these first three chapters I am inquiring into the origins of widely shared female fantasy structures—asking, in effect, where do fantasies come from? Therefore I consider here only novels that girls read early, during childhood and early

adolescence. The theory that the unconscious can assimilate new fantasy structures holds good for adult readers as well. In the concluding chapter I try out the theory of unconscious reading outlined here on mature readers of *The Color Purple*.

2. For a more comprehensive treatment of the vexed question of what an image is, see the work of Marshall Alcorn, W. T. Mitchell, Ulric Neisser, and Mardi Jon Horwitz. Mitchell has graphed "the incredible variety of things that go by this name" (504), each with its own complicated and contradictory conceptual history. Neisser describes the phenomenology of mental images. Alcorn presents a virtually encyclopedic overview of current thinking on image-making (*Narcissism*, 85–90.) I am indebted to his account for references to the theorists mentioned here.

3. Lacan's discussion of an unconscious that is "structured like a language" has given rise to conflicting interpretations. In my view Lacan does not mean that the unconscious is constructed, like the conscious mind, by language and its ideological structures. If the unconscious operates by means of signifiers, as Lacan says, those signifiers "are elements drawn from the realm of the imaginary" (Laplanche and Leclaire, 162)—words or, more often, images, that represent unconscious desires. Language does not impose its structures on the unconscious mind. Nor do signifiers in the unconscious behave like words in a linguistic network. Rather, once signifiers become attached to drive energies, they join the dance of condensation and displacement that makes up the combinatory logic peculiar to the unconscious. For a more complete discussion of Lacan's views on language and the unconscious and various critics' interpretations of them, see note 6 to the Introduction, above.

4. Nancy Miller is surely right to point out that Freud is inconsistent when he attributes primarily erotic fantasies to women. If, as he says in "Creative Writers and Daydreaming," "unsatisfied wishes are the driving power behind phantasies" (147), then women should fabricate fantasies of power, not love. Pleasing and being lovable are fully accepted impulses in young girls and women; it is their desire for power that must be suppressed in a male-dominant society (Miller, 41).

5. The Red Room is also associated with female sexuality through its vaginal imagery, as Elaine Showalter has shown (114–15). She regards Jane's incarceration there as a rite of initiation into womanhood, coinciding with the onset of menstruation. The deep-red velvet draperies and fawn-colored walls suggest the folds and flesh of female genitalia; and the jewels enclosed in a jewel box hidden within a secret drawer in the wardrobe of a locked room suggest the penetralia of female sexual anatomy. The fear associated with the Red Room, later displaced onto the room where the mature sexual woman Bertha rages in mad passion, can then serve as a vehicle for a girl reader's dread of female sexuality—starting with her own.

6. I am indebted to Arthur Marotti's article on countertransference and reader response both for this quotation and for references to Ehrenzweig and Noy. Marotti uses countertransference as an analogy for the circuit of communication between reader's and author's unconscious.

7. Alcorn and Bracher describe another psychological mechanism for integrating literary patterns. Correcting Holland's exclusive emphasis on projection, they point out that "projection is never merely projective; it also involves an introjec-

tive moment" ("Literature," 351). The configuration of words in a text exerts a counterpressure on the emotion injected into them by the reader, tending to mold that emotion into the shape presented by the fiction; the reader then receives the projected emotion back in a more concrete and presumably usable shape. Hanns Sachs has hypothesized a similar meeting between a reader's inchoate unconscious emotion and a literary form that allows the reader "to adopt the emotional content of the work as his own, . . . deciphering—not intellectually, but by way of response from the unconscious—the hieroglyphic symbols. . . . The particular emotional situation which it permits us to experience for the first time has always been potentially in our possession. . . . Yet, it was not within our unaided power to make it really our own, to possess it as a recognizable part of our personality" (197–202). Wolfgang Iser agrees with Sachs: upon meeting the literary form of a particular emotion, "a layer of the reader's personality is brought to light which had hitherto remained hidden in the shadows." That potentiality is given form by the shape that configures the emotion in the text. "Thus each text constitutes its own reader" (*Act*, 157).

Chapter 3

1. I have chosen to treat *Little Women*, part 1, as a complete novel because it was written as one. Alcott finished it in August 1868, published it in October 1868, and only began the sequel—*Good Wives*, or *Little Women*, part 2—in November 1868, at the request of her publisher. As Ruth MacDonald points out, "[*Little Women*] was written without the second part of the book clearly in mind. Without the sequel *Good Wives* . . . the book works as a unified whole" (23). In terms of formal organization, the second Christmas, in the penultimate chapter, restores family unity as it completes the yearly cycle begun with the Christmas of chapter 2. The father's "graduation" speeches to his "little women" complete the pattern of spiritual quest begun by his inspirational letter in chapter 1. Because the edition of *Little Women* I have cited in this essay does not contain part 2, occasional references to *Good Wives* are drawn from a different edition and cited accordingly.

2. Nina Auerbach makes us richly aware that the community of women in *Little Women* is emotionally satisfying in a way that makes marriage—ostensibly the goal of the girls' development—a kind of death, because it breaks up the family: "The world of the March girls is rich enough to complete itself" (55). Auerbach describes how that plenitude is given body by the full description of concrete things in the house: "The physicality of their community is . . . inherent and overflowing" (60). Death (Beth's) and marriage (the other sisters') are parallel, both destroying the fabric of sisterhood rather than leading to something better" (63).

Several other critics have remarked on the tension between *Little Women*'s covert and overt messages. Judith Fetterley says, "The imaginative experience of *Little Women* is built on a paradox: the figure who most resists the pressure to become a little woman is the most attractive and the figure who most succumbs to it dies. Jo is the vital center of Alcott's book, and she is so because she is least a little woman. Beth, on the other hand, is the least vital and the least interesting. . . . In her content, her lack of ambition beyond broom and mop and feather-duster, Beth is the perfect little woman. Yet she dies. Implicitly, a connection is made between the degree to which she fulfills the prescription for being a little woman and the fact that she dies" ("Alcott's Civil War," 379). Elizabeth Langland similarly describes how the novel "opposes a vision of female fulfillment in a community of women to female self-realization in marriage" (112). Patricia Spacks stresses the didactic side of the novel, its ruthless imposition of sex roles and curtailment of female possibilities (120–28). Elizabeth Janeway notices only the other side of the story, the triumph of Jo as "the one young woman in 19th-century fiction who maintains her individual independence, who gives up no part of her autonomy as payment for being born a woman—and who gets away with it" (235).

3. Alcott's choice of storks for this simile may indicate a conscious advocacy of mother-child reciprocity. Traditional animal lore has it that storks "are exceedingly dutiful toward their babies and incubate the nests so tirelessly that they lose their own feathers. What is more, when they have moulted in this way, they in turn are looked after by the babies, for a time corresponding in length to the time which they themselves have spent in bringing up and cherishing their offspring" (White, 117–18). Birds were favorite figures for maternity in Victorian times: notably, "the image of the pelican woman, feeding her brood with her own vital substance dominated Victorian conceptions of the female role" (Rose, *Woman*, 157). It is not implausible that Alcott was acquainted with the folklore on storks as well and consciously used them to replace the image of pelican-mother sacrificing herself for her children.

4. I have chosen to use Kohut's "Forms and Transformations of Narcissism" rather than his later and better-known *Analysis of the Self* and *Restoration of the Self* (New York: International Universities Press, 1971, 1977) because the article explains Kohut's basic theories on the creative uses of narcissism lucidly while avoiding the technical terminology of the later books.

5. Two qualifications are in order here. First, Kohut specifies that making narcissistic impulses available to "goal-directed activities" (253)—that is, to ambitions appropriate to the real world—involves the gradual frustration of infantile illusions of omnipotence. Parents can gently correct the inflations of infantile grandiosity, and for the most part this correction will occur inevitably, through the ordinary frustrations of time and life. Parental assaults on narcissism are superfluous and can be harmful: "if the grandiosity of the narcissistic self . . . has been insufficiently modified because traumatic onslaughts on the child's self esteem have driven the grandiose fantasies into repression, then the adult ego will tend to vacillate between an irrational overestimation of the self and feelings of inferiority" (252). Narcissism will follow its own healthy developmental progress if the mother (or caretaker) does her part in providing an affirmative reflection of the self on display. Second, Kohut's emphasis on the grandiose is age-appropriate; that is, he is advocating an affirmation of a preoedipal child's exhibitionism. Nevertheless his notion that a child's self-esteem and subsequent capacity for effective action in the world stems from an unequivocal reinforcement of its self-worth by loving parents can be extended to later developmental periods. Indeed Kohutian psychotherapy rests on the notion that deficits in early parental mirroring can be

made up by a therapist who bathes his or her adult patients in an atmosphere of unequivocal empathy and support.

In the introduction to *Narcissism and the Text* Lynne Layton and Barbara Schapiro describe various other ways that Kohut's theories bear on psychoanalytic theories of creativity (20–25). See Susan Grayson's essay on Rousseau in the same collection for a precise analysis of how a particular artist's creative production meshes with narcissistic processes. For reflections on the feminist uses of Kohut's ideas see Judith Kegan Gardiner, "Self Psychology as Feminist Theory." Gardiner's recent book *Rhys, Stead, Lessing, and the Politics of Empathy* proposes a Kohutian model of reading, using "the multiple positions of 'narcissistic transferences' as analogies for the many kinds of relationships people establish with literary texts" (5).

6. Elizabeth Keyser remarks on Amy's transformation to "woman as artifact rather than artificer" (456).

7. Carolyn Heilbrun points out the importance to little girls—real and imaginary—of having a room of their own: "Small girls, at least those who grew up to be writers, have early begged for a room of their own, and, we hear, got it" (*Reinventing*, 181). Her examples are Louisa May Alcott and Willa Cather.

Chapter 4

1. Jane Tompkins discusses the problematics of *The Awakening*'s ambivalent narrative stance. Stewart Smith and Ruth Sullivan distinguish a narrative attitude sympathetic to Edna's romantic notions from a more critical realistic narrative voice.

2. Paula Treichler has charted the verbal vaguenesses and ambiguities that attend Edna's awakening with admirable clarity and precision ("Construction"). Patricia Yaeger's inquiry into the languages of *The Awakening* starts with a premise similar to mine but moves in a different direction. "Chopin herself has divided the linguistic topography of *The Awakening* into an extra-linguistic zone of meaning imaged for us at the beginning of the novel in the speech of the parrot, a 'language which nobody understood,' and a countervailing region of linguistic constraints imaged for us in Mr. Pontellier's speech" ("Language," 204). "Edna Pontellier speaks an unfinished discourse that reaches out to be completed by other speaking human beings: her 'lost' speech [is] represented by her own speech fragments, by the sibilant voice of the sea and the chatter of the trilingual parrot" (205). In the beginning, according to Yaeger, Edna pursues her inarticulate feelings; but she lets Robert impose the discourse of romantic cliché on her confused emotions, so that the opening "discontinuous series of images that are promisingly feminocentric" is subsumed into the discourse of romantic love (206). This summary oversimplifies Yaeger's complex account of the interplay between inarticulate desire and conventional language in *The Awakening*.

3. Wolkenfeld has compiled a helpful survey of the conflicting critical positions on Edna's end.

4. Yaeger is more pessimistic about Edna's efforts to construct her own discourse: she foregrounds not Edna's story, but moments when she is inarticulate,

moments when she cannot make a dent on the patriarchal discourse that surrounds her and pins her down. The conflict "between men's speech and the speaking of women" is "articulated as a struggle between men's normative language and
something unvoiced and enigmatic . . . Edna's anger is speechless" ("Language,"
211–12). In Yaeger's interpretation, what *The Awakening* describes is "a frightening antagonism between a feminine subject and the objectifying world of discourse she inhabits" (211). Dale Bauer similarly reads the novel as Edna's failed
attempt to replace the voices of male authority with her own discourse: her culture
offers her no language to define her new self (148), and she is unable to invent
one.

5. Gilbert and Gubar see Edna's interaction with the sea as transformative: "her
swimming immerses Edna in an other element—an element, indeed, of otherness—in whose baptismal embrace she is renewed, reborn" (*No Man's Land*, vol.
2, *Sexchanges*, 103). Like Aphrodite born of the sea's foam, Edna comes to embody the principle of female erotic energy. According to Gilbert and Gubar, Chopin both celebrates this erotic power by clothing Edna in the attributes of Aphrodite and imagines what would "really" happen to a woman who tried to live out
the erotic freedom of Aphrodite in late nineteenth-century society. None of the
activities the social sphere offers her is commensurate with "what is by now quite
clearly Edna's metaphysical desire" (108). Setting Edna's final swim in this mythic
subtext, Gilbert and Gubar see her swimming toward rebirth rather than toward
death—perhaps toward Cyprus or Cythera, but at any rate toward "the mythic, the
pagan, the aphrodisiac" (110). She thus marks out a helpful direction for women,
"toward a genre that intends to propose new realities for women by providing new
mythic paradigms through which women's lives can be understood" (110).

Gilbert and Gubar's account illuminates Chopin's intention by placing *The
Awakening* in historical context, in an alternative nineteenth-century reading of
women's sexuality that advocated erotic freedom for women. Its members in-
cluded George Sand, Victoria Woodhull, Elizabeth Cady Stanton, Edward Car-
penter, and Walt Whitman. "Sharing the views of all these thinkers, Chopin
dreamed of . . . a culture beyond culture whose energy would arise from the
liberation and celebration of female desire" (94).

6. Robert Arner has pointed out that the sea fosters Edna's instinctual processes, "vibrating chords in her unconscious being" (111). He concludes that no
human lover can satisfy Edna's instinctual desires as the sea can, with its affinity to
her inner world and its offer of death and love combined: "In the arms of her
demon lover, the sea, she has satisfied at least the most primitive of organic
instincts, the drive towards death" (118). Anne Goodwyn Jones also describes
Edna and the sea as lovers merging (157). Rosemary Franklin, charting Edna's
progress toward self-awareness through a parallel with the myth of Psyche, aligns
"the magnetic sea" with the lure of the unconscious. Dipping into, even dwelling
in it for a time, is necessary to individuation and full consciousness; but to become
ensnared in a permanent stay there constitutes a false turn, a failure of individuation (516–17, 526).

7. Yaeger comments on this passage: "It is as if Chopin is aware, as Edna is only
naively, that the mind wants to go beyond itself, to go toward extremes, to test the
accuracy of its own boundaries. . . . outside the other's language they enter the

arena of 'Nothing,' of a language which nobody speaks. And yet in talking with Adèle Ratignolle Edna begins to see connections she has not seen before; her thoughts become unsystematic—they go forward before going astray" (214). But this adventure is short-lived, according to Yaeger. Edna allows the romantic discourse of Robert to reduce her yearnings to conventional forms.

8. Several critics draw parallels between the sea's refrain and Walt Whitman's "Song of Myself." Per Seyersted and Lewis Leary claim that the sea's refrain, with its emphasis on awakening to authentic selfhood through sensuality, echoes Whitman's spirit (Seyersted, 151; Leary, 196). Arner finds Swinburne's "Triumph of Time" closer in spirit to the sensuous pull of death implicit in the sea's invitation (105–6).

9. See Kristeva, *La révolution du langage poétique*, 207–39. Margaret Waller's translation, *Revolution in Poetic Language*, includes only the first 205 pages of Kristeva's 646-page work. When I refer to portions of Kristeva's text that appear in the translation, I give the English title and page numbers; otherwise I cite the French title and page numbers. A portion of "Le dispositif sémiotique du texte," which describes specific semiotic disruptions of the symbolic register, is translated in Philip Lewis's "Revolutionary Semiotics." This early review of Kristeva's work remains one of the most helpful explanations of the semiotic.

10. See also Kristeva, "Novel," 168: "Musicating . . . lifts even the signifier/signified censorship."

11. Rachel Blau DuPlessis in *Writing beyond the Ending* and Leslie Rabine in *Reading the Romantic Heroine* describe how narrative inscribes ideological patterns in its readers (DuPlessis, 1–19; Rabine, 3–6) and how disruptive texts subvert these patterns.

12. In *Psyche as Hero* Lee Edwards deals with the contradiction between female sexuality and motherhood in *The Awakening* as well as in other nineteenth-century novels, pointing out that "although indulged sexuality produces children, children inhibit, even destroy, sexuality. . . . their continued 'safe' existence requires a denial of their natural, impulsive origins" (113–15).

13. In the year that *The Awakening* was published Charlotte Perkins Gilman in *Women and Economics* demanded economic independence and moral and mental freedom for women, protesting the infantilization of their dependent position within the family. Even Dorothy Dix, who as advice-to-women columnist could not afford to advocate overthrowing family structure altogether, urged women to take a stand against the tyranny of husbands and children. Culley's edition of *The Awakening* includes excerpts from both.

14. Gilbert and Gubar similarly interpret Edna's end as a transcendence of discursive as well as personal limits: "Edna's supposed suicide enacts not a refusal to accept the limitations of reality but a subversive questioning of both reality and 'realism.' For swimming away from . . . the oppressive imperatives of marriage and maternity, Edna swims, as the novel's last sentence tell us, not into death, but back into her own life, back into the imaginative openness of her childhood" (*No Man's Land*, vol. 2, *Sexchanges*, 109).

Chapter 5

1. Compare the self-naming and self-placing that opens *Robinson Crusoe*: "I was born in the Year 1632, in the City of York, of a good family . . . my mother['s] relations were named Robinson, a very good family in that country, and from whom I was called Robinson . . . Crusoe" (5). *Robinson Crusoe*, of course, makes good on this promise of factuality and substantiality.

2. This fused point of view fits in with the overlapping dimension of character that Joan Lidoff ascribes to "female" novels governed by a lack of ego boundaries: "mothers and daughters . . . are frequently drawn as they exist within the minds and feelings of each other: they are imaged by reflection, without the distinction between them always being clear—to them, to us, to the narrator. The story of one becomes the story of the other with the imperceptible figure-ground reversal of an optical illusion" (44).

3. In Lacan's scheme "imaginary" and "symbolic" are not meant to be stages of development in the sense of Freud's preoedipal and oedipal. Nevertheless, imaginary operations dominate the earliest stages of human life, the time of the infant-mother dyad that Freud labeled preoedipal. The rudiments of the ego are constituted during this period "through a process of identification with images: the images of the other as self (mother) and of the self as other (mirror image)" (Schor, 217 n. 2). Because the ego is originally constituted through the assimilation of others' images, "adults will always be caught up in the spatial lures of identification with their semblables" (Ragland-Sullivan, 27). Lacan's "symbolic" is, like Kristeva's "symbolic," the register of language and culture; it is based on difference (gender difference as well as linguistic difference) and governed by the Law of the Father.

4. Wilden remarks in "Lacan and the Discourse of the Other" that "for Lacan . . . the adult quest for transcendence . . . [and] lost paradises . . . can be reduced, if one wishes, to the question . . . asked by Oedipus: 'Who (or what) am I?'" (*Language*, 166).

5. I am indebted to John Swift for the observation on a reader's response to the "I" in the text that sparked this reflection (conversation at Occidental College, 23 September 1988).

6. Elizabeth A. Meese sees transiency as "an exercise of female autonomy, a necessary outcome of woman's refusal to participate in the socially imposed economy of gender roles" (62). Joan Kirkby understands Ruth's and Sylvie's burning of the house and entry into vagrancy as the culmination of the novel's drive to reject "the patriarchal notion of housebuilding and housekeeping" and the "social vision of the female, the housed woman, the house wife" (106) in favor of an alliance with natural forces. Thomas Foster aligns Ruth's and Sylvie's alternative life-style with Kristeva's description of a third generation of feminism, one that would refuse the limitations of domesticity to insist on an "insertion into history" but would also refuse "the subjective limitations imposed by this history's time on an experiment carried out in the name of irreducible difference" (Kristeva, "Women's Time," 53; quoted in Foster, 77). According to Foster, Ruth and Sylvie practice difference and live out an "alternative, prefigurative practice that comes into contradiction with dominant social forms" (85).

7. Madelon Sprengnether sees in *Housekeeping* "a peculiarly modern Book of Ruth, constructing a fable out of the mother-daughter relationship" (319)—a fable of originary loss, foregrounding the irremediable separation between mother and daughter. As Sprengnether reads this modern Ruth's message, a daughter is always an alien, always cast out of the original maternal plenitude. Ruth's solution is to contemplate, to live within, this state of loss; her reward is a perception of the lost object in all its richness, "as though the fact of loss itself were responsible for its special beauty. . . . 'For when do our senses know anything so utterly as when we lack it?' (152)" (Sprengnether, 317). Life is necessarily haunted, then, by what is absent, lost.

8. This analysis derives from Frege's notion that the negative is always linked to the predicate, not the noun (cited in Kristeva, *Revolution*, 122).

9. The phrase is Rosemary Jackson's, from *Fantasy* (23). Her analysis of disorienting texts has given me a frame of reference and a vocabulary for dealing with these elusive matters.

Chapter 6

1. The cultural directive that a woman must choose between art and love functions as a powerful preserver of the status quo. If women are convinced that pursuing a career of writing or painting means giving up the traditional satisfactions of being a woman—love and family—all but the most independent and self-determining women will be deterred from entering the cultural sphere; that leaves male cultural hegemony intact, with men creating the art works that define cultural expectations and interpret human experience. In *The Madwoman in the Attic* Sandra Gilbert and Susan Gubar present a virtual encyclopedia of male authority figures who deny that the creature without a penis has a right to the pen—a gender assumption that naturally undermines a writing woman's self-confidence and makes her feel "presumptuous," "an intruder on the rights of men" (Finch, 100; quoted in Gilbert and Gubar, 3–7.) Rachel Blau DuPlessis takes Avis's words in Elizabeth Phelps Dodge Ward's *The Story of Avis* to represent the nineteenth-century assumption that there is only enough energy to power one female activity, not two: "Whether [a woman] paints a picture or loves a man, there is no division of labor possible in her economy. To the attainment of any end worth living for, a symmetrical sacrifice of her nature is compulsory upon her" (Ward, 126; quoted in DuPlessis, 89–90). My idea of a conservation of energy principle operating in female artist novels came from DuPlessis's analysis of Ward's novel. Susan Suleiman finds among women writers who are also mothers a common fantasy powered by maternal guilt: "With every word I write . . . with every act of genuine creation, I hurt my child" ("Writing," 374). Or, as Ursula LeGuin condenses the maternal version of the either-or imperative: "I create / you are destroyed" (231).

Joanna Frye presents the female author confronted by an equally rigid choice between opposites. A woman writer can swerve from tradition to set her female protagonist in a "male paradigmatic story" governed by ambition, but then she cannot touch on issues concerning the female body or female socialization. If she chooses a "female" plot line, on the other hand, she has to leave out everything but "passivity and self-denial, . . . the self existing only in relationship" (3). Frye attributes this inflexibility to cultural pressures: "Because the conventional assumptions of the novel as narrative form share in a dominant sexual ideology, they act to limit the possibilities for novels" (5). That is, gender expectations become plot expectations. But the inflexibility Frye attributes to female authors, the arbitrary quality of a bipolar opposition that rules out any intermediate solutions, suggests the pressure of an unconscious structuring principle.

Like the present study, Frye's book foregrounds contemporary novels that attempt to work through this oppositional psychology toward more integrative solutions. She too uses Godwin's *Violet Clay* to illustrate the dilemma of a woman who would also be an artist: she describes Violet's oscillation between woman and artist scripts (notably her flight from painting to wifehood, then back again from marriage to career) (120–22). "The problem, of course, derives from the inevitable falseness of the plots themselves, particularly from their insistence that as a woman [Violet] must make an either/or choice between her femaleness and her ambition. She has no available pattern for narrative connections that include both work and womanhood" (122). While my analysis focuses on Violet's working out new possibilities for herself through painting, Frye's analysis focuses on Violet's position as narrating subject. "Violet Clay [learns] not so much the art of painting as the art of narrating the self": through telling her own story Violet releases herself from predetermined cultural plots and creates her own open-ended "ever-changing destiny" (130).

Phyllis Rose links the conflict that Lily in *To the Lighthouse* feels between "being a woman and being an artist" to conflicts between altruism and achievement suffered by women generally (*Woman*, 153–73). Rose ties Virginia Woolf's responses to cultural ideology to the emotional patterns inscribed by her personal relations with her mother and father. My reading of *To the Lighthouse*, below, has been greatly enriched by Rose's discussion of Woolf's images.

2. Perry's elaboration of the creative possibilities of Winnicott's transitional space was very helpful to me in thinking through these issues.

3. Both Rose, in *Parallel Lives*, and Knoepflmacher, in "On Exile and Fiction," have vividly interpreted the story of George Eliot's "birth." I return to it here because it encapsulates better than any fictional story I know the creative possibilities of transitional space and the theme of sexuality nurturing creativity.

4. Flax argues that because a number of factors related to the overvaluation of males and undervaluation of females in patriarchy lead to maternal ambivalence about parenting girls, daughters often do not get the unconditional nurturance they need during preoedipal times. Consequently a girl arrives at the stage of individuation "less likely [than her male counterpart] to have had an adequate symbiotic experience, [so that] her needs for a sense of fusion . . . remain strong" ("Conflict," 178). The girl's ambivalence about moving away from the symbiotic relation with her mother is compounded by her mother's reluctance to lose the one relationship that has been feeding her own unsatisfied need for fusion. Abandonment of close relationship seems certain to be read as rejection by the mother and to lead to her rejection of the daughter in turn. Nurturance seems to be the price of autonomy ("Conflict," 171–89).

5. *To the Lighthouse* is moving largely because Woolf seems to have retained in all

their immediacy both preoedipal feelings of adoration for an omnipotent mother and the oedipal anguish of separating from the mother in order to define the self differently. Sometimes one can see through Lily's self-doubts the original mother-or-me issue that I claim underlies the arbitrary choice between love and art that structures most female artist novels. When she actually sets brush to canvas, Lily doubts that she can paint and "had much ado to control her impulse to fling herself (thank Heaven she had always resisted so far) at Mrs. Ramsay's knee and say to her . . . 'I'm in love with you? . . . I'm in love with this all?'" (32). The opposition between getting Mrs. Ramsay's love and painting a picture is not a logical one: there is no reason to regard these as mutually exclusive alternatives. Rather, Woolf seems to draw here on the original anguished choice between a nurturing closeness to the mother (at her knee) and the lonely autonomous space where the artist works. Phyllis Rose says that this passage reflects "a fundamental ambivalence between a desire for self-definition and a desire for self-surrender, an almost childlike yearning for dependency" on the mother (*Woman*, 167). Rose develops, with brilliant clarity, all the levels on which departing from the maternal model in order to be a writer divided Woolf from her mother and her mother's affections (*Woman*, 157–72).

6. In a later essay Chodorow clarifies her position. The crucial early period of a girl's gender formation is not conflicted, she says: "Female identification and the assumption of core gender identity are straightforward." Conflict comes only "later in development," after a girl's core identity is already established. "[Difficulties] arise from identification with a negatively valued gender category, and an ambivalently experienced maternal figure. . . . Conflicts here arise from questions of relative power, and social and cultural value . . . and are less pervasively determining of psychological life for women than are masculine conflicts around core gender identity and gender difference" ("Gender," 14). Chodorow tends to think of cultural factors as relatively superficial, mere add-ons to the crucial patterning of the unconscious through very early relations. I differ from her in thinking that the social devaluation of women does enter into the crucial patterning of both a girl's identity and her gender identity, through the emotional recoil from a derogated mother who is also, from earliest times, part of the self.

7. Lynn Sukenick coined the term "matrophobia" in "Feeling and Reason in Doris Lessing's Fiction," 519. The definition here is Rich's, from *Of Woman Born*, 237.

8. Both Roberta Rubenstein and Elaine Tuttle Hansen comment on the meaning of this transfer of maternal power. Rubenstein sees the flashback to her mother's and grandmother's linked hands as Rennie's integration of what had been "missing" in herself and a turn away from the neutrality and "objectivity" that Rennie now sees is complicit with the violence all around her. "The ability . . . to connect to another person in empathetic touch, is the only real antidote to the deadening objectification that allows one person to see others as mere bodies to which violence may be done" ("Pandora's Box," 133–34). Hansen connects the hands of mother and grandmother to a Caribbean grandmother in the novel who has the gift of healing hands. The transfer of power from the doctor's to the mother's hands is a reappropriation "of the female powers of healing that male specialists have taken over from women" (15). Recovering her connection to a

female tradition of power is also a recovery of agency: Rennie moves from the position of naive, passive, childlike woman who can only wait, even in the jail cell, for the doctor to come and fix things, to the position of "midwife and mother" who "takes charge, takes care," and "delivers" Lora from death into life (16). By comparing the parallel narratives of Lora and Rennie to the telling and listening of women's consciousness-raising groups, Hansen brings out the novel's structural implication that personal stories make sense "only as they are shared and connected, and as they thus interrupt and shatter a paralyzing self-absorption" (11).

9. Gubar argues that female modernists like Katherine Mansfield and Virginia Woolf use the *Künstlerroman* to "salvage uniquely female images of creativity" (27) from their mothers' lives, redefining creativity to encompass their mothers' domestic arts. They can then embed their own form of art in a maternal creative tradition.

DuPlessis similarly claims that twentieth-century artist novels heal the rift between art and love by constructing a continuity between daughter-artist and loving mother: what the mother created in unacknowledged (domestic) forms of art, the daughter-protagonist will display in the dominant forms (writing, painting) that the world recognizes as art; her inspiration arises from her mother's domestic creativity. I differ from DuPlessis in distinguishing two different traditions, one reflecting the values of white middle-class family life and one the values of black American family life. African American women writers (and Alice Walker is in fact DuPlessis's principal example of an artist claiming continuity with maternal creativity) are reflecting a family tradition that attributes strength and influence to the mother as the central power in the family; an ambitious girl need not break off with such a mother in order to win a measure of dignity and autonomy. (See chapters 9 and 10 and Conclusion, below, for a discussion of African American family patterns and how they affect the fantasies of their daughters.) The artist fantasies of white middle-class authors, on the other hand, reflect a daughter's need to separate from a serviceable and subordinate mother in order to grasp the power to write or paint.

Many of the works by white women authors that DuPlessis herself analyzes, as well as those in the present chapter and those in Grace Stewart's survey of female artist novels, *A New Mythos*, picture the artist-daughter defining herself in opposition to the mother figure through the body of the work; reconciliation between mother and daughter comes only at the end, in an epiphany that represents more a consummation devoutly to be wished than an ongoing matrix of relationship that nurtures creativity.

10. Gubar, 48. Gubar understands Lily's final stroke of the brush as "a moment of ecstatic union [with the mother figure] which implies on the one hand that mother-daughter eroticism predates heterosexuality for women and on the other hand that the daughter's celebration of the dead mother serves as recompense for a life that repudiates the strictures that structured the mother's" (47–48).

11. The same could be said of the documentary film that Molly makes about her mother in Rita Mae Brown's *Rubyfruit Jungle*. Molly's book-long effort to leave her mother behind ends when Molly films her mother talking about her daily life. The movie, like Lily's painting, is made by Molly yet filled with her mother, reconstituting transitional space in concrete form.

12. Some of Rich's own poems, as well as Audre Lorde's, support the idea that an affirmation of love for women leads to a release of creative energy. Their poems escape the unalterable opposition of sexuality and art that patterns white heterosexual women's artist novels. In their poems the creation of art is, rather, infused with erotic energy. In Lorde's "Recreation," making love blurs into writing poetry: each lover makes the other's body into a poem. In "Transcendental Etude" Rich finds in "two women, eye to eye measuring each other's spirit, each other's limitless desire," "a whole new poetry beginning here" (76). For a history of the term "lesbian" as a metaphor for autonomous female creativity see Marilyn F. Farwell, "Toward a Definition."

13. The idea that creative artists often inhabit a transitional zone like that shared by mother and baby is widely accepted by psychoanalytic critics of art. Oremland locates creativity squarely within transitional modes of perception: "Creative people seem to be those singular few individuals who maintain an extraordinary kinship to, or in fact maintain developmental continuances of, transitional phenomena" (427–28). By likening the stages of an artist's relation to his or her creation to the stages of a mother-infant relation, Anton Ehrenzweig implies that a loosening of ego boundaries between the artist and the work in process is necessary for artistic production to take place at all (102–20). Arthur Marotti enlarges on this idea: "As in the infant-mother situation, loosened ego-boundaries are a precondition for growth, communication, and the enlargement of the area of creative perception." "The artist must, in effect, do for himself what the infant's emotionally nurturing mother does for him . . . : freely accept the material of the unconscious in its rawest form and thus provide the favorable conditions for its integration and translation onto a higher, more conscious level" (483). Ernst Kris and Brewster Ghiselin similarly maintain that a return to earlier, less differentiated states of mind is the prerequisite for creating something new. Kris describes the initial stage of creativity as "regression in the service of the ego," a strategic return to primary-process thinking. Ghiselin speaks of a lapse into an "unfocused" state of mind, with "attention diverted from the too-assertive contours of any particular scheme and dispersed" over a range of "ill-defined impulses" as the necessary precondition to "yielding to the indeterminate within," opening up to new and inchoate ideas from the unconscious. Without some such lapse into primary-process modes, Ghiselin says, the conscious mind will reduce any vague hunch or intimation from less structured levels of the mind to its own iron structures (14, 25).

14. The view of maturation elaborated here rests on Nancy Chodorow's "Gender, Relation, and Difference in Psychoanalytic Perspective" and Jessica Benjamin's "A Desire of One's Own." Chodorow emphasizes that "true differentiation, true separateness, cannot be simply a perception of self-other. . . . It must precisely involve two selves, two presences, two subjects" (7). "Differentiation is not distinctness and separateness, but a particular way of being connected to others" that enables one to recognize them as subjects in their own right (11). Benjamin elaborates Winnicott's notion that "really recognizing the other as existing outside the self and not just as a bundle of my own projections, is the decisive aspect of differentiation" (93). (She refers here to Winnicott's "Use of an Object.")

Chapter 7

1. Joanne Creighton likewise suggests that "she and James indulge in an oral fantasy in which James is the loving mother and she the helpless infant who is tied absolutely to his solicitous care" (58).

2. In *Reading the Romantic Heroine* Leslie Rabine comments on this displacement of erotic focus to the word: "In Brontë's novels erotic feeling emanates from talking, and is communicated along with the dialogue. . . . What Robert Heilman calls 'erotic energy' forms that atmosphere in which words are suspended" (Rabine, 126).

3. Although James's fantasy life is beyond the scope of this chapter, the contours of his desire can be glimpsed through his words and actions: he is drawn to the overheated, womblike room with its centerpiece of childbirth and nursing; he participates insofar as he can in the oral relations between mother and infant, eating "with avidity Bianca's disgusting tepid baby food, scraping out her abandoned plates of cereal and bone broth" (220). If we accept Freud's hypothesis that adult love grows out of infantile projection, we can see why the maternal scene so attracts James: he spent his early childhood on his mother's bed, listening to her endless amorous telephone conversations. It is his good luck that Jane is compliant to his wishes, willing to assent to the command: "'You are my prisoner here, in this bed'" (39). Thus James gets to replay the fantasy of attending mother in bed, with the added feature that he controls her presence there. (Eleanor Skoller, 127, posits James's identification with the baby Jane has just borne, which enables him to recapture the "desperate paradise" of oneness with his own mother.)

4. If sexual repression worked for the other Jane, keeping her kinship with Bertha under wraps and her love story pure, this twentieth-century Jane's sexuality refuses repression, demands integration: "Her sexual beauty. . . had seemed to her . . . wild like an animal, that could not be let loose, so she had denied it. . . . but now, for all that, it sat there by her bedside, . . . existent, alive, despite the dark years of its captivity" (37–38). Initially split off and projected onto a wild animal shape like Bertha's, Jane Gray's sexuality refuses to stay safely contained in a separate room: it moves into Jane's bedroom—or, more precisely, Jane herself moves into Bertha's third-story cell, a hot, close room with insistently female sexual connotations on the upper story of a dusty Victorian mansion. Refusing to continue her "years" of "dark captivity" in a subplot, Bertha demands inclusion in Jane's story.

5. Carol Gilligan shows how the debate that Jane engages in with Maggie revolves around issues relevant to women now, as in Victorian times. Like Maggie, Jane tries to dodge the accusation of selfishness and longs for innocence, but in spite of the "longings after perfect goodness" (Eliot, *Mill*, 500) that Jane shares with Maggie, she is not ready to renounce herself and her love for some abstract virtue. She has to create "a new virtue" that can include "activity, sexuality, and survival without abandoning the old virtues of responsibility and care" (Gilligan, 131). I would add to Gilligan's analysis the idea of a dialogic process in which Jane's embrace of a position of supreme selfishness—"I had not cared who should drown, as long as I should reach the land" (Drabble, 160)—is not her final word,

but an initial gambit in a moral debate: she speaks in reaction to Maggie's equally extreme solution—self-sacrifice—to the ethical dilemma of being able to get what you want only by taking it away from others. The dialogue continues throughout the novel, with Jane occupying various ethical positions, often in relation to Maggie's choices.

Nancy Rabinowitz explores similar ethical issues in the parallel between Jane and Maggie. She claims that Jane "almost willfully misunderstands *The Mill on the Floss*," attributing a global passivity to Maggie when Maggie actually develops from the passivity imposed by sexual love to the assertiveness of her final act, when she commands her own boat and goes to save her brother. In fact, Rabinowitz argues, Maggie's progress from passivity to activity parallels Jane's (239).

6. Joanne Frye's *Living Stories, Telling Lives* explores the ways the first-person narrative voice enables women to escape the cultural definition of woman-as-object and establish themselves as subjects capable of autonomous self-definition.

7. Ellen Cronan Rose identifies the third-person narrative with "Jane, the woman," whose experience is liquid and formless, and the first-person narrative with "Jane Gray, the artist [who gives] form, order and shapeliness to that experience" (91). The drama of *The Waterfall*, then, lies in the reconciliation of the two aspects, the transformation of the writer into "a woman writer" who finds a form to encompass the fluidity of her sexual experience. Frye sees the oscillation between first- and third-person narrators as a split between the woman ("she") contained in the "femininity text" of the culture, who is defined exclusively in terms of her body—she "drowns" first in childbirth, then in sexuality—and the "assertive I," the "agent-self," "the judging, questioning mind" (154) that dissents from such self-objectification. Like Rose, though, Frye acknowledges that "making the connections finally is the effort of the whole novel. . . . The connections must acknowledge the complexity of experience . . . her autonomy and her relationality, her questioning mind and her female body" (158).

8. As Eleanor Honig Skoller points out, there is no such line in Brontë, although there are addresses in plenty to the reader. The closest is "Reader, I married him" (Brontë, 452). Skoller takes this misquotation as one proof among many that the references to *Jane Eyre* are a false front concealing the real Jane who lies behind Jane Gray: Lady Jane Grey. Skoller interprets *The Waterfall* through a focus on Drabble's wordplay. Thus she sees a sentence describing Jane's mother's snobbish humiliation at misspelling the name of a student's titled parent as "a play of words of outlandish proportions." The passage reads, "I saw her hair turn gray, for a G where there should have been an H" (Drabble, 61). Skoller claims that Drabble's word games license her reading of this sentence as a clue that Grey lurks behind Eyre: "I saw her (Brontë's) (h)Eyre turn Gray" (Skoller, 129).

9. On the influence of Byron on Brontë's imagination see Moglen (26–33, 67–73).

10. Montrelay claims that women suffer from the absence of an unconscious representation of their genitalia. Parents' own fixations often prevent their acknowledging key events in their daughters' sexual maturation. Daughters, for example, usually escape prohibitions on masturbation. They do not therefore repress images of the genitals, as boys do. When parents neither prohibit nor rein-

force aspects of their daughters' sexuality, but simply censor it, girls grow up with a blank where a representation of their own sexual body might be. Or if they manage to repress an unconscious representation of very early sensual experience, that archaic representation is displaced when the girl accedes to a phallocentric ordering of the unconscious. Because of this long exclusion from systems of representation, the description of their sexuality evokes erotic pleasure. Montrelay cites M. Torok, one of the authors of *Recherches psychanalytiques nouvelles sur la sexualité féminine* (Payot, 1964), who reports that his female patients often dream they have an orgasm following sessions where he names their sexuality for them. Erotic pleasure follows not from the release of repression, but from repression itself, in the sense of substituting the word—the unconscious representation—for the body. The analyst's word, since it is produced from his listening-place, is not "a mirror" of the patient's sexual experience, but "a metaphor" for it. Montrelay does not speculate on the uses of her theory for literary criticism. But her hypothesis suggests that transposing one's sexual experience into the field of words might yield a specifically female *jouissance* of the kind that makes itself felt in Jane's overflowing metaphors ("Inquiry into Femininity," 87–97).

11. Gayle Greene also sees Jane's creation of her own metaphor as evidence of her taking control of her text—of her sexuality and its expression. "Jane re-combines and redefines the cluster of words relating to limits, boundaries, possession, in an evocation of an undiscovered country with 'no sign of an ending.' . . . The passage rings changes on the novel's water imagery, transforming the waterfall . . . to the more impressive, encompassing sea. . . . Drabble's 'illimitable, circular, inexhaustible sea' resembles the 'ocean' Cixous associates with female libido to suggest energies not confined by 'boundaries' or 'limits'" ("New Morality," 63).

12. Lorna Irvine understands Drabble's refusal of closure as an endorsement of the continuum of life over the isolated "significant moment" and of the survivor over the victim (both revisions of nineteenth-century literary conventions). Jane's freedom to change her mind about the direction of her story up until the last is an index of Drabble's faith in the freedom and responsibility of individual choice, as opposed to an authorial teleology that would function like predestination, directing the plot toward an ending known in advance.

Chapter 8

1. Because my analysis is thus limited to one part of the novel, it leaves out the complexity of *The Golden Notebook*'s overall structure, which Lessing herself says is central to her meaning (xiv). For an analysis of the complex interrelations between structure and meaning, see Joanne Frye, Judith Kegan Gardiner (*Rhys*), Molly Hite (*Other Side*), Joseph Hynes, Martha Lifson, Marjorie Lightfoot, Herbert Marder, and Roberta Rubenstein (*Novelistic Vision*). Gardiner's description of the novel's "paradoxical self-enfolding structure" as a reflection of Anna's identity—always in process but never finished, blurring the border between inside and outside (*Rhys*, 148)—is relevant to my emphasis on Anna's involvement in a pre-oedipal kind of thinking.

2. I am indebted to Ellen Morgan for focusing my attention on Lessing's ability to articulate the structural disadvantages of a male-dominant heterosexual model that "pits the interests of women and men against each other, women being driven to need and grasp for security and protection and men resisting being drawn into the restrictive role of provider" (478).

3. Jones is summarizing the views expressed by Lacan in *Encore: le Séminaire XX*, 90.

4. See Melanie Klein, "Some Theoretical Conclusions." Dorothy Dinnerstein's *Mermaid and the Minotaur* contains a helpful description of splitting (96–97). Bruno Bettelheim points out that the split between fairy godmother and bad stepmother in fairy tales reflects the split between good and bad mothers (68–69). See also Susan Suleiman's useful survey of the psychoanalytic literature in "On Maternal Splitting," 27–28.

5. Betsy Draine points out that Saul's "schizophrenic leaping from role to role has been just the sort of madness calculated to cure Anna's excessive sanity. She has always kept herself within the confines of a few narrow roles; she has divided her perceptions into separate notebooks; she has made a false dichotomy between fiction and reportage. Saul forces her into a chaotic state of dreams and vision, where she embraces the fullness of her experiences, including, at last, all the roles she has denied herself" (84). Draine's analysis always keeps in view the dialectic between chaos and form through which "chaos . . . continually destroys forms while moving itself to create new ones" (70).

Similarly, Molly Hite views Anna's breakdown with Saul as "an educational process, a 'breaking through,' which Anna undertakes by deciding to enter into Saul Green's 'madness.' . . . the aim of the educational process is to dissolve boundaries and to enable possible future selves to break through" (*Other Side*, 93). Hite ties issues of personal coherence and fragmentation in Lessing's characters to Lessing's experiments with form, with "'cracking' and 'splitting' the containing form" of the traditional novel.

Roberta Rubenstein calls into question Saul's independent existence: "he participates in that blurring of the distinctions between 'reality' and 'fiction' that makes it impossible to ascertain whether *any* character exists outside Anna's fictions" (*Novelistic Vision*, 104–5). In this perspective, Saul is just a split-off fragment of Anna's personality, so that the "breakdown into each other" (Lessing, vii) that Draine and Hite suggest makes way for new forms of consciousness becomes just another twist on Anna's solipsism. Rubenstein invokes Jung's *animus* as a way of understanding the function of Saul in Anna's psychic life (81–82).

6. Gayle Greene emphasizes the connection between Anna's break with outworn forms in her life and her break into new forms in her art. "It is only when she can cast off conventional roles in her life that she can take comparable chances in her fiction—risks that enable the creation of 'something new' (Lessing, 61, 472–73, 479). Her search requires her to 'break . . . [her] own form, as it were' (Lessing, 466) and to forge a new shape for her life and her art which is a surrender neither to conventional form nor to formlessness" ("Women and Men," 286–87; references to Lessing are Greene's).

7. John Carey (444–51) describes Anna's need to "name" things prematurely,

to sort them into manageable categories, and her subsequent breakthrough into an acceptance of disorder.

8. While Anna's guilt is related to the Marxist aesthetic of the 1950s—"true art was bound up with the external world and with social change" (Hite, *Other Side*, 57)—Lessing's relationship to the Marxist line on art is more complex and critical. See Molly Hite's useful exposition of the orthodox Marxist aesthetic, together with a discussion of Lessing's complicated relation to it, in *The Other Side of the Story*. Marxist Raymond Williams's praise for the kind of novel that combines the personal and the political clarifies my point that centering a novel on the position of an Algerian soldier might make it possible for Anna to write without social guilt. Williams admires "the kind of novel which creates and judges the quality of a whole way of life in terms of the qualities of persons. . . . Every aspect of personal life is radically affected by the quality of general life, yet the general life is seen at its most important in completely personal terms" (Williams, *Revolution*, 278, quoted in Hite, 59).

9. See also Joanne Frye (163–66) for a useful review of feminist criticisms and feminist approbations of *The Golden Notebook*.

10. See the articles on *The Waterfall* by Virginia K. Beards and Marion Vlastos Libby.

Chapter 9

1. See Marilyn Frye's witty and disturbing exposition (esp. 156–57) of what gets excluded from the category of sexuality by dictionary definitions that tie sexuality to intercourse and intercourse to penile penetration and ejaculation.

2. Lesbian relationships in themselves "call into question society's definition of woman at its deepest level," as Barbara Christian points out. "By being sexually independent" of men, lesbians undermine the phallocentric definition of woman as dependent on man (199). Christian also characterizes the quality of Celie's and Shug's relationship to each other as maternal: "these two women nurture each other," Celie taking care of Shug as if she were a baby and Shug in turn "becoming the mother that Celie never had" (194).

3. Molly Hite says that Shug's gesture, together with Celie's response—"Way after while, I act like a little lost baby too" (109)—gives their erotic relationship a maternal dimension from the start: "Celie's love affair with Shug begins from an erotic exchange that is poignantly figured as a mutual reparenting" (*Other Side*, 124).

4. Gates points out that Celie's gradual self-creation through writing echoes Janie's self-creation through oral narrative in *Their Eyes Were Watching God*; both women "speak themselves into being" (243) in vivid black dialect. Shug herself seems to be a portrait of Hurston (254). And *The Color Purple* reflects key metaphors from *Their Eyes Were Watching God*, so that Walker's text is always talking to Hurston's text.

5. Benjamin elaborates a concept of "recognition" on the basis of Winnicott's observation that seeing the other as that other exists in the here and now requires a

destruction of one's fantasy image of her or him: "One destroys the object in fantasy and discovers that it still exists in reality; it survives, setting a limit to the power of fantasy and self. To me it seems that the clarity of such a moment, the heightened awareness of both self and other, the reciprocal recognition that intensifies the self's freedom of expression, is actually the goal of erotic union" (93).

6. The various creations in *The Color Purple* fit DuPlessis's description of the fictive art works in women's novels, "fabricated from and immersed in the temporal, social and psychic conditions of muted female life" (103), perhaps even better than the examples that she herself discusses.

7. Freud mentions only in passing the idea that shared work might create libidinal bonds between the workers and that work might offer "the possibility . . . of displacing a large amount of libidinal components, even erotic [ones], on to professional work and on to the human relations connected with it" (*Civilization*, 80 n. 1). He does not develop the idea. Pessimism combines with his habit of bipolar thinking to relegate pleasure and reality to mutually exclusive categories (Keller, 101), and because work more than any other activity demands an adherence to the reality principle, it must rest on a repression of erotic pleasure. It remained for Herbert Marcuse and, more recently, Audre Lorde to assert the fulfillments of work powered by the erotic. Against Freud's notion that sexuality is inexorably opposed to the interests of civilization, Marcuse argues for the possibility of "civilization evolving from and sustained by free libidinal relations" (207). Sexual energy, released from its artificial confinement to genital activity, would inform every area of the body, so that people would find pleasure and satisfaction in a variety of activities beyond sexual intercourse, including work: "If work were accompanied by a reactivation of pregenital polymorphous eroticism, it would tend to become gratifying in itself without losing its *work* content" (215). Lorde redefines the erotic in the largest possible sense, as the source of authentic self-knowledge and as a fund of creative energy that empowers a variety of activities, including work: "Within the celebration of the erotic in all our endeavors, my work becomes a conscious decision—a longed-for bed which I enter gratefully and from which I rise up empowered" (*Uses of the Erotic*, 3).

8. In *Revolution in Poetic Language* Kristeva, following Lautréamont, makes laughter "the symptom of rupture" (223); laughter is a manifestation of that other self, heterogeneous to the subject inscribed in the symbolic order—a self that doesn't follow (or even know) the rules, that breaks out of symbolic enclosures. Laughter "designates an irruption of the drives against symbolic prohibition" (222).

9. The female community that builds up inside the structure of the patriarchal family and finally replaces it has its counterpart in the society of women within the male-dominant tribe of the Olinka described in Nettie's letters. In the male-centered world of the Olinka the women, like Celie in her oppressed state, have no identity outside that defined by their relations to men: "a girl is nothing to herself; only to her husband can she become something" (144). But the women live and work and have their being in an alternative community based on sharing work and sharing child care with other women: "It is in work that the women get to know and care about each other. . . . The women are friends and will do anything for

one another . . . they giggle and gossip and nurse each other's children" (153). As in Celie's world, taking care of each other's children is a mark of the women's vital connection to each other.

10. As Elizabeth Meese points out, "the system of sexual dominance entrapping Celie depends upon the repression, the concealment of woman's messages to her sister" (126); in order for the exploitation of women to be complete, they must be isolated from their sisters' support. Once she repossesses the letters and knowledge/power they contain, "Celie possesses herself" and so breaks free of patriarchal control (126).

11. I share Molly Hite's amazement and dismay at the way Stephen Spielberg's movie of *The Color Purple* reappropriates for patriarchy the alternative community and alternative religion created by the novel. The film gives Shug a wholly gratuitous father who does not exist in the book, and a preacher-father at that: at the end Shug leads the whole alternative community constructed around the Celie-Shug couple back into the patriarchal enclave of her father's church, where their song blends into the official hymn and their company is engulfed by the congregation; they all stand listening humbly to the father's Word. "Spielberg unerringly provides climax and denouement by restoring the patriarchal status quo" (Hite, "Writing," 141 n. 22).

Chapter 10

1. One could argue that references to *Mrs. Dalloway* and Kate's preparations for the party—buying flowers, choosing a dress—make this scene a revision of Mrs. Dalloway's party. "'Go and arrange the flowers,' said Ruth. 'That's what people are supposed to do before parties.' Ruth was doing *Mrs. Dalloway* for A level" (248). In an interview with Diana Cooper-Clark, Drabble described the closing party as "a literary joke, a Mrs. Dalloway–type party" (75); but in a conversation with me (MLA convention, New Orleans, 29 December 1988) Drabble affirmed that *To the Lighthouse* was the model, conscious or unconscious, for Kate's gathering. To the question, "Did you have *To the Lighthouse* in mind when you wrote about family at the end of *The Middle Ground*?," Margaret Drabble answered, "Oh, yes, David Lodge said that, and I thought, 'That's absolutely right.' " Whether it is Mrs. Dalloway or Mrs. Ramsay that Drabble had in mind, she evokes Woolf's celebration of communal gatherings that connect disparate persons.

Pamela Bromberg stresses the embrace of diversity that characterizes the final party. Against the violence precipitated by difference throughout the novel— "strife among classes and among ethnic, racial and nationalist groups"—Drabble "places friendship, loyalty, and parental love—the capacity to imagine and accept otherness" (477). Bromberg's analysis of what she sees as *The Middle Ground*'s deliberate structurelessness makes intelligible Drabble's resistance, often explicitly stated in the novel, to all the formal limitations associated with novel writing— including the seemingly inescapable storyteller's task of choosing some, rather than other, aspects of her characters' lives to write about.

2. The exact age of the baby is not given; she was nine months old just before

Sethe escaped from Sweet Home (223) and not yet two when she died (4). As she is always referred to as "crawling already" just before her death, and no more than three months can have elapsed between Sethe's leaving Sweet Home and the infanticide, I put her age at a little over one year.

3. Although as a ghost Beloved would "naturally" feel anxious about her insubstantiality, the forms her ontological insecurity takes match fantasies attributed by Lacan and Klein to preoedipal children. Lacan attributes a fantasy of the "body-in-pieces" to pre-mirror-stage infants ("Aggressivity," 4). The fear of being swallowed up is the other side of an infant's impulse to give free rein to its greed and devour the mother's breast: the baby fears that "the bad breast will devour him in the same greedy way as he desires to devour it" (Klein, 200–201).

4. Nancy Chodorow, for example, writes: "Women as wives and mothers reproduce people . . . psychologically in their emotional support of husbands and their maternal relation to sons and daughters. . . . in the family as it is currently constituted no one supports and reconstitutes women affectively and emotionally" (*Mothering*, 36).

5. Sarah Elbert remarks that "it was never clear . . . whether Bronson was unable to make money or simply refused to do so (perhaps feeling that charity bestowed by more worldly friends was evidence of his own saintliness)" (53–54).

6. Elbert describes Bronson as habitually "assuming an idealistic distance from [his family's] real needs" (80).

7. Ruth MacDonald sums up Louisa's response to her father's distance and irresponsibility thus: "From the time of the Fruitlands experiment it was clear to the young Louisa that her father was not a reliable supporter of his family, either financially or emotionally. . . . the fact that he was willing to abandon them, albeit for philosophical purposes and with their discussion of the matter, combined with his unresponsive, almost comatose presence after the nervous breakdown, served only to underscore the man's distance from and irresponsibility about his dependents. It became clear to Louisa that her mother relied on her not only for the emotional support that a wife might otherwise have expected from her husband, but also, as Louisa became older, for financial support" (3).

8. See Louisa's letter of 1845—"I have been thinking about my little room which I suppose I never shall have" (Myerson and Shealy, 6)—and the triumphant journal entry of 1846: "I have at last got the little room I have wanted so long, and am very happy about it" (Cheney, 47–48).

9. Several sociological studies describe the strong role of the mother in African American families and daughters' corresponding lack of ambivalence. Joyce Ladner's study of young African American women cites their respect for maternal strength: "All of these girls had been exposed to women who played central roles in their households . . . women were expected to be strong, and parents socialized their daughters with this intention" (Ladner, 127, 131; cited by N. Tanner, 151). Similarly, Gloria Joseph ties daughters' respect for their mothers' "strength, honesty, and ability to overcome difficulties" to the socialization of daughters to "become strong, independent women" (94–95; quoted in Gardiner, "Self Psychology," 778).

10. Child care in the societies that Chodorow covers is shared by wide networks

of family and friends like the one in *The Color Purple*. In cultures that offer mothers strong support from other women—where mothers cooperate and visit on a daily basis—women are less dependent on their children for emotional sustenance. Their relational needs satisfied by others, they can accept and encourage their daughters' moves toward individuation. Because they have the support of other women, they are also less prone to depression than mothers isolated in nuclear families. So they can offer their daughters a positive image of female vitality and self-confidence. A daughter can also negotiate differentiation from her mother more easily if she is surrounded by her mother's friends. Loosening her ties with her mother need not include a rejection of her gender identity when she has continuing attachments to other adult women (Chodorow, "Family Structure," 65–66).

11. DuPlessis ascribes to twentieth-century female artist novels a "domestic poetics" that, by inserting the artist into the family group, does away with both the cliché of the artist as isolated genius and the distinction between high art and domestic crafts (103–4).

Conclusion

1. Hamida Bosmajian makes this point in an essay that vividly describes the contrasts between the vast and threatening spaces of the prairie and the "felicitous space" inside the little house.

2. Perhaps the fantasy of a room of one's own that strikes a responsive chord in many women is a derivative of the "holding fantasy." In a room of one's own one is safe from intrusion, free to pursue one's thoughts wherever they take one—in directions both risky and creative. To what extent does that security depend on the sense of an overarching, protective parental structure? The attic room where Jo writes in *Little Women* is apart from, yet part of, a warmly supportive female household. That fantasy recaptures in architectural terms the paradox of Winnicott's infantile space, in which being alone is possible because of a larger sense of being together. See also Benjamin, 97.

3. Norman Holland likewise cites these figures of speech as evidence that reading is first and foremost an act of oral fusion; but he sees this phenomenon as the psychological basis for a reader's passive immobility, for the willing suspension of disbelief that enables him or her to "take in" the story (*Dynamics*, 73–79). I find it more fruitful to explore the active aspect of the drive for oral incorporation. Ernst Schachtel imputes to children a native curiosity, a drive to reach out into the world and enfold things in a kind of total attentiveness that is a more mature and other-directed version of the oceanic desire to merge (182, 252). In his comprehensive analysis of narcissism in reading Marshall Alcorn ascribes to all readers a degree of narcissistic deficit, a basic sense of insufficient or tenuous selfhood. By reading, readers can add to a precarious sense of existence a "supplementation of being" (*Narcissism*, 7).

Bibliography

Adams, Maurianne. "*Jane Eyre*: Woman's Estate." In *The Authority of Experience: Essays in Feminist Criticism*, edited by Arlyn Diamond and Lee Edwards, 137–59. Amherst: University of Massachusetts Press, 1977.

Adorno, Theodor W. "Cultural Criticism and Society." In *Prisms*. London: Neville Spearman, 1967.

Alcorn, Marshall. *Narcissism in the Text: Reflections on the Semiotic Transfer of Ideals.* Forthcoming.

———. "Rhetoric, Projection, and the Authority of the Signifier." *College English* 49 (February 1987): 137–57.

Alcorn, Marshall, and Mark Bracher. "Literature, Psychoanalysis, and the Re-Formation of the Self: A New Direction for Reader Response Theory." *PMLA* 100 (May 1985): 342–54.

Alcott, Louisa May. *Little Women*. New York: Puffin Books, 1978.

———. *Little Women*, part 2, *Good Wives*. Boston: Little, Brown, 1896.

Allen, Priscilla. "Old Critics and New: The Treatment of Chopin's *The Awakening*." In *The Authority of Experience: Essays in Feminist Criticism*, edited by Arlyn Diamond and Lee Edwards, 224–38. Amherst: University of Massachusetts Press, 1977.

Althusser, Louis. "Ideology and Ideological State Apparatuses (Notes towards an Investigation)." In *Lenin and Philosophy*, 127–86. Translated by Ben Brewster. New York and London: Monthly Review Press, 1971.

Arms, George. "Contrasting Forces in the Novel." From his "Kate Chopin's *The Awakening* in the Perspective of Her Literary Career." In *Essays on American Literature in Honor of Jay B. Hubbell*, edited by Clarence Gohdes, 215–28. Durham: Duke University Press, 1967. Reprinted in Chopin, *The Awakening*, 175–80.

Arner, Robert. "The Art of Kate Chopin: Apprenticeship and Achievement," chapter 6, *"The Awakening." Louisiana Studies* 14 (Spring 1975): 105–18.

Atwood, Margaret. *Bodily Harm*. New York: Simon & Schuster, 1982.

Auerbach, Nina. *Communities of Women*. Cambridge: Harvard University Press, 1978.

Bakhtin, Mikhail. *Problems of Dostoevsky's Poetics*. Edited and translated by Caryl Emerson. Berlin, New York, and Amsterdam: Mouton, 1984.

Bauer, Dale M. *Feminist Dialogics: A Theory of Failed Community*. Albany: State University of New York Press, 1988.

Baum, L. Frank. *The Wizard of Oz*. Chicago: Reilly & Lee, 1939.

Beards, Virginia. "Margaret Drabble: Novels of a Cautious Feminist." *Critique* 15 (1973): 35–47.

Beebe, Maurice. *Ivory Towers and Sacred Founts: The Artist as Hero in Fiction from Goethe to Joyce*. New York: New York University Press, 1964.

Beers, Patricia. *Reader, I Married Him*. New York: Harper & Row, 1974.

Belsey, Catherine. *Critical Practice*. London and New York: Methuen, 1980.

Bem, Sandra L. "Gender Schema Theory: A Cognitive Account of Sex Typing." *Psychological Review* 88 (1981): 354–64.

Benjamin, Jessica. "A Desire of One's Own: Psychoanalytic Feminism and Intersubjective Space." In *Feminist Studies/Critical Studies*, edited by Teresa de Lauretis, 78–101. Bloomington: Indiana University Press, 1986.

Bettelheim, Bruno. *The Uses of Enchantment: The Meaning and Importance of Fairy Tales*. New York: Random House, 1977.

Bosmajian, Hamida. "Vastness and Contraction of Space in *Little House on the Prairie*." *Children's Literature* 11 (1983): 49–63.

Bracher, Mark. "Lacan's Theory of the Four Discourses." *Prose Studies* 11 (December 1988, special issue on *Lacanian Discourse*, edited by Marshall Alcorn, Mark Bracher, and Ronald Corthell): 32–49.

Braudy, Susan. "A Day in the Life of Joan Didion." *Ms.*, 8 February 1977, 109.

Bromberg, Pamela. "Narrative in Drabble's *The Middle Ground*: Relativity versus Teleology." *Contemporary Literature* 24 (Winter 1983): 463–79.

Broner, E. M. *A Weave of Women*. New York: Holt, Rinehart & Winston, 1978.

Brontë, Charlotte. *Jane Eyre*. New York: New American Library, 1960.

Brown, Rita Mae. *Rubyfruit Jungle*. New York: Bantam, 1983.

Brownstein, Rachel. *Becoming a Heroine*. New York: Random House, 1982.

Carey, John. "Art and Reality in *The Golden Notebook*." *Contemporary Literature* 14 (Autumn 1973): 437–56.

Chaffin, Roger, and Mary Crawford. "The Reader's Construction of Meaning: Cognitive Research on Gender and Comprehension." In *Gender and Reading*, edited by Elizabeth Flynn and Patrocinio Schweickart, 3–30. Baltimore and London: The Johns Hopkins University Press, 1986.

Chametzky, Jules. "Edna and the Woman Question." From "Our Decentralized Literature." In *Jahrbuch für Amerikastudien* (1972): 56–72. Reprinted in Chopin, *The Awakening*, 200–201.

Chaucer, Geoffrey. "The Wife of Bath's Tale." In *The Canterbury Tales*, edited by E. T. Donaldson, 218–30. New York: The Ronald Press, 1975.

Cheney, Ednah D., ed. *Louisa May Alcott: Her Life, Letters and Journal*. Boston: Roberts Brothers, 1890.

Chodorow, Nancy. "Family Structure and Feminine Personality." In *Woman, Culture, and Society*, edited by Louise Lamphere and Michelle Rosaldo, 43–66. Stanford: Stanford University Press, 1974.

———. "Gender, Relation, and Difference in Psychoanalytic Perspective." In *The Future of Difference*, edited by Hester Eisenstein and Alice Jardine, 3–19. New Brunswick: Rutgers University Press, 1985.

———. *The Reproduction of Mothering*. Berkeley and Los Angeles: University of California Press, 1978.

Chopin, Kate. *The Awakening*. Edited by Margaret Culley. New York: Norton Critical Editions, 1976.

Christian, Barbara. *Black Feminist Criticism: Perspectives on Black Women Writers*. New York: Pergamon Press, 1986.

Cixous, Hélène. "Castration or Decapitation?" Translated by Annette Kuhn. *Signs* 7 (Autumn 1981): 41–55.

———. "La fiction et ses fantômes: une lecture de l'Unheimliche de Freud." *Poétique* 10 (1973): 199–216.

———. "The Laugh of the Medusa." Translated by Keith Cohen and Paula Cohen. *Signs* 1 (Summer 1976): 875–93.

Cohen, Ira H. *Ideology and Unconsciousness: Reich, Freud and Marx*. New York: New York University Press, 1982.

Contratto, Susan. "Father Presence in Women's Psychological Development." In *Advances in Psychoanalytic Sociology*, edited by Jerome Rabow, Gerald Platt, and Marion Goldman, 138–57. Malabar, Fla.: Krieger, 1987.

———. "Maternal Sexuality and Asexual Motherhood." In *Women: Sex and Sexuality*, edited by Catharine Stimpson and Ethel Person, 224–40. Chicago: University of Chicago Press, 1980.

Cooper-Clark, Diana. "Margaret Drabble: Cautious Feminist." *Atlantic Monthly*, November 1980, 72–82.

Coward, Rosalind, and John Ellis. *Language and Materialism: Developments in Semiology and the Theory of the Subject*. Boston and London: Routledge & Kegan Paul, 1977.

Creighton, Joanne. *Margaret Drabble*. London and New York: Methuen, 1985.

de Beauvoir, Simone. *The Second Sex*. Translated by H. M. Parshley. New York: Random House, 1974.

Defoe, Daniel. *Robinson Crusoe*. New York: W. W. Norton, 1975.

de Lauretis, Teresa. *Alice Doesn't: Feminism, Semiotics, Cinema*. Bloomington: Indiana University Press, 1984.

de Rougemont, Denis. *Love in the Western World*. New York: Doubleday, 1957.

Deutsch, Helene. *Psychology of Women*. New York: Grune & Stratton, 1944.

Dinnerstein, Dorothy. *The Mermaid and the Minotaur: Sexual Arrangements and Human Malaise*. New York: Harper & Row, 1976.

Dix, Dorothy. "The American Wife." Excerpted in Chopin, *The Awakening*, 129–30.

Donaldson, Laura. "The Miranda Complex: Colonialism and the Question of Feminist Reading." *Diacritics* 18 (Fall 1988): 67–77.

Drabble, Margaret. *The Middle Ground*. New York: Bantam Books, 1982.

———. *The Waterfall*. New York: Fawcett, 1977.

Draine, Betsy. *Substance under Pressure*. Madison: University of Wisconsin Press, 1983.

DuPlessis, Rachel Blau. *Writing beyond the Ending: Narrative Strategies of Twentieth-Century Women Writers*. Bloomington: Indiana University Press, 1985.

Eagleton, Terry. *Myths of Power: A Marxist Study of the Brontës*. London: Macmillan, 1975.

Edwards, Lee R. *Psyche as Hero: Female Heroism and Fictional Form*. Middletown, Conn.: Wesleyan University Press, 1984.

Ehrenzweig, Anton. *The Hidden Order of Art*. Berkeley and Los Angeles: University of California Press, 1967.

Elbert, Sarah. *A Hunger for Home: Louisa May Alcott and Little Women*. Philadelphia: Temple University Press, 1984.

Eliot, George. "How I Came to Write Fiction." In *The George Eliot Letters*, edited by Gordon S. Haight, 2:406–10. New Haven: Yale University Press, 1954.

———. *The Mill on the Floss*. New York: New American Library, 1965.

Erikson, Erik. *Insight and Responsibility*. New York: W. W. Norton, 1964.

Farwell, Marilyn R. "Toward a Definition of the Lesbian Literary Imagination." *Signs* 14 (Autumn 1988): 100–118.

Féral, Josette. "The Powers of Difference." In *The Future of Difference*, edited by Hester Eisenstein and Alice Jardine, 88–94. New Brunswick: Rutgers University Press, 1985.

Fetterley, Judith. "*Little Women*: Alcott's Civil War." *Feminist Studies* 5 (Summer 1979): 369–83.

———. *The Resisting Reader*. Bloomington: Indiana University Press, 1978.

Field, Joanna [Marion Milner]. *On Not Being Able to Paint*. Los Angeles: Jeremy P. Tarcher, 1957.

Finch, Anne. "The Introduction." In *The Norton Anthology of Literature by Women*, edited by Sandra M. Gilbert and Susan Gubar, 100–102. New York and London: W. W. Norton, 1985.

Firestone, Shulamith. *The Dialectic of Sex*. New York: Bantam, 1970.

Fish, Stanley. *Is There a Text in This Class?* Cambridge: Harvard University Press, 1980.

Flax, Jane. "The Conflict between Nurturance and Autonomy in Mother-Daughter Relationships and within Feminism." *Feminist Studies* 4 (June 1978): 171–89.

———. "The Family in Contemporary Feminist Thought." In *The Family in Political Thought*, edited by Jean Bethke Elshtain, 223–53. Amherst: University of Massachusetts Press, 1982.

Flieger, Jerry Aline. "Ignorance Is Bliss: *Jouissance* and the Refusal of the Symbolic in French Feminist Theory." Paper presented at the MLA convention, New Orleans, 28 December 1988.

Ford, Karen. "'The Yellow Wallpaper' and Women's Discourse." *Tulsa Studies in Women's Literature* 4 (Fall 1985): 309–14.

Foster, Thomas. "History, Critical Theory, and Women's Social Practices: 'Women's Time' and *Housekeeping*." *Signs* 14 (Autumn 1988): 73–99.

Franklin, Rosemary F. "*The Awakening* and the Failure of Psyche." *American Literature* 56 (December 1984): 510–26.

Freud, Sigmund. "A Case of Homosexuality in a Woman." *The Standard Edition of the Complete Psychological Works of Sigmund Freud* (SE). Translated from the German under the general editorship of James Strachey. Vol. 18 (1920): 146–72. London: Hogarth Press.

———. "A Child Is Being Beaten." *SE*, 17 (1919): 175–204.

———. *Civilization and Its Discontents*. SE, 21 (1930): 57–115.

———. "Creative Writers and Day-Dreaming." *SE*, 9 (1908): 141–53.

———. "The Ego and the Id." *SE*, 19 (1923): 1–66.

———. "An Example of Psychoanalytic Work." *SE*, 23 (1940): 183–94.

———. "Female Sexuality." *SE*, 21 (1931): 221–43.

———. "Fetishism." *SE*, 21 (1927): 147–57.

———. "Negation." *SE*, 19 (1925): 233–39.

———. "On the Universal Tendency to Debasement in the Sphere of Love." *SE*, 11 (1912): 177–90.

———. *An Outline of Psycho-analysis. SE*, 23 (1940): 139–207.

———. "Repression." *SE*, 14 (1915): 141–58.

———. "The Unconscious." *SE*, 14 (1915): 159–215.

Frye, Joanne. *Living Stories, Telling Lives: Women and the Novel in Contemporary Experience*. Ann Arbor: University of Michigan Press, 1986.

Frye, Marilyn. "To Be and Be Seen: The Politics of Reality." In *The Politics of Reality: Essays in Feminist Theory*, 152–74. Freedom, California: Crossing Press, 1983.

Gallop, Jane. *The Daughter's Seduction: Feminism and Psychoanalysis*. Ithaca: Cornell University Press, 1982.

Gardiner, Judith Kegan. *Rhys, Stead, Lessing and the Politics of Empathy*. Bloomington: Indiana University Press, 1989.

———. "Self Psychology as Feminist Theory." *Signs* 12 (Summer 1987): 761–80.

Gates, Henry Louis, Jr. *The Signifying Monkey: A Theory of Afro-American Literary Criticism*. New York and Oxford: Oxford University Press, 1988.

Gérin, Winifred. "General Introduction." In Charlotte Brontë, *Five Novelettes*, edited by Winifred Gérin, 7–23. London: Folio Press, 1971.

Ghiselin, Brewster. "Introduction." In *The Creative Process*, edited by Brewster Ghiselin, 11–31. New York: New American Library, 1952.

Gilbert, Sandra, and Susan Gubar. *The Madwoman in the Attic: The Woman Writer and the Nineteenth-Century Literary Imagination*. New Haven and London: Yale University Press, 1979.

———. *No Man's Land: The Place of the Woman Writer in the Twentieth Century*, vol. 2, *Sexchanges*. New Haven and London: Yale University Press, 1989.

Gilligan, Carol. *In a Different Voice: Psychological Theory and Women's Development*. Cambridge and London: Harvard University Press, 1982.

Gilman, Charlotte Perkins Stetson. *Women and Economics: A Study of the Economic Relation between Men and Women as a Factor in Social Evolution*. Boston: Small, Maynard, 1899. Excerpted in Chopin, *The Awakening*, 134–38.

Godwin, Gail. *Violet Clay*. New York: Warner Books, 1978.

Grayson, Susan. "Rousseau and the Text as Self." In *Narcissism and the Text: Studies in Literature and the Psychology of Self*, edited by Lynne Layton and Barbara Ann Schapiro, 78–96. New York and London: New York University Press, 1986.

Greene, Gayle. "Feminist Fiction and the Uses of Memory." *Signs* (in press).

———. "Margaret Drabble's *The Waterfall*: New System, New Morality." *Novel* (Fall 1988): 45–65.

———. "Women and Men in Doris Lessing's *Golden Notebook*: Divided Selves." In *The (M)other Tongue*, edited by Shirley Nelson Garner, Claire Kahane, and Madelon Sprengnether. Ithaca: Cornell University Press, 1986, 280–305.

Gubar, Susan. "The Birth of the Artist as Heroine: (Re)production, the *Künstlerroman* Tradition, and the Fiction of Katherine Mansfield." In *The Representation of Women in Fiction: Selected Papers from the English Institute, 1981*, edited by Carolyn G. Heilbrun and Margaret R. Higonnet, 19–59. Baltimore and London: The Johns Hopkins University Press, 1983.

Hansen, Elaine Tuttle. "Fiction and (Post) Feminism in Atwood's *Bodily Harm*." *Novel* 19 (Fall 1985): 5–21.

Hardin, Nancy. "An Interview with Margaret Drabble." *Contemporary Literature* 14 (Autumn 1973): 273–95.

Hartmann, Heidi I. "The Family as the Locus of Gender, Class, and Political Struggle: The Example of Housework." *Signs* 3 (Spring 1981): 366–94.

Hartsock, Nancy C. M. *Money, Sex and Power: Toward a Feminist Historical Materialism*. New York and London: Longman, 1983.

Heilbrun, Carolyn G. *Reinventing Womanhood*. New York: W. W. Norton, 1979.

––––––. *Writing a Woman's Life*. New York: W. W. Norton, 1988.

Hirsch, Marianne. "Spiritual *Bildung*: The Beautiful Soul as Paradigm." In *The Voyage In: Fictions of Female Development*, edited by Elizabeth Abel, Marianne Hirsch, and Elizabeth Langland, 23–48. Hanover and London: University Press of New England, 1983.

Hite, Molly. *The Other Side of the Story: Structures and Strategies of Contemporary Feminist Narratives*. Ithaca and London: Cornell University Press, 1989.

––––––. "Writing—and Reading—the Body: Female Sexuality and Recent Feminist Fiction." *Feminist Studies* 14 (Spring 1988): 121–42.

Hochschild, Arlie. *Second Shift: Inside the Two-Job Marriage*. New York: Viking, 1989.

Holland, Norman. *The Dynamics of Literary Response*. New York and London: W. W. Norton, 1975.

––––––. "Gothic Possibilities." In *Gender and Reading*, edited by Elizabeth Flynn and Patrocinio P. Schweickart, 215–33. Baltimore and London: The Johns Hopkins University Press, 1986.

––––––. "Unity Identity Text Self." *PMLA* 90 (1975): 813–22.

Horwitz, Mardi Jon. *Image Formation and Psychotherapy*. New York and London: Jason Aronson, 1983.

Hurston, Zora Neale. *Their Eyes Were Watching God*. Urbana: University of Illinois Press, 1978.

Hynes, Joseph. "The Construction of *The Golden Notebook*." *Iowa Review* 4 (1973): 100–113.

Irigaray, Luce. "And the One Doesn't Stir without the Other." Translated by Hélène Vivienne Wenzel. *Signs* 7 (Autumn 1981): 60–67.

––––––. "The 'Mechanics' of Fluids." Translated by Catherine Porter. In *This Sex Which Is Not One*, 106–18. Ithaca: Cornell University Press, 1985.

Irvine, Lorna. "No Sense of an Ending." In *Critical Essays on Margaret Drabble*, edited by Ellen Cronan Rose, 73–86. Boston: G. K. Hall, 1985.

Iser, Wolfgang. *The Act of Reading*. Baltimore: The Johns Hopkins University Press, 1978.

––––––. "The Reading Process: A Phenomenological Approach." In *Reader-Response Criticism*, edited by Jane Tompkins, 50–69. Baltimore: The Johns Hopkins University Press, 1980. Reprinted from *The Implied Reader: Patterns in Communication in Prose Fiction from Bunyan to Beckett*, 274–94. Baltimore: Johns Hopkins University Press, 1974.

Jackson, Rosemary. *Fantasy: The Literature of Subversion*. London and New York: Methuen, 1981.

Jameson, Fredric. "Reification and Utopia in Mass Culture." *Social Text* 1 (1979): 130–48.

Janeway, Elizabeth. *Between Myth and Morning: Women Awakening*. New York: William Morrow, 1975.

Jehlen, Myra. "Archimedes and the Paradox of Feminist Criticism." In *Feminist Theory: A Critique of Ideology*, edited by Barbara Gelpi, Nannerl Keohane, and Michelle Rosaldo, 189–215. Chicago: University of Chicago Press, 1982.

Johnson, Mark. *The Body in the Mind*. Chicago: University of Chicago Press, 1987.

Jones, Anne Goodwyn. *Tomorrow Is Another Day: The Woman Writer in the South, 1859–1936*. Baton Rouge: Louisiana State University Press, 1981.

Jones, Ann Rosalind. "Inscribing Femininity: French Theories of the Feminine." In *Making a Difference*, edited by Gayle Greene and Coppelia Kahn, 80–112. London and New York: Methuen, 1985.

———. "Writing the Body: Toward an Understanding of l'Ecriture Féminine." In *The New Feminist Criticism*, edited by Elaine Showalter, 361–77. New York: Pantheon Books, 1985.

Joseph, Gloria. "Black Mothers and Daughters: Their Roles and Functions in American Society." In *Common Differences: Conflicts in Black and White Feminist Perspectives*, edited by Gloria Joseph and Jill Lewis, 75–126. Garden City, New York: Doubleday, Anchor Press, 1981.

Keller, Evelyn Fox. *Reflections on Gender and Science*. New Haven and London: Yale University Press, 1985.

Kernberg, Otto F. "Boundaries and Structure in Love Relations." *American Psychoanalytic Association Journal* 25 (1977): 81–114.

Keyser, Elizabeth. "Alcott's Portraits of the Artist as Little Woman." *International Journal of Women's Studies* 5 (1982): 445–59.

Kirkby, Joan. "Is There Life after Art? The Metaphysics of Marilynne Robinson's *Housekeeping*." *Tulsa Studies in Women's Literature* 5 (Spring 1986): 91–109.

Klein, Melanie. "Some Theoretical Conclusions Regarding the Emotional Life of the Infant." In Melanie Klein, Paula Heimann, Susan Isaacs, and Joan Riviere, *Developments in Psycho-Analysis*, 198–236. London: Hogarth Press, 1952.

Knoepflmacher, U. C. "On Exile and Fiction: The Leweses and the Shelleys." In *Mothering the Mind*, edited by Ruth Perry and Martine Watson Brownley, 102–21. New York: Holmes & Meier, 1984.

Koestler, Arthur. "Bisociation in Creation." In *The Creativity Question*, edited by Albert Rothenberg and Carl R. Hausman, 108–13. Durham: Duke University Press, 1976. Reprinted from *The Act of Creation*. New York: Macmillan, 1965.

Kohut, Heinz. "Forms and Transformation of Narcissism." *Journal of the American Psychoanalytic Association* 14 (1966): 243–72.

Kris, Ernst. *Psychoanalytic Explorations in Art*. New York: International Universities Press, 1952.

Kristeva, Julia. "The Bounded Text." In *Desire in Language: A Semiotic Approach to Literature and Art*, translated by Thomas Gora, Alice Jardine, and Leon S. Roudiez, edited by Leon S. Roudiez, 36–63. New York: Columbia University Press, 1980.

———. "From One Identity to Another." In *Desire in Language*, 124–47.

———. "The Novel as Polylogue." In *Desire in Language*, 159–209.

———. *Polylogues*. Paris: Editions du Seuil, 1977.

———. *La révolution du langage poétique*. Paris: Editions du Seuil, 1974.

———. *Revolution in Poetic Language*. Translated by Margaret Waller. New York: Columbia University Press, 1984.

———. "Women's Time." In *Feminist Theory: A Critique of Ideology*, edited by Barbara Gelpi, Nannerl Keohane, and Michelle Rosaldo, 31–54. Chicago: University of Chicago Press, 1982. Reprinted from *34/44: Cahiers de recherche de sciences des textes et documents* 5 (Winter 1979): 5–19.

Lacan, Jacques. "The Agency of the Letter in the Unconscious, or Reason since Freud." Translated by Alan Sheridan. In *Ecrits: A Selection*, 146–78. New York and London: W. W. Norton, 1977.

———. "Aggressivity in Psychoanalysis." Translated by Alan Sheridan. In *Ecrits: A Selection*, 8–29.

———. *Encore: le Séminaire XX, 1972–1974*. Paris: Seuil, 1975.

———. "L'envers de la psychanalyse: le Séminaire XVIII, 1969–1970." Typescript.

———. *The Four Fundamental Concepts of Psycho-Analysis*. Translated by Alan Sheridan. New York and London: W. W. Norton, 1981.

———. "Intervention on Transference." Translated by Jacqueline Rose. In *Feminine Sexuality: Jacques Lacan and the Ecole Freudienne*, edited by Juliet Mitchell and Jacqueline Rose, 61–73. New York and London: W. W. Norton, 1985.

———. *The Language of the Self: The Function of Language in Psychoanalysis*. Translated by Anthony Wilden. Baltimore: The Johns Hopkins University Press, 1968.

———. "A Love Letter." Translated by Jacqueline Rose. In *Feminine Sexuality: Jacques Lacan and the Ecole Freudienne*, edited by Juliet Mitchell and Jacqueline Rose, 149–61. New York and London: W. W. Norton, 1985.

———. "The Meaning of the Phallus." Translated by Jacqueline Rose. In *Feminine Sexuality: Jacques Lacan and the Ecole Freudienne*, 74–85.

———. "The Mirror-Stage as Formative of the Function of the I." Translated by Alan Sheridan. In *Ecrits: A Selection*, 1–7.

———. "The Phallic Phase and the Subjective Import of the Castration Complex." Translated by Jacqueline Rose. In *Feminine Sexuality: Jacques Lacan and the Ecole Freudienne*, edited by Juliet Mitchell and Jacqueline Rose, 99–122. New York and London: W. W. Norton, 1982.

———. "The Subversion of the Subject and the Dialectic of Desire in the Freudian Unconscious." Translated by Alan Sheridan. In *Ecrits: A Selection*, 292–325.

Ladner, Joyce. *Tomorrow's Tomorrow: The Black Woman*. Garden City, N.Y.: Doubleday, 1971.

Langland, Elizabeth. "Female Stories of Experience: Alcott's *Little Women* in Light of *Work*." In *The Voyage In: Fictions of Female Development*, edited by Elizabeth Abel, Marianne Hirsch, and Elizabeth Langland, 112–27. Hanover and London: University Press of New England, 1983.

Laplanche, Jean, and Serge Leclaire. "The Unconscious: A Psychoanalytic Study." Translated by Patrick Coleman. *Yale French Studies* 48 (1972): 118–75.

Laplanche, Jean, and Jean-Bertrand Pontalis. "Fantasy and the Origins of Sexuality." In *Formations of Fantasy*, edited by Victor Burgin, James Donald, and Cora Kaplan, 5–34. London and New York: Methuen, 1986. Reprinted from *The International Journal of Psychoanalysis* 49 (1968), part 1.

————. *The Language of Psychoanalysis*. Translated by Donald Nicholson-Smith. New York and London: W. W. Norton, 1973.

Lawrence, D. H. *Lady Chatterley's Lover*. New York: New American Library, 1959.

Layton, Lynne, and Barbara Ann Schapiro. "Introduction." In *Narcissism and the Text: Studies in Literature and the Psychology of Self*, edited by Lynne Layton and Barbara Ann Schapiro, 1–35. New York and London: New York University Press, 1986.

Lazarre, Jane. "Charlotte's Web: Reading *Jane Eyre* over Time." In *Between Women*, edited by Carol Ascher, Louise DeSalvo, and Sara Ruddick, 221–35. Boston: Beacon Press, 1984.

Leary, Lewis. "Kate Chopin and Walt Whitman." In *Southern Excursions: Essays on Mark Twain and Others*, 169–74. Baton Rouge: Louisiana State University Press, 1971. Reprinted in Chopin, *The Awakening*, 195–99.

LeGuin, Ursula K. *Dancing at the Edge of the World*. New York: Grove Press, 1989.

Lessing, Doris. *The Golden Notebook*. New York: Bantam, 1973.

Lewis, Philip E. "Revolutionary Semiotics." *Diacritics* 4 (Fall 1974): 28–32.

Libby, Marion Vlastos. "Fate and Feminism in the Novels of Margaret Drabble." *Contemporary Literature* 16 (Spring 1975): 175–92.

Lidoff, Joan. "Virginia Woolf's Feminine Structures: The Mother-Daughter World of *To the Lighthouse*." *Literature and Psychology* 32 (1986): 43–57.

Lifson, Martha. "Structural Patterns in *The Golden Notebook*." *Michigan Papers in Women's Studies* 2 (1978): 95–108.

Lightfoot, Marjorie. "Breakthrough in *The Golden Notebook*." *Studies in the Novel* 7 (1975): 277–85.

Loewald, Hans. "Ego and Reality." *International Journal of Psychoanalysis* 32 (1951): 10–18.

Lorde, Audre. "The Master's Tools Will Never Dismantle the Master's House." In *This Bridge Called My Back*, edited by Cherrie Moraga and Gloria Anzaldua, 98–101. Watertown, Mass.: Persephone Press, 1981.

————. "Recreation." In *The Norton Introduction to Poetry*, 2d ed., edited by J. Paul Hunter, 20–21. New York and London: W. W. Norton, 1981.

————. *Uses of the Erotic: The Erotic as Power*. Trumansburg, N.Y.: Out and Out Books, 1978.

MacDonald, Ruth. *Louisa May Alcott*. Twayne's United States Authors Series. Boston: G. K. Hall, 1983.

McLellan, David. *Karl Marx*. New York: Viking, 1975.

Marcus, Jane. *Art and Anger: Reading like a Woman*. Columbus: Ohio State University Press, 1988.

Marcuse, Herbert. *Eros and Civilization*. Boston: Beacon Press, 1955.

Marder, Herbert. "The Paradox of Form in *The Golden Notebook*." *Modern Fiction Studies* 26 (Spring 1980): 48–54.

Marotti, Arthur. "Countertransference, the Communication Process, and the Dimensions of Psychoanalytic Criticism." *Critical Inquiry* 4 (Spring 1978): 471–89.

Martineau, Harriet. *Autobiography* [1877]. Excerpted in Ellen Moers, *Literary Women*, 9. Garden City, N.Y.: Doubleday, 1977.

Meese, Elizabeth A. *Crossing the Double-Cross: The Practice of Feminist Criticism*.

Chapel Hill: University of North Carolina Press, 1986.

Miller, Alice. *Prisoners of Childhood: The Drama of the Gifted Child and the Search for the True Self.* New York: Basic Books, 1981.

Miller, Nancy. "Emphasis Added: Plots and Plausibilities in Women's Fiction." *PMLA* 96 (January 1981): 36–48.

Mitchell, Juliet. "Introduction I." In *Feminine Sexuality: Jacques Lacan and the Ecole Freudienne,* edited by Juliet Mitchell and Jacqueline Rose, 1–26. New York: Norton, 1982.

————. *Psychoanalysis and Feminism.* New York: Random House, 1975.

Mitchell, W. T. "What Is an Image?" *New Literary History* 15 (Spring 1984): 503–38.

Modleski, Tania. *Loving with a Vengeance.* Hamden, Conn.: Shoe String Press, 1968.

Moers, Ellen. *Literary Women.* Garden City, N.Y.: Doubleday, 1977.

Moglen, Helene. *Charlotte Brontë: The Self Conceived.* New York and London: W. W. Norton, 1976.

Montrelay, Michelle. "Inquiry into Femininity." Translated by Parveen Adams. *m/f* 1 (1978): 83–101. Reprinted in *French Feminist Thought: A Reader,* edited by Toril Moi, 227–49. Oxford and New York: Basil Blackwell, 1987.

Morgan, Ellen. "Alienation of the Woman Writer in *The Golden Notebook.*" *Contemporary Literature* 14 (Autumn 1973): 471–80.

Morrison, Toni. *Beloved.* New York: Alfred A. Knopf, 1987.

Murdoch, Iris. *The Sovereignty of Good.* New York: Schocken, 1971.

Myerson, Joel, and Daniel Shealy. *The Selected Letters of Louisa May Alcott.* Boston and Toronto: Little, Brown, 1987.

Neisser, Ulric. "The Processes of Vision." In *The Nature of Human Consciousness,* edited by Robert Ornstein, 195–210. San Francisco: W. H. Freeman, 1973.

Newton, Judith. *Women, Power, and Subversion: Social Strategies in British Fiction, 1778–1860.* Athens, Ga.: University of Georgia Press, 1981.

Newton, Niles. "Interrelationships between Sexual Responsiveness, Birth, and Breast-Feeding." In *Contemporary Sexual Behavior: Critical Issues in the 1970's,* edited by Joseph Zubin and John Money, 77–98. Baltimore: The Johns Hopkins University Press, 1973.

Noy, Pinchas. "A Revision of the Psychoanalytic Theory of the Primary Process." *International Journal of Psycho-analysis* 50 (1969): 155–78.

Nye, Andrea. "Woman Clothed with the Sun: Julia Kristeva and the Escape from/ to Language." *Signs* 12 (Summer 1987): 664–86.

Oremland, Jerome D. "Michelangelo's *Ignudi,* Hermaphroditism, and Creativity." *Psychoanalytic Study of the Child* 40 (1985): 399–433.

Perry, Ruth. "Introduction." In *Mothering the Mind: Twelve Studies of Writers and Their Silent Partners,* edited by Ruth Perry and Martine Brownley, 3–24. New York and London: Holmes & Meier, 1984.

Pratt, Annis. *Archetypal Patterns in Women's Fiction.* Bloomington: Indiana University Press, 1981.

Rabine, Leslie W. *Reading the Romantic Heroine: Text, History, Ideology.* Ann Arbor: University of Michigan Press, 1985.

Rabinowitz, Nancy. "Talc on the Scotch: Art and Morality in Margaret Drabble's *The Waterfall*." *International Journal of Women's Studies* 5 (1982): 236–45.

Radway, Janice. *Reading the Romance: Women, Patriarchy, and Popular Literature.* Chapel Hill: University of North Carolina Press, 1984.

Ragland-Sullivan, Ellie. *Jacques Lacan and the Philosophy of Psychoanalysis.* Urbana and Chicago: University of Illinois Press, 1986.

Rich, Adrienne. *The Dream of a Common Language.* New York and London: W. W. Norton, 1978.

_____. "It Is the Lesbian in Us. . . ." In *On Lies, Secrets, and Silences: Selected Prose, 1966–1978*, 199–202. New York and London: W. W. Norton, 1979.

_____. "Jane Eyre: The Temptations of a Motherless Woman." In *On Lies, Secrets, and Silences*, 89–106.

_____. *Of Woman Born.* New York and London: W. W. Norton, 1976.

Richards, I. A. *Principles of Literary Criticism.* New York: Harcourt, Brace, 1959.

Robinson, Marilynne. *Housekeeping.* New York: Bantam Books, 1982.

Rose, Ellen Cronan. "Feminine Endings—and Beginnings: Margaret Drabble's *The Waterfall*." *Contemporary Literature* 21 (1980): 81–99.

Rose, Jacqueline. "Introduction II." In *Feminine Sexuality: Jacques Lacan and the Ecole Freudienne*, edited by Juliet Mitchell and Jacqueline Rose, 27–57. New York: W. W. Norton, 1982.

Rose, Phyllis. *Parallel Lives: Five Victorian Marriages.* New York: Knopf, 1983.

_____. *Woman of Letters: A Life of Virginia Woolf.* New York: Oxford University Press, 1978.

Rossi, Alice. "Maternalism, Sexuality and the New Feminism." In *Contemporary Sexual Behavior: Critical Issues in the 1970's*, edited by Joseph Zubin and John Money, 145–73. Baltimore: The Johns Hopkins University Press, 1973.

Rothenberg, Albert. "The Process of Janusian Thinking in Creativity." In *The Creativity Question*, edited by Albert Rothenberg and Carl R. Hausman, 311–27. Durham: Duke University Press, 1976.

Rowe, Karen. "'Fairy-Born and Human Bred': Jane Eyre's Education in Romance." In *The Voyage In: Fictions in Female Development*, edited by Elizabeth Abel, Marianne Hirsch, and Elizabeth Langland, 69–89. Hanover: University Press of New England, 1983.

Rubenstein, Roberta. *Boundaries of the Self: Gender, Culture, Fiction.* Urbana: University of Illinois Press, 1987.

_____. *The Novelistic Vision of Doris Lessing: Breaking the Forms of Consciousness.* Urbana: University of Illinois Press, 1979.

_____. "Pandora's Box and Female Survival: Margaret Atwood's *Bodily Harm*." *Revue d'études canadiennes* 20 (Spring 1985): 120–35.

Rubin, Gayle. "The Traffic in Women: Notes on the 'Political Economy' of Sex." In *Toward an Anthology of Women*, edited by Rayna Reiter, 157–210. New York and London: Monthly Review Press, 1975.

Ruddick, Sara. "Maternal Thinking." In *Women and Values: Readings in Recent Feminist Philosophy*, edited by Marilyn Pearsall, 340–51. Belmont, Calif.: Wadsworth, 1986.

Sachs, Hanns. *The Creative Unconscious: Studies in the Psychoanalysis of Art*. Cambridge, Mass.: Sci-Art, 1942.

Sadoff, Dianne. *Monsters of Affection*. Baltimore: The Johns Hopkins University Press, 1982.

Schachtel, Ernst. *Metamorphosis*. New York: Basic Books, 1959.

Schneiderman, Stuart. *Returning to Freud: Clinical Psychoanalysis in the School of Lacan*. Translated and edited by Stuart Schneiderman. New Haven: Yale University Press, 1980.

Schor, Naomi. "*Eugénie Grandet*: Mirrors and Melancholia." In *The (M)other Tongue*, edited by Shirley Nelson Garner, Claire Kahane, and Madelon Sprengnether, 217–37. Ithaca: Cornell University Press, 1985.

Seyersted, Per. "Kate Chopin and the American Realists." In *Kate Chopin: A Critical Biography*. Baton Rouge: Louisiana State University Press, 1969. Reprinted in Chopin, *The Awakening*, 180–86.

Showalter, Elaine. *A Literature of Their Own*. Princeton: Princeton University Press, 1977.

Silhol, Robert. "Language and the Unconscious." *Prose Studies* 11 (December 1988, special issue on *Lacanian Discourse*, edited by Marshall Alcorn, Mark Bracher, and Ronald Corthell): 21–29.

Skoller, Eleanor Honig. "The Progress of a Letter: Truth, Feminism, and *The Waterfall*." In *Critical Essays on Margaret Drabble*, edited by Ellen Cronan Rose, 119–33. Boston: G. K. Hall, 1985.

Smith, David. "Incest Patterns in Two Victorian Novels." *Literature and Psychology* 15 (Summer 1965): 135–44.

Smith, Stewart, and Ruth Sullivan. "Narrative Stance in Kate Chopin's *The Awakening*." *Studies in American Fiction* 1 (Spring 1973): 62–75.

Spacks, Patricia Meyer. *The Female Imagination*. New York: Avon Books, 1976.

Spangler, George M. "The Ending of the Novel." From "Kate Chopin's *The Awakening*: A Partial Dissent." *Novel* 3 (Spring 1970): 249–55. Reprinted in Chopin, *The Awakening*, 186–89.

Speed, Harold. *The Practice and Science of Drawing*. New York: Seeley Service, 1935.

Spivak, Gayatri. "Three Women's Texts and a Critique of Imperialism." *Critical Inquiry* 12 (1985): 243–61.

Sprague, Claire. *Rereading Doris Lessing: Narrative Patterns of Doubling and Repetition*. Chapel Hill: University of North Carolina Press, 1987.

Sprengnether, Madelon. "(M)other Eve: Some Revisions of the Fall in Fiction by Contemporary Women Writers." In *Psychoanalysis and Feminism*, edited by Richard Feldstein and Judith Roof, 298–322. Ithaca and London: Cornell University Press, 1989.

Spyri, Johanna. *Heidi*. Translated by Helen B. Dole. New York: Grosset and Dunlap, 1945.

Stack, Carol B. "Sex Roles and Survival Strategies in the Urban Black Community." In *Woman, Culture, and Society*, edited by Michelle Rosaldo and Louise Lamphere, 113–28. Stanford: Stanford University Press, 1974.

Stewart, Grace. *A New Mythos: The Novel of the Artist as Heroine, 1877–1977*. Montreal: Eden Press Women's Publications, 1981.

Sukenick, Lynn. "Feeling and Reason in Doris Lessing's Fiction." *Contemporary Literature* 14 (Autumn 1973): 515–35.

Suleiman, Susan Rubin. "On Maternal Splitting: A propos of Mary Gordon's *Men and Angels.*" *Signs* 14 (Autumn 1988): 25–41.

_____. "Writing and Motherhood." In *The (M)other Tongue*, edited by Shirley Nelson Garner, Claire Kahane, and Madelon Sprengnether, 352–77. Ithaca: Cornell University Press, 1985.

Tanner, Nancy. "Matrifocality in Indonesia and Africa and among Black Americans." In *Woman, Culture, and Society*, edited by Louise Lamphere and Michelle Rosaldo, 129–57. Stanford: Stanford University Press, 1974.

Tanner, Tony. *Adultery in the Novel*. Baltimore and London: The Johns Hopkins University Press, 1979.

Tennyson, Alfred, Lord. "Mariana." In *Victorian Poetry*, edited by E. K. Brown and J. O. Bailey, 2. New York: The Ronald Press, 1962.

Tompkins, Jane P. "*The Awakening*: An Evaluation." *Feminist Studies* 3 (Spring–Summer 1976): 22–29.

Treichler, Paula. "The Construction of Ambiguity in *The Awakening*: A Linguistic Analysis." In *Women and Language in Literature and Society*, edited by Sally McConnell-Ginet, Ruth Borker, and Nelly Furman, 239–56. New York: Praeger, 1980.

_____. "Escaping the Sentence: Diagnosis and Discourse in 'The Yellow Wall-paper.'" *Tulsa Studies in Women's Literature* 3 (1984): 61–77.

_____. "The Wall behind the Yellow Wallpaper: Response to Carol Neely and Karen Ford." *Tulsa Studies in Women's Literature* 4 (Fall 1985): 323–29.

Walker, Alice. *The Color Purple*. New York: Washington Square Press, 1982.

_____. "In Search of Our Mothers' Gardens." In *In Search of Our Mothers' Gardens*, 231–43. New York: Harcourt, Brace, 1983.

Ward, Elizabeth Stuart Phelps. *The Story of Avis*. Boston: James R. Osgood, 1877.

Washington, Mary Helen. "I Sign My Mother's Name: Alice Walker, Dorothy West, Paule Marshall." In *Mothering the Mind*, edited by Ruth Perry and Martine Brownley, 142–63. New York and London: Holmes & Meier, 1984.

Wheeler, Otis B. "The Five Awakenings of Edna Pontellier." *Southern Review* 11 (Winter 1975): 119–28.

White, T. H., ed. *The Bestiary: A Book of Beasts, Being a Translation from a Latin Bestiary of the Twelfth Century*. New York: Putnam/Capricorn, 1960.

Wilden, Anthony. *System and Structure: Essays in Communication*. New York: Barnes & Noble, 1972.

Wilder, Laura Ingalls. *Little House in the Big Woods*. New York: Harper & Row, 1971.

_____. *Little House on the Prairie*. New York: Harper & Row, 1971.

Williams, Raymond. *The Long Revolution*. London: Chatto & Windus, 1961.

_____. *Marxism and Literature*. Oxford and New York: Oxford University Press, 1977.

Winner, Ellen. *Invented Worlds: The Psychology of the Arts*. Cambridge: Harvard University Press, 1982.

Winnicott, D. W. "The Capacity to Be Alone." In *The Maturational Processes and the Facilitating Environment*, 29–36. New York: International Universities Press, 1965.

———. "Mirror-Role of Mother and Family in Child Development." In *Playing and Reality*, 111–18. London: Tavistock, 1971.

———. "The Theory of the Parent-Infant Relationship." In *Maturational Processes*, 37–55.

———. "Transitional Objects and Transitional Phenomena." In *Playing and Reality*, 1–25.

———. "The Use of an Object and Relating through Identifications." In *Playing and Reality*, 86–94.

Wolff, Cynthia Griffin. "Thanatos and Eros: Kate Chopin's *The Awakening*." *American Quarterly* 25 (October 1973): 449–71. Reprinted in Chopin, *The Awakening*, 206–18.

Wolkenfeld, Suzanne. "Edna's Suicide: The Problem of the One and the Many." In Chopin, *The Awakening*, 218–24.

Woolf, Virginia. *Mrs. Dalloway*. New York and London: Harcourt, Brace, 1925.

———. *To the Lighthouse*. New York and London: Harcourt, Brace, 1927.

Wyatt, Jean. "Avoiding Self-Definition: In Defense of Women's Right to Merge (Julia Kristeva and *Mrs. Dalloway*)." *Women's Studies* 13 (1986): 115–26. Reprinted in *The Female Imagination and the Modernist Aesthetic*, edited by Sandra Gilbert and Susan Gubar, 115–26. New York and London: Gordon & Breach, 1988.

Yaeger, Patricia. *Honey-Mad Women: Emancipatory Strategies in Women's Writing*. New York: Columbia University Press, 1988.

———. "'A Language Which Nobody Understood': Emancipatory Strategies in *The Awakening*." *Novel* 20 (Spring 1987): 197–219.

Index